Interest Groups and Trade Policy

Interest Groups and Trade Policy

Gene M. Grossman
and
Elhanan Helpman

.

Princeton University Press
Princeton and Oxford

Published by
Princeton University Press
41 William Street, Princeton
New Jersey 08540

In the United Kingdom:
Princeton University Press
3 Market Place,
Woodstock, Oxfordshire OX20 1SY

Full-Service Production:
NOVA Graphic Services, Ft. Washington, PA

Library of Congress Cataloging-in-Publication Data

Interest groups and trade policy / Gene M. Grossman and Elhanan Helpman
    p. cm.
  Includes bibliographical references and index.
  ISBN 0-691-09596-5 (alk. paper)—ISBN 0-691-09597-3 (pbk. alk. paper)
    1. Commercial policy. 2. Pressure groups. 3. United States—Commercial
policy. 4. Pressure group—United States. I. Grossman, Gene M.
II. Helpman, Elhanan.

  HF1411 .I414 2002
  382'.3'0973—dc21   2001055190

British Library Cataloging-in-Publication Data is available

This book has been composed in New Baskerville

Printed on acid-free paper. ∞

www.puppress.princeton.edu

Printed in the United States of America

10 9 8 7 6 5 4 3 2 1

Contents

Introduction   1
  1 Special Interest Politics   2
  2 Articles in this Collection   7
    2.1 Part I: Methodology   7
    2.2 Part II: Applications to Trade Policy   11
  3 Empirical Validation   17
  References   21

Part I: Instruments of Influence   23

**1. Common Agency and Coordination: General Theory
and Application to Government Policy Making**   25
with Avinash Dixit
  1 Introduction   25
  2 General Theory   28
    2.1 Equilibrium   28
    2.2 Truthful Equilibria   32
    2.3 Quasi-Linear Preferences   34
  3 Application to Government Policy Making   35
  References   41

2. Electoral Competition and Special Interest Politics   43
  1 Introduction   43
  2 Related Literature   45
  3 The Model   47
    3.1 The Voters   47
    3.2 The Parties and the Government   49
    3.3 The Special Interests   50
    3.4 Political Equilibrium   52
    3.5 Functional Forms   54
  4 Equilibrium with One Lobby   54
    4.1 Contributions with Only an Influence Motive   56
    4.2 When Is an Electoral Motive Operative? 59
  5 Equilibrium with Several Lobbies   61
  6 Summary   67
  APPENDIX   69
    Strict Majority Rule   69
  References   71

3. Competing for Endorsements   **73**
1 The Literature on Political Endorsements   77
2 The Model and a Benchmark   79
3 A Neutrality Result   84
4 Effective Endorsements   85
   4.1 Mechanical Endorsements   86
   4.2 Strategic Endorsements   92
5 Welfare   95
6 Conclusions   98
APPENDIX   100
   Statement and Proof of Proposition 4   100
   Proof of Proposition 5   104
References   107

Part II: Trade Policy   **109**

4. Protection for Sale   **111**
1 Overview   114
2 Formal Framework   116
3 The Structure of Protection   119
4 Political Contributions   126
5 Why Lobbies May Prefer Trade Policies   132
6 Summary and Extensions   134
References   136

5. Trade Wars and Trade Talks   **139**
1 Introduction   139
2 Model Outline and Relation to the Literature   141
3 The Formal Model   143
4 Trade Wars   147
5 Trade Talks   157
6 Conclusions   168
References   170

6. Politics and Trade Policy   **173**
1 Introduction   173
2 Political Economy Approaches   175
   2.1 Direct Democracy   175
   2.2 Political Support Function   178
   2.3 Tariff-Formation Function   180
   2.4 Electoral Competition   184
   2.5 Influence-Driven Contributions   186

3 Double-Edged Diplomacy   191
  3.1 Trade Wars   192
  3.2 Trade Talks   193
  3.3 Free Trade Agreements   194
References   197

7. The Politics of Free Trade Agreements   **199**
1 Analytical Framework   201
  1.1 Objectives of Economic and Political Agents   202
  1.2 The Political Game   204
  1.3 Economic Equilibria Under an FTA   205
  1.4 Effects of an FTA on Economic Interests   207
2 Unilateral Stances   208
3 Equilibrium Agreements   212
4 Industry Exclusions   219
  4.1 Unilateral Stances   219
  4.2 Bargaining over Industry Exclusions   224
5 Conclusions   228
APPENDIX   229
  Contributions to Foreign Governments   229
References   232

8. Foreign Investment with Endogenous Protection   **233**
1 Introduction   233
2 Basic Model   236
  2.1 Consumption and Production   237
  2.2 The Special Interest Group and the Government   239
  2.3 Multinationals   242
3 DFI and Protection   243
  3.1 Tariff Response Curves   243
  3.2 Profit Differential Curves   244
  3.3 Entry   244
  3.4 Equilibrium DFI and Protection   246
4 Does DFI Benefit the Average Voter?   249
5 Workers Versus Capitalists   251
6 Conclusions   255
References   255

Index   **257**

Introduction

Interest groups play a prominent political role in all democratic societies. Their activities are many and varied. They lobby politicians. They educate the public about issues and candidates. They participate in demonstrations. They contribute to campaigns. And they encourage participation in elections, especially by their members and others sympathetic to their cause. By these means and more, the groups seek to influence the political process in ways that further the interests of their members. Sometimes their actions also serve the general public. Other times, they do not.

By all indications, the participation of interest groups in the policy process has been growing by leaps and bounds in the United States and elsewhere. The number of organizations that engage representatives in Washington, Brussels, and other capital cities has exploded in recent years. So too has the number of registered lobbyists. Spending on lobbying has grown precipitously in the United States, as has the total amount of campaign contributions by Political Action Committees (PACs). Political advertising appears to be on the rise. And the media report ever more frequently on the alleged influence of special interest groups and on the need for campaign reform. It seems critical that economists and political scientists come to understand better the role that interest groups play in the policy-making process. This has been the main focus of our research for several years, as it has been for many others.

This book collects eight of our previously published papers. We are reprinting these papers to provide a companion to our recently published treatise, *Special Interest Politics* (MIT Press, 2001). Whereas *Special Interest Politics* considers the various mechanisms by which interest groups influence policy decisions, this collection mostly contains applications of the theory to an important policy area. More specifically, five of the articles investigate how trade policies are determined in response to competing political pressures, and how private and public actors behave in the light of political realities. We envision the two books together providing complementary material for graduate-level courses in political science and political economics, while this collection of articles can also serve as supplementary reading in graduate courses on international trade theory.

We have three objectives in the remainder of this introductory chapter. First, we aim to provide an overview of the contents of *Special Interest Politics* and to explain how the current collection of articles relates to the material in the monograph. Second, we will describe the questions that are addressed in the articles reprinted here and preview some of the main findings. Finally, we will describe some recent empirical studies that make use of our approaches and argue that the abstract theories we have developed find support in the conduct of trade policy.

1 Special Interest Politics

As noted above, our monograph *Special Interest Politics* examines the various mechanisms by which interest groups affect policy outcomes. We focus on three distinct roles that interest groups and their members play in the political process. Groups act as voters, as purveyors of information, and as contributors to political campaigns. These various roles define the three parts of our book.

After an introductory chapter that provides data on the activities of special interest groups and that previews the book's content, we begin the substantive analysis in *Special Interest Politics* with a discussion of voting and elections. We start with a selective review of the voting literature, much of which ascribes little or no role to special interests. There are three reasons why certain groups of like-minded voters—even ones who are not organized and thus take no collective action—may fare especially well in representative democracies. First, groups differ in their participation rates in elections. We argue that voter turnout is best explained as a group social norm, and discuss the reasons why such a norm may be more effective in promoting participation in certain groups of voters than in others. Second, members of different interest groups have access to different amounts of information about the candidates in an election and the policy issues to be resolved. We show that in some settings, the policies implemented by elected candidates will favor better-informed groups of voters, while in other settings they may not. Finally, interest groups differ in their partisanship. A partisan voter is one who has a strong allegiance to a particular political party based on its ideological or fixed positions, and who is likely to vote for that party unless its rival promises a much more favorable platform on the new and pliable issues being contested in the election. Groups with few partisan voters fare especially well in electoral contests, because the parties either concede or take for granted the votes from groups with many partisan members while they compete vigorously for support among groups with large fractions of swing voters.

Part II of *Special Interest Politics* focuses on the use of information by organized special interest groups. There are at least two reasons why organized groups may be well placed to deal in information. First, the members of an interest group are likely to gain expertise about many of the policy matters that concern them in the course of their everyday participation in an industry, profession, or hobby. For example, doctors and hospital administrators are bound to know more about the details of the issues to do with health care reform than do most politicians, let alone the typical members of the voting public. Second, interest group members can pool their resources to gather information that bears on their collective interests. Since information has the properties of a public good—once collected, it can be used by many without diminishing its value—there are good reasons for members of organized groups to share the fixed costs of gathering it.

Interest groups provide information to both politicians and voters, so we examine educational activities aimed at each of these audiences. In a chapter on "lobbying" we study the attempts by one or more knowledgeable groups to educate a less well-informed politician about the policy environment. The setting for this analysis is one in which the interests of the groups and the politician are imperfectly aligned. We model the act of lobbying as "cheap talk." That is, the lobbyists can convey information costlessly to a politician who has no independent means to verify their claims. A sophisticated politician will discount what she hears in such circumstances unless the self-interested lobbyists can offer persuasive arguments. We evaluate the persuasiveness of a lobbyist's arguments by considering the incentives he has to speak honestly when he expects his words to be taken at face value. With cheap talk, a lobbyist representing a single interest group can communicate some information about the policy environment, but the communication is bound to contain less detail than what the interest group actually knows. With several lobbying groups competing for the politician's favor, there is the possibility that the policy maker can use each group as a foil for the others. Surprisingly, a lobby group may fare better when there is another with opposing views to discipline its remarks than when its claims to the politician go unchallenged.

A second chapter in Part II of *Special Interest Politics* investigates situations in which lobbying is costly. Lobbying may be costly either because groups incur unavoidable expenses when gathering and presenting information, or because the groups choose to bear avoidable costs as a way to lend credibility to their arguments. The economic literature on "signaling" provides valuable insights that shed light on costly lobbying. Lobbying is more effective when it is costly than when talk is cheap, because the groups use their willingness to bear the cost as an indication that the conditions truly warrant a significant policy response. And with freedom to vary the size of a lobbying campaign, a group is able to convey much more information to the politician than is possible when the cost of lobbying is fixed. We also examine the idea that politicians may impose access fees (in the form of campaign contributions) as an additional cost of lobbying. Politicians may charge for access for one of three reasons. They may need resources to run their election campaigns and be willing to sacrifice some valuable information in order to obtain these funds. Or they may view their time as a scarce resource and wish to limit visits from groups that have relatively little valuable information to share. Or they may use the access charges as a way to screen lobbyists in situations in which they are unsure about the biases and preferences of the various represented groups.

In Part II of *Special Interest Politics*, we also examine the efforts by interest groups to educate voters. Interest groups attempt to inform the public in order to win greater sympathy for their policy views. They also seek to educate their members, so that these members will be better able to cast their ballots in support of the group's common cause. But, as with lobbying, the statements from an interest group cannot be taken by voters at face value. Before the candidates have announced their positions, the interest groups have an incentive to exaggerate in order to induce voters to believe that the group's own preferred policies are socially desirable ones. If they are successful in doing so, the competition for votes between candidates will lead them to adopt positions more to the group's liking. Even after the candidates have staked their positions, a group has reason to exaggerate its claims, because at this stage it wants to maximize the prospect of victory for the candidate or party whose position is more favorable to its cause. An organized interest group typically will face a credibility problem even in its efforts to communicate with its own members, because the organization will want to convince as many of these individuals as possible to vote for the candidate whose platform best serves the average member, whereas some of the members may have partisan preferences that incline them to vote differently.

The third part of *Special Interest Politics* deals with campaign giving by special interest groups. In addition to buying access, groups may use their contributions as a means to influence policy makers' decisions and to improve the electoral prospects for their favorite candidates and parties. We consider the incentives that interest groups have to purchase influence and to invest in their preferred candidates in a variety of political settings. We also investigate what happens when several or many interest groups vie for influence and favors.

We begin with influence seeking by a single interest group. Such a group may be able to communicate to a policy maker its willingness to pay for different policy options. A potential contributor confronts the politician with a menu of offers. These offers, which need not be explicit, associate different sizes of contribution with different policy alternatives. Politicians value contributions for their potential usefulness in financing campaigns, but many also wish to enact policies that benefit the public in order to improve their popularity among the well informed or to fulfill their sense of social responsibility. How should the interest group structure its offers? How does the politician trade off the desire for contributions against the desire to do good? What policies result from an optimal schedule of offers by the interest group and an optimal response by the politician? These are the questions that are the subject of our analysis.

We proceed to examine competition between interest groups. The form of such competition resembles an economic problem of "common agency." In a principal–agent relationship, the principal must design incentives for the agent to induce her to take actions that reflect the principal's interests. In a situation of common agency, an act by an agent affects the well-being of several principals simultaneously. Then they each must offer incentives, and the agent must balance the benefit from weighing the interest of some more heavily than others. Similarly, in pressure politics, the politician takes policy actions that will affect several interest groups, as well as the general public. The groups offer contributions as a way to induce the politician to favor their interests relative to those of the others. An equilibrium in a game of common agency is a set of incentive schedules, one for each principal, with the property that each schedule is best for the principal that offers it, given the schedules of the others and the anticipated optimal response by the agent. An equilibrium in our contribution game also takes this form. Each group designs an optimal response to the anticipated offers of other groups, recognizing that the politician ultimately will choose the policy that maximizes her own political welfare.

The quest for influence becomes more complicated when decisions are taken by the members of a legislative body who are not subject to strong party discipline. In Part III of *Special Interest Politics*, we extend the common agency approach to allow for situations in which there is no unified party in power. After describing some alternatives, we model a legislature that will choose by majority rule either a policy proposed by an agenda setter or a given status quo. The agenda setter is a member of the body who has the authority to propose legislation. For example, the members of the Senate Finance Committee have such authority in the U.S. Senate for policy areas that fall under its jurisdiction. The competition for influence involves bids by the interest groups for consideration by the agenda setter, and further bids by these groups for the votes of the elected representatives on the floor of the chamber. By the time a bill has been proposed, some groups may wish to see it passed and will offer contributions to those who are willing to vote in favor, while others prefer the status quo and seek the bill's defeat. But those on the side that ultimately will win do not wish to pay for more votes than are needed to ensure their political victory. And those who ultimately will lose do not wish to buy votes that will do them no good. So the game has an interesting structure in which it often will be necessary for the interest groups to randomize their strategies. This randomization makes uncertain the prospects of passage for any given bill. The agenda setter will need to factor in this uncertainty when deciding what bill to propose, and the interest groups will need to consider it when deciding how they might choose to influence the agenda setter.

The final chapter of *Special Interest Politics* investigates the incentives for interest group giving during an election campaign. The interest groups may give to the parties in order to influence their policy positions. They may also contribute to a party without strings attached to further its electoral prospects. The parties choose their platforms to woo the well-informed voters. But they also take into account the contribution offers, because the funds can be used for campaign spending that can attract impressionable voters. An equilibrium in this case is a set of contribution schedules that are best responses for the interest groups to the offers of the others, and a pair of platforms for each party that maximizes its chance of being elected in view of the contribution offers it faces and the platform it anticipates from its rival. We derive a number of predictions about the pattern of giving by interest groups to the two political parties, about how unlikely it is that groups will perceive an electoral motive for giving, and about the possibility of a bandwagon in which many groups give generously to a certain party because they expect that others will do likewise.

2 Articles in this Collection

The articles reprinted here fall into one of two categories. The first part of the book contains papers that show how interest groups can use certain tools at their disposal to influence and shape the policy process. These are papers that formed the basis for some of the modeling in *Special Interest Politics* and, in some cases, provide more detail than it was possible to include in the monograph. The second part of the book contains applications of the theory to issues of international economic policy. These papers show how the tools described in Part I and in *Special Interest Politics* can be put to productive use. Of course, the results in these articles are of substantive interest in their own right, inasmuch as they offer predictions about the structure of trade protection, the outcome of trade negotiations, and the response of trade flows and direct foreign investment to politically motivated trade policies.

2.1 Part I: Methodology

In "Common Agency and Coordination: General Theory and Application to Government Policy Making" (Chapter 1), we collaborated with Avinash Dixit to extend the theory of common agency under complete information to settings with nontransferable utilities. As we noted above, the theory of common agency provides a useful tool for examining the competition between interest groups for political influence. The theory—as developed by Bernheim and Whinston (1986)—assumes that monetary transfers enter additively into the utility functions of the agent and all principals. In other words, the players all have constant marginal utilities of income. This assumption is quite reasonable for many of the industrial organization applications that Bernheim and Whinston had in mind. However, it is a problematic one for key issues in redistributive politics. Such politics involves the determination of taxes and transfers that are bound to have general equilibrium implications that may change the marginal utilities of income in non-negligible ways.

Our extension of the theory retains much of the flavor of the Bernheim-Whinston analysis. Specifically, we imagine a setting of perfect information in which an agent must take some actions that will bear on the welfare of several principals. Each principal designs a payment schedule to induce the agent to act on his behalf. The schedules indicate non-negative transfers that the principals will pay to the agent for each action the agent might take. An equilibrium is a set of payment schedules that are mutual best responses when the principals expect the agent to take her utility maximizing action in response to all the offers. We depart from Bernheim and

Whinston only in assuming that the utility functions of the principals and the agent are general, nonlinear functions of the actions and the transfers.

In this setting, we are able to establish many of the same results as Bernheim and Whinston. Our characterization of equilibrium is similar to theirs. Also, we can show that a principal's best response set contains a payment schedule that is "truthful" in the sense that Bernheim and Whinston used the term, and that we have designated as "compensating" in *Special Interest Politics*. When all principals employ incentive schedules that are compensating, the resulting equilibrium is efficient from the point of view of the set of principals and the agent taken together.

The application to government policy making comes from assuming that the principal is a politician whose welfare depends on her policy actions and on the contributions she receives, and the principals are interest groups whose welfare depends on the policies and their pay-outs. This specification forms the basis for our analysis in Chapters 7 and 8 of *Special Interest Politics*. In the article with Dixit, we derived an important result for the case in which the politician's welfare depends on the policies only through their effects on the welfare of the members of the polity. As long as the politician's welfare increases with the utility of every individual in the society, a truthful (or compensating) equilibrium of the contribution game must be efficient for society as a whole. In other words, there is no other set of campaign contributions and policies different from those in a truthful equilibrium that would make the politician or some member of the public better off than in the equilibrium, without making another worse off. An immediate implication is that if the government can effect income redistribution with lump-sum transfers, it will not be induced to use distorting instruments such as production subsidies, consumption taxes, or trade policies in a political equilibrium. When the government does use these instruments, it means either that lump-sum transfers are infeasible or that the political rules have set to eliminate such transfers as a policy option.

Our paper on "Electoral Competition and Special Interest Politics" (Chapter 2) presents the original ideas that were subsequently modified and refined in Chapter 10 in *Special Interest Politics*. In the paper, we develop a model of the interactions between voters, interest groups, and political parties. The interest groups offer contributions to the parties in order to influence their policy positions and perhaps to help their preferred party to gain more votes. The parties set their positions on a set of pliable policy issues with an eye to attracting contributions from the interest groups and to capturing the votes of informed voters. In this paper, we assume that their goal is to maximize their vote tally. Finally, there are informed voters who cast their ballots to maximize their expected utility, and impressionable voters who respond to campaign spending by the parties.

In the model, the interest groups confront the political parties with contribution schedules, each one linking the choices of platforms on the pliable issues to potential campaign gifts. In other words, we treat the relationship between the parties and the interest groups as one of common agency. The organizations represent groups of voters who share common preferences over the pliable policy issues but may have differing opinions about another set of fixed policies. If, in equilibrium, the interest group contributes to a party exactly what is needed to induce it to choose a particular platform, we say that the group has exercised only an "influence motive" for campaign giving. If, instead, it contributes something more than this minimum, we say that it has also exercised an "electoral motive" for giving. One of the main concerns of the paper is to understand when each of these motives is operative.

This first attempt to model the complete set of interactions between interest groups, political parties, and voters yields some interesting conclusions. First, we derive conditions under which the parties behave in equilibrium as if they were maximizing an objective function that includes the total amount of campaign contributions and the aggregate welfare of society as additive arguments. This justifies the reduced-form welfare function for the politician that we have used in many of our papers (and in the monograph) in cases where we do not formally model the voters and the election. Second, we identify the determinants of the relative weights that the politicians give to campaign contributions and aggregate welfare in their political objective functions. The weight that a party places on contributions is greater, the greater is the fraction of impressionable voters, the more effective is campaign spending in attracting these voters, the more diverse are the opinions of the informed voters about the relative desirability of the parties' fixed positions, and the more popular is a party's set of fixed positions relative to those of its rival.

When many interest groups compete for influence, there is little incentive for them to exercise an electoral motive for giving. In fact, at most one interest group that prefers a given party will have an incentive to give to it more than what is needed to influence its platform. In the equilibrium, most groups exercise only an influence motive and give to both political parties. The groups give more to the party that they expect to win a majority of the votes. But since the groups cannot coordinate their campaign giving, it is possible that their collective actions will make a winner of the party that is the ex ante underdog. Then their independent decisions to target their most generous giving to the expected majority winner become a self-fulfilling prophecy.

In "Competing for Endorsements" (Chapter 3), we consider the use of information by an interest group as a tool for political influence. We imagine a two-party election in which the parties announce policy positions but the voters do not understand the pliable issue well enough to know for sure which of the positions would provide them with greater welfare. A subset of the voters are members of an interest group, and the organization of the group knows how the members' common interest in the pliable policy would be served by the different policy options. To convey information to its members, the interest group can "endorse" one of the parties as its favorite in the election.

We assume that the political parties anticipate the organization's actions when setting their platforms. In some circumstances, an endorsement by the interest group would win votes for the named party. Then the parties will cater to the interest group in the hopes of winning its endorsement. By inducing competition for the endorsement, an interest group sometimes can tilt the political process in favor of its members.

Endorsements are not always effective as a tool for influence. If, for example, the average ideal policy in the voting population of interest group members and non-members is independent of the unknown (to the voters) state of the world, then the parties' platforms with endorsements will be the same as when endorsements are not possible. In such circumstances, a party that caters to the interest group by choosing a position more to its liking indeed will be successful in capturing the group's endorsement. The endorsement will lead members of the group to realize that the party's position is closer to their ideal, and so some of them will shift their votes to the party that has catered. But, the voters who are not members of the interest group will recognize that what is good for the group members is not on average good for them. So an endorsement by the interest group would cause a loss of votes among those who are not group members. In the benchmark case under discussion, an endorsement has no effect on the total vote count. Then there is no reason for the parties to compete for the endorsement.

Much of our paper focuses on a case in which the ideal pliable policy for a typical voter who is not a member of the interest group is statistically independent of the group's ideal policy. In this case, the members of an interest group do benefit from the ability of their organization to issue an endorsement, as the political parties cater to the group in an effort to win its verbal support. For a range of values of the underlying random variable that describes the voters' uncertainty, the parties both announce the interest group's ideal pliable policy as their position on this issue, and interest group members are able to surmise in equilibrium exactly what policy is best for them. If the organization's information indicates an extreme policy option as the one that is best for the members of the interest group, the parties will not offer the members their ideal policy. Still, the policy outcome will be better for the group members (and worse for the average voter who is not a member of the interest group) than the one that would result if the organization had no chance to issue an endorsement.

The endorsement is but one example of an interest group using its superior information to further its political ends. In Chapter 6 of *Special Interest Politics* we study a whole range of messages that an interest group might send to its members and to other voters. These messages might contain more detail than a simple "vote for *A*" or "vote for *B*," if for example they are conveyed via issue advertising or by more lengthy reports in newsletters and trade publications. In the monograph, we consider both situations in which the group can issue its report before the parties have announced their positions and situations—as with an endorsement—in which the message comes after the parties' positions are known. Surprisingly, the most information that can be credibly communicated by an interest group after the parties' positions have been announced is equivalent to what could be conveyed by its choosing one of two one-word messages. Thus, an endorsement does as well as a much lengthier report in educating voters, once the credibility constraints are taken into account.

2.2 Part II: Applications to Trade Policy

In the papers reprinted in Part I, and especially in our monograph *Special Interest Politics*, we have developed a set of tools that can be used for analyzing the political influence of special interest groups. Of course, the value of these tools can only be judged from their usefulness in specific applications. In Part II, we have collected five papers that address issues regarding the formation of foreign economic policy. Here, the models yield specific predictions that can be subjected to empirical scrutiny.

"Protection for Sale" (Chapter 4) was our first foray into political economics. We were motivated to write this paper by our observation that so many of the prescriptions of normative trade theory bear little resemblance to what governments actually do in practice. While we were hardly the first to make this observation, we were dissatisfied with the modeling of those who preceded us, which typically treated the political process as a "black box." Our approach was to posit the existence of politicians who value both campaign contributions and aggregate welfare and to investigate their interaction in a common agency relationship with groups representing industry interests.

The application of a political model to trade policy (or any other specific issue) requires a detailed specification of the economic environment. Chapter 4 considers a small open economy with many industries and many factors. In one sector, output is produced from labor alone, with constant returns to scale. In all other industries, output is produced by labor and a sector-specific input. A set of organized groups represent

the special interests of the owners of some (perhaps all) of these specific factors. Each group offers a contribution schedule to the policy
maker in an effort to influence her choice of import tariffs and export
subsidies.

Our model yields several testable predictions about the cross-sectional
structure of trade protection. The political equilibrium is characterized
by positive rates of protection for all industries that are represented by
organized groups and negative protection for those that have no political representation. Rates of protection are higher for organized industries the greater is the value placed by the policy maker on political
contributions and the smaller is the fraction of the population that is represented by some organized group or another. Protection will be particularly high in those industries with a high ratio of domestic output to
trade volume and in those in which trade flows are relatively unresponsive to the domestic price. This pattern of protection reflects the policy
maker's effort to obtain a given amount of campaign financing at the least
social cost.

Although all organized industries succeed in buying protection, it does
not follow that all interest groups must benefit from their pursuit of political influence. A case in point is the situation that arises when every individual belongs to an organized group. Then the resource allocation in
the political equilibrium mirrors that under free trade. But the groups
achieve this political stalemate only by making costly contributions to
the policy maker, which means that every individual (except the politician) is worse off in equilibrium than he or she would be if contributions
were impossible. The organized groups pay tribute to the policy maker
to induce a set of neutral trade policies, because the outcome would be
still worse for them if they were to refrain from such giving.

In "Trade Wars and Trade Talks" (Chapter 5) we extend the analysis
to a setting with two large countries. Here, domestic politics interact with
foreign relations. In each country, the policy maker receives offers of
contributions from domestic special interests. These offers interact with
her concern for aggregate welfare to induce preferences over vectors of
tariffs and export subsidies. In a "trade war," the policy makers set their
nations' trade policies noncooperatively, each maximizing a political
objective function while taking as given the anticipated behavior of the
other. When there are "trade talks," the policies are chosen cooperatively
so as to be jointly efficient for the pair of politicians. We assume that the
interest groups know whether policies will be set noncooperatively or
cooperatively, and design their contribution schedules accordingly.

In a noncooperative policy equilibrium, the formula for the trade policy that applies to a given industry has two components. One component
is the same as in Chapter 4; it reflects a balancing of the political bene-

fits and economic costs perceived by the policy maker when she extends protection to a particular industry, given the international price of the industry's output. The other component is the inverse of the elasticity of the foreign country's import demand or export supply. This term is well known from the normative theory of trade, as it represents the "optimal tariff" for a large country with a benevolent government. The model predicts a rate of protection for each industry that is simply the sum of the protection that would result with fixed terms of trade from political competition in the country and the policy that optimally exploits the country's monopoly power in the world market. We predict larger tariffs and smaller export taxes in politically organized industries than would result from a trade war between welfare-maximizing governments.

Our analysis suggests a "political" explanation for trade negotiations. Typically, multilateral negotiations are seen as a response to the economic inefficiencies that result when countries exploit their monopoly power in world trade. But in our model, the politicians who conduct trade talks are only partly concerned with aggregate welfare. They are keen to negotiate nonetheless, because the noncooperative equilibrium is politically inefficient for them; that is, it is possible to find alternative trade policies to the ones that result from a trade war with the property that they yield higher political welfare to at least one policy maker while causing no harm to the other. When the policy makers enter a negotiation with preferences that have been shaped by domestic interest groups, the outcome in each sector reflects the relative political power of the industry groups in the two countries. An interest group is powerful in our sense if it could achieve a high level of protection in the political equilibrium of a small economy.

"Politics and Trade Policy" (Chapter 6) presents a comparison of five alternative approaches to modeling tariff formation. The alternatives include our own model of common agency, along with Mayer's (1984) model of policy formation by direct democracy, Hillman's (1982) specification of a "political support function," Findlay and Wellisz's (1982) specification of a "tariff-formation function," and Magee, Brock, and Young's (1989) model of electorally motivated campaign contributions. To effect a meaningful comparison, the various formulations of the political process have been grafted to a common specification of the economy. The economic model is the same as the one we used in Chapter 4; it posits a small country with many industries, all but one of which produce output with labor and an industry-specific factor of production.

In a direct democracy, policies are determined by the preferences of the median voter. The voting equilibrium affords positive protection to all industries with median holdings of the specific input in excess of the average holding and negative protection to industries where the opposite is true. With many sectors and concentrated factor ownership, this will imply negative protection for most if not all industries. Hillman's political support function (based on Stigler [1971], and Peltzman [1976]) is a reduced form for the policy maker's political well-being. It includes the profits of some or all industries and aggregate welfare as arguments. In maximizing such a function, the politician trades off the extra profits that can be awarded to a supportive industry via protectionist policies against the loss of aggregate welfare that results from the price distortion. The model predicts a positive level of protection for all industries that receive a positive weight in the politician's political support function, and a zero rate of protection for all industries that receive no weight in this function.

The tariff-formation approach posits a reduced-form relationship between the protection afforded to an industry and the resources that are used in lobbying for and against protection. The lobbying expenditures in turn are the solution to a noncooperative game between interest groups that favor and oppose protection. A positive rate of protection is provided in equilibrium to industries in which the marginal rate of substitution between the spending of pro- and anti-protection forces in the tariff-formation function exceeds one. In our model with industry-specific factors, this means positive protection for all organized industries and negative protection for those that are not organized.

The Magee et al. model of electoral competition fits less easily into the common framework of the others. In their model, two parties vie for election. They assume that one party is aligned with an interest group that favors an import tariff, while the other is aligned with a group that prefers an export subsidy. The parties first commit to policy positions, then the interest groups can contribute to their political partner to alter the election odds. The probability of election for a party increases with the amount of contributions it collects relative to the amount amassed by its rival. This model generates some counterfactual predictions, which are discussed in Chapter 6.

The political viability of bilateral trade treaties is the subject of "The Politics of Free Trade Agreements" (Chapter 7). We consider agreements that would conform to Article XXIV of the General Agreement on Tariffs and Trade, which allows preferential policies only in cases in which the participants eliminate substantially all barriers to their bilateral trade. A free trade agreement (FTA) presumably would be favored by some industry interest groups and opposed by others. We ask, Will two small countries be able to conclude such an agreement, if the agreement must be acceptable to the policy maker in each country and if the policy makers are subject to political pressures from their organized interest groups?

We begin by considering the viability of an FTA with no excluded sectors. If the agreement comes to pass, the countries will allow duty-free access to their markets for all goods emanating from their FTA partner that satisfy rules of origin. Meanwhile, they continue to levy their status quo tariffs on imports from outside the bloc. The alternative to the agreement is continued application of the status quo tariffs on a most-favored-nation (MFN) basis.

The distinctive feature of this political environment is the binary nature of the policy choice. Either the policy maker takes a stance in favor of the agreement, or else she opposes it. We define a pressured stance as one that a policy maker adopts in response to offers of campaign contributions. If a policy maker expects the other country's government to oppose the agreement, then she will take whatever position maximizes her contributions, because her own stance will not alter the fate of the proposal. In these circumstances, the interest groups would be foolish to offer any positive contributions. The more interesting case arises when a policy maker expects the other government to support an agreement. Then an equilibrium exists in which the policy maker takes a pressured stance in favor of the FTA if and only if a weighted sum of aggregate welfare and the welfare of all industry interest groups (including those in favor of the agreement and those opposed to it) would be higher under an FTA than in the status quo.

Next we examine how the properties of the status quo trade equilibrium affect the likelihood that both policy makers would support an agreement in political equilibrium. First we show that if one of the potential parties to the FTA has uniformly higher tariff rates than the other, the proposed agreement stands no chance of being approved. In the high tariff country, an FTA would cause a loss of tariff revenue without creating any offsetting benefit to domestic interest groups. Then the policy maker would surely oppose the proposal, since it would produce an aggregate welfare loss and there would be no pressures for it.

When each country has lower tariffs in some industries and higher tariffs in others, there is some chance that an FTA could be successfully negotiated. The organized groups representing low tariff industries would support the proposal, because an FTA would allow them to export within the bloc under preferential terms. Since internal prices initially are higher in the FTA partner country than at home, the agreement actually would enhance protection for these producers. We find that a bilateral agreement can be viable if and only if the status quo trade between the potential partners is sufficiently "balanced." The acceptability of an FTA to both policy makers requires a sufficient volume of trade diversion, which means that agreements are most likely to be viable when they are socially harmful.

In the last section of Chapter 7, we examine the prospects for an agreement that excludes a small number of industries. Such exclusions exist in many bilateral agreements, and similar effects are achieved by long phase-in periods for certain industries. We show that exclusions can make an agreement politically viable that otherwise would not be. The common agency approach also yields predictions about which sectors will be excluded from a bilateral free trade agreement, the details of which are given in the chapter.

The last paper, "Foreign Investment with Endogenous Protection" (Chapter 8), deals with multinational investment that may take place in anticipation of protectionist policies. Bhagwati (1987) coined the term "quid pro quo foreign investment" for this sort of activity and has used it to describe the motivation for much of the direct foreign investment by Japanese firms in the United States and Europe during the 1980s. Our paper develops a formal model of this phenomenon to understand when it might occur and what effect it has on aggregate welfare.

In our model, foreign firms can locate production facilities in the home market or serve the market by exporting. To operate in the home market, they must bear an extra fixed cost as well as some extra production costs. But it may nonetheless prove profitable for them to do so if the home government decides to protect the home market. The foreign firms make their separate location decisions based on their forecasts of the policies of the home government. The policy maker in turn chooses a policy response to contribution offers from domestic interest groups, taking into account, of course, her concern for domestic welfare. Since domestic welfare varies with the number of foreign firms operating in the home market, the policy decision varies with the investment choices of the foreign firms. In equilibrium, the foreign investment behavior must be optimal, given rational expectations of the home government's policy response, and the tariffs must be optimal for the home policy maker given the contributions that are offered by the domestic interest groups.

We suppose to begin that a group representing the domestic industry is the only one to offer contributions in order to influence trade policy decisions. Then there are several different types of equilibria that may arise, including equilibria in which foreign firms are indifferent about the location of their production and a fraction of these firms decide to invest abroad while the remainder produce at home. In these equilibria, the extent of multinational activity depends inter alia on the policy maker's taste for campaign contributions. When the policy maker places a high value on contributions, the foreign firms expect that tariffs will be high unless relatively many of them choose to operate in the home country. In this case, anticipatory foreign investment flourishes. But then the equilibrium tariff rate may not be so high when the policy maker's taste for contributions is great, because the preemptive foreign investment serves to moderate the protectionist demands by domestic producers.

In this setting, foreign investment may raise domestic welfare by a mechanism that is not often recognized in the literature. The potential benefit of such activity derives from the equilibrium response of the domestic government. To the extent that quid pro quo investment wards off high tariffs, it generates consumer gains that have little to do with the usual reasons why home production by foreign firms may be good for domestic residents.

The last part of the paper deals with the case in which both domestic shareholders and workers with industry-specific skills are organized as interest groups. The two groups share similar interests as far as the tariff rate is concerned. But they have opposing interests concerning restrictions on direct foreign investment. We describe the trade-offs and show how the political pressures play out under these more complex conditions.

3 Empirical Validation

Our models of political economy yield precise predictions about the pattern of trade protection and other aspects of trade policy. It should be possible, therefore, to evaluate the theoretical tools by examining the extent to which these predictions are borne out in the actual practice of trade policy. A number of recent studies have attempted to do just that. Here we provide a brief introduction to these papers.[1]

The starting point for much of this work has been our model of the determination of the structure of protection in a small economy (Chapter 4). Our analysis yields a formula relating the tariff rate in industry i to the ratio of output to imports in industry i, the elasticity of import demand in industry i, and a dummy variable indicating whether the owners of specific factors employed in industry i are politically organized or not. The parameters in the formula reflect the weight that the policy maker attaches to campaign contributions in her political objective function and the share of the population that belongs to an organized interest group.

Goldberg and Maggi (1999) were the first to estimate an empirical model based on this formula, using U.S. data for 1983. Since U.S. tariffs have been set in the course of several rounds of multilateral trade negotiations, they used the coverage ratio of non-tariff barriers (the fraction of sub-categories within a trade category for which a non-tariff barrier is in place) as a proxy for the discretionary protection afforded to an industry.

---

[1] See Gawande and Krishna (2002) for a recent survey of empirical research on the political economy of trade policy, which covers in greater detail the studies described below.

Goldberg and Maggi regressed the product of this variable and the import demand elasticity on the ratio of output to imports in the industry and on this same variable interacted with a dummy variable indicating whether the industry was politically organized or not in 1983. A politically organized industry was defined as one with Political Action Committees that spent more than a threshold fraction of industry revenues on campaign contributions. The model predicts a positive sign in this regression for the coefficient on the product of the dummy variable and the ratio of sales to imports, a negative sign for the coefficient on the ratio variable alone, and a positive sign for the sum of these two coefficients. Goldberg and Maggi found this pattern to be borne out in the data. Moreover, when they added additional regressors chosen from among those that are often included in empirical models of the structure of U.S. protection, they found that these additional regressors lack any explanatory power. Importantly, they note that previous findings of a positive relationship between protection and the import penetration ratio (the ratio of imports to domestic production plus imports) are misleading. The model in Chapter 4 suggests that this relationship ought to be different in industries that are politically organized than in industries that are not. The regressions of Goldberg and Maggi confirm this prediction. Previous empirical researchers have not made any such distinction, however. This means that their estimated relationship is misspecified and difficult to interpret.

The regression coefficients estimated by Goldberg and Maggi allowed them to compute estimates of the structural parameters of the model— specifically, the weight placed by the policy maker on campaign contributions and the fraction of the population that is represented by an interest group. They estimate that the policy maker attaches between 50 and 70 times as much weight on aggregate welfare as on contributions and that between 84 and 88 percent of the population is represented by an interest group. These findings are troubling, because the figures seem implausibly high.

A closely related study was conducted by Gawande and Bandyopadhyay (2000). They, too, used the coverage ratio for non-tariff barriers as a proxy for industry protection, but they identified politically organized industries somewhat differently. They considered as organized those industries in which there has been a positive relationship between PAC contributions and trade flows.

There are two major differences between the Gawande-Bandyopadhyay study and the Goldberg-Maggi study. First, Gawande and Bandyopadhyay extended the model of tariff formation to allow for conflict between importers of intermediate inputs and producers of these goods. Second, they used the model to estimate not only the determinants of trade protection but also the determinants of industry contributions.

Like Goldberg and Maggi, Gawande and Bandyopadhyay find support for the theory's predictions that organized industries with high ratios of output to imports will enjoy greater protection than those with low ratios, and that the comparison runs the other way around for industries that are not active in influence seeking. Their extended theory also predicts a positive link between the rate of protection afforded the producer of a final good and the rate that applies to intermediate inputs. This prediction, too, is supported by the data.

In their investigation of the pattern of campaign contributions, Gawande and Bandyopadhyay find that PAC spending rises with the size of the deadweight loss that results from protection of the industry, and rises with the share of an industry's output that is used by downstream industries with political representation. Both of these findings accord well with the theory. The authors also fail to find a significant role for a number of additional variables in explaining the pattern of protection, although industries with high concentration ratios do seem to fare especially well in the political game. As with the Goldberg-Maggi study, some of the parameter values computed by Gawande and Bandyopadhyay have implausible magnitudes, even if they do have the predicted signs.

Mitra, Thomakos, and Ulubaşoğlu (2002) have examined the pattern of protection in Turkey for a number of different years between 1983 and 1990. They use not only coverage ratios to measure industry protection, but also the nominal and effective rates of tariff protection. With their several years of data, they are able to exploit panel data techniques in estimating the model and to compare protective rates across different political regimes. Lacking data on campaign contributions, these authors classify sectors as organized or not based on whether they are members of the Turkish Industrialists and Business Association.

Like the others, these authors find support for the model in the sign pattern of the coefficient estimates. Moreover, the weight that the policy maker places on aggregate welfare compared to contributions is estimated to be much greater during times of democracy than in times of military dictatorship. The fraction of the population that belongs to an interest group is estimated to be lower in a regime of democracy. This finding supports a prediction of Mitra (1999), who extended the model of Chapter 4 to allow endogenous formation of interest groups. Mitra showed that fewer groups will organize when the policy maker's taste for contributions declines, as there is less to be gained from influence seeking.

A further study conducted along similar lines is McCalman's (2002) investigation of the pattern of protection in Australia. McCalman used industry tariff rates for Australia covering the period from the late 1960s to the early 1990s. The author was particularly interested to see if the political economic approach could explain the sharp decline in rates of protection that Australia has witnessed during this period. He argues that trade liberalization has reflected a marked increase in the fraction of individuals represented by organized interest groups and a secular increase in the weight that politicians in Australia attach to aggregate welfare.

Finally, Gawande, Krishna, and Robbins (2001) have extended the model of Chapter 4 to allow for contributions by foreign interest groups. A prediction of the extended model is that protection should be lower in industries in which a foreign organized group is active in seeking to influence U.S. trade policy than in industries in which this is not the case. Using a recently compiled data set on foreign lobbying presence in the United States, the authors find confirmation of this prediction and broad support for the extended theory. Thus, foreign interest groups do seem to play a significant role in American trade politics.

In a different vein, Gawande, Sanguinetti, and Bohara (2001) have assessed empirically some of the predictions of the model presented in Chapter 7 about the pattern of industry exclusions from a preferential trade agreement. Using data from the Mercosur trade agreement between Argentina, Brazil, Paraguay, and Uruguay, the authors find support for the model's prediction that exclusions will go to politically organized industries that have high ratios of domestic output to imports and low import demand elasticities. The authors conclude that a trade agreement between Argentina and Brazil would not have been possible but for the exclusions and that the excluded industries were chosen primarily to generate political support for the agreement in Argentina.

Finally, Branstetter and Feenstra (1999) have used the framework of Chapter 8 as a basis for studying the inter-provincial patterns of direct foreign investment in China. They find that the parsimonious model of the political economy can explain much of the variation between provinces in flows of direct foreign investment. Their estimates indicate that the Chinese government places a weight on consumer welfare in its objective function that is only half as large as the weight it places on the profits of state-owned enterprises.

Although much remains to be done in squaring the theories with the evidence, the results to date are encouraging. It seems that a parsimonious model of the political forces that shape trade policy yields predictions that are broadly consistent with observed policies in a number of different countries at different times and under different political regimes. Apparently, some features of reality are missing from the models, because the observed rates of protection tend to be lower than what would be predicted by the theories for reasonable parameters describing the policy maker's objective function and the fraction of the population that is represented in the political contest. Perhaps the observed

barriers reflect the fruits of trade negotiations, which are predicted by
the model of Chapter 5 but which have played little role in the empirical research to date. In any case, we feel vindicated in our thinking that
policy makers can be modeled as maximizing agents, and that attempts
to understand the incentives they face can give rise to reasonable predictions about policy outcomes.

References

Bernheim, B. Douglas, and Whinston, Michael D. (1986). Menu auctions, resource allo-
cation, and economic influence. *Quarterly Journal of Economics* 101 (February): 1–31.
Bhagwati, Jagdish N. (1987). Quid pro quo DFI and VIEs: A political-economy theoretic
analysis. *International Economic Journal* 1 (spring): 1–14.
Branstetter, Lee, and Feenstra, Robert C. (1999). Trade and FDI in China. Working Paper
No. 7100. National Bureau of Economic Research.
Findlay, Ronald, and Wellisz, Stanislaw. (1982). Endogenous tariffs and the political economy
of trade restrictions and welfare. In Jagdish Bhagwati, ed., *Import Competition and Response*
(Chicago: University of Chicago Press for the National Bureau of Economic Research).
Gawande, Kishore, and Bandyopadhyay, Usree (2000). Is protection for sale? A test of the
Grossman-Helpman theory of endogenous protection. *Review of Economics and Statistics*
89 (March): 139–152.
Gawande, Kishore, and Krishna, Pravin (2002). The political economy of trade policy:
Empirical approaches. In James Harrigan, ed., *Handbook of International Trade* (Oxford
and Malden, Mass.: Blackwell Publishers).
Gawande, Kishore, Krishna, Pravin, and Robbins, Michael (2001). Foreign lobbies and U.S.
trade policy. University of New Mexico, Manuscript.
Gawande, Kishore, Sanguinetti, Pablo, and Bohara, Alok K. (2001). Exclusions for sale: Evi-
dence on the Grossman-Helpman theory of free trade agreements. University of New
Mexico, Manuscript.
Goldberg, Pinelopi K., and Maggi, Giovanni (1999). Protection for sale: An empirical
investigation. *American Economic Review* 89 (December): 833–850.
Hillman, Arye L. (1982). Declining industries and political support protectionist motives.
American Economic Review 72 (December): 1180–1187.
Magee, Stephen P., Brock, William A., and Young, Leslie (1989). *Black hole tariffs and endoge-
nous policy theory: Political economy in general equilibrium* (London: Cambridge University
Press).
Mayer, Wolfgang (1984). Endogenous tariff formation. *American Economic Review* 74
(December): 970–985.
McCalman, Philip (2002). Protection for sale and trade liberalization: An empirical inves-
tigation. *Review of International Economics*, forthcoming.
Mitra, Devashish (1999). Endogenous lobby formation and endogenous protection: A
long-run model of trade policy determination. *American Economic Review* 89 (December):
1116–1134.
Mitra, Devashish, Thomakos, Dimitrios D., and Ulubaşoğlu, Mehmet A. (2002). Protection
for sale in a developing country: Democracy versus dictatorship. *Review of Economics and
Statistics*, forthcoming.
Peltzman, Sam (1976). Towards a more general theory of regulation. *Journal of Law and
Economics* 19 (August): 211–240.
Stigler, George J. (1971). The theory of economic regulation. *Bell Journal of Economics and
Management Science* 2 (spring): 3–21.

Part One

Instruments of Influence

One

Common Agency and Coordination: General Theory and Application to Government Policy Making

1 Introduction

Common agency is a multilateral relationship in which several principals simultaneously try to influence the actions of an agent. Such situations occur frequently, particularly in the political processes that generate economic policies. For example, legislators respond to many diverse pressures, including those from voters, contributors, and party officials. Administrative agencies, formally responsible to the lawmakers, are in practice influenced by the courts, the media, and various interest and

By Avinash Dixit, Gene M. Grossman, and Elhanan Helpman. Originally published in *Journal of Political Economy* 105 (August 1997): 752–769. Copyright © 1997 by the University of Chicago Press. Reprinted with permission. We thank Timothy Besley, Stephen Coate, Chaim Fershtman, Giovanni Maggi, David Pines, and a referee for their comments on earlier versions of this paper and the National Science Foundation and the Israel-U.S. Binational Science Foundation for financial support.

advocacy groups. In the European Union, several sovereign governments deal with a common policy-making body in Brussels. And in the United States, the devolution of economic power to the states and localities may give governments at these levels the standing of principals in relation to the federal government.

Information asymmetries are important in a common agency just as in an agency with a single principal. However, even with complete information, the existence of multiple principals introduces the new issues of whether they can achieve an outcome that is efficient for the group of players (the principals and the agent together) and how the available surplus gets divided among players. Bernheim and Whinston (1986) show that a noncooperative menu auction among the principals does have an efficient equilibrium. Their model has found many applications, including the study of lobbying for tariffs (Grossman and Helpman [1994]) and for consumer and producer taxes and subsidies (Dixit [1996]).

However, the Bernheim-Whinston model assumes quasi-linear preferences, so monetary transfers are equivalent to transferable utility among the principals and their common agent. This is usual and acceptable in the partial equilibrium analysis of industrial organization for which the Bernheim-Whinston model was originally designed, but it is generally inappropriate in most other economic settings, which require a more general equilibrium analysis. In models of economic policy, whether normative or positive, the most important drawback of quasi linearity is that it gives incomplete or implausible answers to distributional questions. For example, consider a policy maker who has a Benthamite (additive) social welfare function as part of his objective. Then since quasi linearity implies constant marginal utilities of income, the policy maker can have no concern for distribution per se. In reality, leaders do often care about income inequality. Next, in the common agency framework of recent political economy models, where the politically organized interest groups are the principals and the government is the agent, the government's implied objective is a weighted sum of utilities in which favored or organized groups get a higher weight. Then a government that has access to efficient means of transfer will drive the less favored or unorganized groups down to their minimum subsistence utility levels, whereas distribution among the favored or organized groups will be indeterminate; both features are unrealistic. (See Dixit [1996] for further discussion of this.) Finally, quasi linearity makes the agent's actions independent of the distribution of payoffs among the principals.[1] In short, the assumption of quasi linearity

---

[1] Note the parallel with the Coase theorem, where under quasi-linear utility (no income effects on the activities in question) resource allocation is independent of distribution.

makes the model unsuitable for analyzing distribution and transfer policies that are of the essence in public finance and political economy.

In most economic applications, money is indeed transferable, but the players' payoffs are not linear in money. The strict concavity of utilities in money incomes makes the levels of transfers in the political equilibrium determinate and nonextreme. In this paper we generalize the theory of common agency to handle such situations. We thereby hope to enlarge the scope of applicability of the theory.

We begin by characterizing equilibria for the general common agency problem. We proceed to show that, even when utility is not transferable across players, the agent's actions in equilibrium achieve an efficient outcome for the group of players (principals and agent). Of course, the actions are no longer independent of the distribution of payoffs among the players, and in equilibrium the two sets of magnitudes must be determined simultaneously.[2]

We then consider a political process of economic policy making in the common agency framework. A subset of all individuals is allowed to lobby the government and promise contributions in return for policy favors. The government cares for social welfare defined over the utilities of all individuals (lobbying or not) and for its receipts from the lobbyists. The efficiency theorem then says that the government uses the available policy instruments in a Pareto-efficient manner.

To clarify the implications of our analysis, we apply the results to a positive model of the formation of tax policy. Our model is analogous to the familiar normative model of Diamond and Mirrlees (1971). The policy instruments we allow are commodity tax or subsidy policies and individualized lump-sum transfers, and the political process admits lobbying of the sort described above. Here the efficiency result implies that only the nondistorting lump-sum transfers are used in the political equilibrium, not consumption or production taxes or subsidies. However, the game of lobbying for transfers turns into a prisoners' dilemma for the lobbyists. Indeed, under mild additional assumptions, we find that the government captures all the gains that exist in the common agency relationship. This suggests that if the lobbies could commit ex ante to a "constitution" for lobbying, they would all agree not to lobby for lump-sum transfers. This opens the way for the use of economically inferior instruments such as production subsidies, with an attendant violation of production efficiency in the political equilibrium, contrary to an important general feature of the normative optimum (Diamond and Mirrlees [1971]).

[2] The parallel with the Coase theorem or the core with nontransferable utility should again be apparent. However, we should stress that ours is an equilibrium of a noncooperative game, not a cooperative solution concept.

2 General Theory

Consider the following problem. There is a set L of principals. For each $i \in L$, principal i has continuous preferences $U^i(\mathbf{a}, c_i)$, where the vector $\mathbf{a}$ denotes the agent's action and the scalar c_i denotes principal i's payment to the agent. Each principal's preference function is declining in his payment to the agent. The agent's continuous preference function is $G(\mathbf{a}, \mathbf{c})$, where $\mathbf{c}$ is the vector of the principals' payments. The function G is increasing in each component of $\mathbf{c}$. Thus, for any given action, each principal dislikes making contributions and the agent likes receiving them; their preferences with regard to actions are not restricted in general, but we shall place some specific restrictions for particular results below. We refer to the values of the functions $U^i(\mathbf{a}, c_i)$ and $G(\mathbf{a}, \mathbf{c})$ as the utility levels of the principals and the agent, respectively.

Principal i can choose a payment function $C_i(\mathbf{a})$ from a set $\mathscr{C}_i$, and the agent can choose $\mathbf{a}$ from a set $\mathscr{A}$. The sets $\mathscr{C}_i$ and $\mathscr{A}$ describe feasibility and institutional constraints. For example, from feasibility considerations, $\mathscr{C}_i$ may consist only of functions that provide principal i with a nonnegative income. Or it may consist only of nonnegative functions, implying that the principal can pay the agent but not the reverse. This would describe an institutional constraint. And it may contain only functions with an upper bound on payments, thereby describing another institutional constraint. Similarly, $\mathscr{A}$ may describe institutional or feasibility constraints on the actions of the agent. If, for example, an element of $\mathbf{a}$ equals one plus an ad valorem tax rate, then feasibility requires $\mathscr{A}$ to contain only nonnegative vectors.

Throughout, we maintain the following assumption on the sets of feasible payment functions.

ASSUMPTION 1. Let $C_i \in \mathscr{C}_i$. Then $C_i(\mathbf{a}) \geq 0$ for all $\mathbf{a} \in \mathscr{A}$, and every payment function C_i^* that satisfies (i) $C_i^*(\mathbf{a}) \geq 0$ for all $\mathbf{a} \in \mathscr{A}$ and (ii) $C_i^*(\mathbf{a}) \leq C_i(\mathbf{a})$ for all $\mathbf{a} \in \mathscr{A}$ also belongs to $\mathscr{C}_i$.

Explanation. Payments from the principals to the agent have to be nonnegative, and if a payment function is feasible, all "smaller" payment functions are also feasible. This conforms to the requirements of most relevant economic applications.

2.1 Equilibrium

Our aim is to construct and study a concept of equilibrium for a two-stage game. In the second stage, the agent chooses an action optimally, given the payment functions of all the principals. In the first stage, each principal chooses a payment schedule, knowing that all the other principals are

simultaneously and noncooperatively choosing their own payment schedules and looking ahead to the response of the agent in the second stage.

We shall denote magnitudes pertaining to an equilibrium by the
superscript °. Since the game is noncooperative, we shall have to start with
a "candidate" for such an equilibrium and study the consequences of
allowing the strategies to deviate from this, one player at a time. For this
purpose we establish the following notation: $\mathbf{C}°(\mathbf{a})$ will denote the vector
of contributions with components $C_j°(\mathbf{a})$, for all $j \in L$; $(\{C_j°(\mathbf{a})\}_{j \neq i}, c)$ will
denote the vector in which the ith component is replaced by c, and all
the other components $j \neq i$ are held fixed at $C_j°(\mathbf{a})$. Sometimes c itself
may be the value of another payment function $C_i(\mathbf{a})$ for principal i.

We begin by defining the principals' best-response strategies.

DEFINITION 1. A payment function $C_i° \in \mathscr{C}_i$ and an action $\mathbf{a}_i° \in \mathscr{A}$ are
a best response of principal i to the payment functions $\{C_j°\}_{j \in L, j \neq i}$ of the
other principals if

$$\mathbf{a}_i° \in \underset{\mathbf{a} \in \mathscr{A}}{\mathrm{argmax}} \; G[\mathbf{a}, \mathbf{C}°(\mathbf{a})]$$

and there does not exist a payment $C_i \in \mathscr{C}_i$ and an action $\mathbf{a}_i \in \mathscr{A}$ such that
(i) $U^i[\mathbf{a}_i, C_i(\mathbf{a}_i)] > U^i[\mathbf{a}_i°, C_i°(\mathbf{a}_i°)]$ and (ii) $\mathbf{a}_i \in \mathrm{argmax}_{\mathbf{a} \in \mathscr{A}} \; G[\mathbf{a}, (\{C_j°(\mathbf{a})\}_{j \neq i},$
$C_i(\mathbf{a}))]$.

Explanation. The best-response calculation of principal i holds fixed the
simultaneously chosen strategies (payment functions) of all the other
principals at their candidate equilibrium positions but recognizes that in
the second stage the agent will optimize with respect to these payment
functions along with any deviated function proposed by principal i. If
principal i cannot find another feasible payment function that yields a
better outcome for him, taking into account the agent's anticipated
response, then the original candidate payment function $C_i°$ is a best
response for principal i to the candidate functions $C_j°$ of all the other principals. If the agent's best response is nonunique, we allow the principal
i to designate an action in the agent's set of best responses.

Next we define equilibrium. This is the standard definition of a subgame perfect Nash equilibrium for this two-stage game; in the case of
nonuniqueness mentioned just above, for equilibrium we require that all
principals be willing to designate the same action $\mathbf{a}°$.

DEFINITION 2. An equilibrium of the common agency problem consists
of a vector of feasible payment functions $\mathbf{C}° = \{C_i°\}_{i \in L}$ and a policy vector
$\mathbf{a}°$ such that, for every $i \in L$, the payment function $C_i°$ and action $\mathbf{a}°$ are
a best response of principal i to the payment functions $\{C_j°\}_{j \in L, j \neq i}$ of the
other principals.

The following result provides a characterization of an equilibrium.

Proposition 1. A vector of payment functions $\mathbf{C}^\circ = \{C_i^\circ\}_{i \in L}$ and a policy vector $\mathbf{a}^\circ$ constitute an equilibrium if and only if (i) $C_i^\circ \in \mathcal{C}_i$ for all $i \in L$; (ii) $\mathbf{a}^\circ = \text{argmax}_{a \in \mathcal{A}} G[\mathbf{a}, \mathbf{C}^\circ(\mathbf{a})]$; and (iii) for every $i \in L$,

$$[\mathbf{a}^\circ, C_i^\circ(\mathbf{a}^\circ)] \in \underset{(\mathbf{a}, \, c)}{\text{argmax}} \; U^i(\mathbf{a}, c) \tag{1}$$

subject to $\mathbf{a} \in \mathcal{A}$, $c = C_i(\mathbf{a})$ for some $C_i \in \mathcal{C}_i$, and

$$G[\mathbf{a}, (\{C_j^\circ(\mathbf{a})\}_{j \neq i}, c)] \geq \sup_{\mathbf{a}' \in \mathcal{A}} G[\mathbf{a}', (\{C_j^\circ(\mathbf{a}')\}_{j \neq i}, 0)]. \tag{2}$$

Explanation.[3] Observe that conditions (i) and (ii) must be satisfied by all payment schedules and actions that are best responses. Requirement (iii) is the key aspect of proposition 1: it focuses on the relationship between the agent and one of the principals and helps determine how the potential gains from this relationship get allocated between them in equilibrium.

Examine the situation from the perspective of principal i. He takes as given the strategies of all other principals $j \neq i$ and contemplates his own choice. He must provide the agent at least the level of utility that the agent could get from his outside option, namely by choosing a best response to the payment functions offered by all the other principals when principal i offers nothing. This is what constraint (2) expresses. Subject to this constraint, principal i can propose to the agent an action and a feasible payment that maximizes his own utility. That is the content of equation (1). Then proposition 1 says that such constrained maximization by each principal is equivalent to equilibrium as previously defined.

The intuition behind our result can be appreciated with the aid of Figure 1. Suppose for the sake of illustration that the action is a scalar. Curve $G_i G_i$ depicts combinations of the action $\mathbf{a}$ (on the horizontal axis) and payments c_i by principal i (on the vertical axis) that give the agent a fixed level of utility when the contribution functions of the other principals are given. The particular indifference curve shown in the figure depicts the highest welfare the agent can attain when principal i makes no contribution whatsoever (his payment function coincides with the horizontal axis); the agent then chooses the action associated with the point labeled A_{-i}. The shaded rectangle depicts the combinations of feasible actions and feasible payment levels (there is an upper bound on payments, payments must be nonnegative, and the action is bounded below and above). When the agent's option to take action A_{-i} is considered, the best the principal i can do is to design a payment schedule that induces the agent

---

[3] To conserve space, we provide here only verbal and intuitive explanations of the propositions; more formal proofs are in our working paper (Dixit, Grossman, and Helpman, [1996]).

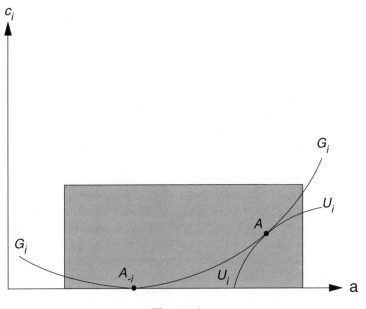

Figure 1

to choose a point in the shaded area that lies above or on the indifference curve $G_i G_i$. Suppose that the principal's welfare is increasing in the action. Then his indifference curves are upward sloping. In the event, he will choose the feasible point on the rising portion of $G_i G_i$ that gives the principal the highest welfare level, namely the tangency point A between his indifference curve $U_i U_i$ and $G_i G_i$. It is easy to see from the figure how the principal can construct a payment schedule that induces the agent to choose point A. For example, he might offer a schedule that coincides with the horizontal axis until some point to the right of A_{-i} and then rises to a tangency with $G_i G_i$ at A without ever crossing that curve.

Corollary to Proposition 1. Let $(\mathbf{C}^\circ, \mathbf{a}^\circ)$ be an equilibrium. Then, for each $i \in L$,

$$G[\mathbf{a}^\circ, \mathbf{C}^\circ(\mathbf{a}^\circ)] = \sup_{\mathbf{a} \in \mathscr{A}} G[\mathbf{a}, (\{C_j^\circ (\mathbf{a})\}_{j \neq i}, 0)].$$

Explanation. This says that the utility level of the agent in equilibrium is the same as what he would get if any one of the principals were to contribute zero whereas all others maintained their equilibrium payment *functions*, and the agent then chose his optimum action in response to this deviation. The intuition is implicit in our discussion of condition (iii) of the proposition.

Each principal must ensure that the agent gets a utility equal to his outside opportunity; it is not in the principal's interest to give the agent any more.

2.2 Truthful Equilibria

The model above can have multiple subgame perfect Nash equilibria, some of which can be inefficient. As in Bernheim and Whinston (1986), we now develop a refinement that selects equilibria that implement Pareto-efficient actions (the concept of Pareto efficiency is of course constrained by the set of available actions).

We consider equilibria that can arise when each principal offers the agent a payment function that is *truthful*. A truthful payment function for principal i rewards the agent for every change in the action that is exactly the amount of change in the principal's welfare, provided that the payment both before and after the change is strictly positive. In other words, the shape of the payment schedule mirrors the shape of the principal's indifference surface. Then the principal gets the same utility for all actions **a** that induce positive payments $C_i(\mathbf{a}) > 0$; the payment is just the compensating variation. We show that the common agency game has an equilibrium in which all the principals follow truthful strategies and that such an equilibrium is Pareto-efficient. We call such an equilibrium a *truthful equilibrium*.

Focus on truthful equilibria may seem restrictive but can be justified in several ways. First, for any set of feasible strategies of the $L - 1$ principals other than i, the set of best-response strategies for principal i contains a truthful payment function. Thus each principal bears essentially no cost from playing a truthful strategy, no matter what he expects from the other players. Then the result that an equilibrium in truthful strategies implements a Pareto-efficient action may make such strategies focal for the group of principals. Second, since the setting has no incomplete information, the players have "nothing to hide" and truthful strategies provide a simple device to achieve efficiency without any player conceding his right to grab as much as he can for himself.

Notice too that we do not restrict the space of feasible payment functions to truthful ones at the outset; in a truthful equilibrium, each principal's truthful strategy is a best response to his rivals even when the space of feasible payment functions is the larger one of assumption 1. Thus we have an equilibrium in the full sense, where the strategies happen to be truthful.

We now proceed to formalize the idea and the results.

DEFINITION 3. A payment function $C_i^T(\mathbf{a}, u_i^*)$ for principal i is *truthful* relative to the constant u_i^* if

$$C_i^T(\mathbf{a}, u_i^*) \equiv \min\{\bar{C}_i(\mathbf{a}), \max[0, \varphi_i(\mathbf{a}, u_i^*)]\} \text{ for all } \mathbf{a} \in \mathcal{A}, \qquad (3)$$

where φ_i is implicitly defined by $U^i[\mathbf{a}, \varphi_i(\mathbf{a}, u_i^*)] = u_i^*$ for all $\mathbf{a} \in \mathcal{A}$, and
$\bar{C}_i(\mathbf{a}) = \sup\{C_i(\mathbf{a}) \mid C_i \in \mathcal{C}_i\}$ for all $\mathbf{a} \in \mathcal{A}$.

Explanation. The definition of φ_i is the basic concept of the compensating variation. Equation (3) merely serves to ensure that the truthful payment function also satisfies the upper and lower bounds on feasible payments. Note that a competition in truthful strategies boils down to noncooperative choices of the constants $\{u_j^*\}_{j \in L}$, which determine the equilibrium payoffs of the principals.

Proposition 2. The best-response set of principal i to payment functions $\{C_j^\circ(\mathbf{a})\}_{j \in L, \; j \neq i}$ of the other principals contains a truthful payment function.

Explanation. The result can be illustrated in the aforementioned Figure 1. The principals other than i induce in the agent the indifference curve $G_i G_i$ with their payment offers. These offers might be truthful or not. In any event, the best-response set for principal i includes all payment functions that induce the action and contribution associated with point A. A truthful strategy in this set is the payment function that coincides with the horizontal axis from the origin until its intersection with $U_i U_i$ and coincides with $U_i U_i$ thereafter.

DEFINITION 4. A *truthful equilibrium* is an equilibrium in which all payment functions are truthful relative to the equilibrium welfare levels.

Proposition 3. Let $(\{C_i^T\}_{i \in L}, \mathbf{a}^\circ)$ be a truthful equilibrium in which u_i° is the equilibrium utility level of principal i, for all $i \in L$. Then $(\{u_i^\circ\}_{i \in L}, \mathbf{a}^\circ)$ is characterized by (i) $\mathbf{a}^\circ = \text{argmax}_{\mathbf{a} \in \mathcal{A}} \, G[\mathbf{a}, \{C_i^T(\mathbf{a}, u_i^\circ)\}_{i \in L}]$ and (ii) for every $i \in L$,

$$G[\mathbf{a}^\circ, \{C_i^T(\mathbf{a}^\circ, u_i^\circ)\}_{i \in L}] = \max_{\mathbf{a} \in \mathcal{A}} G[\mathbf{a}, (\{C_j^T(\mathbf{a}, u_i^\circ)\}_{j \neq i}, 0)].$$

Explanation. This is just a restatement of the corollary to proposition 1, for the case of truthful equilibria, and the explanation given above applies. The added advantage lies in actual use. If we tried to use that corollary to determine equilibria, we would have to solve the conditions simultaneously for all the payment *functions*, which is a complicated fixed-point problem and has a large multiplicity of solutions. The corresponding set of equations in proposition 3 involves the equilibrium utility *numbers*; therefore, they constitute a simpler simultaneous equation problem with solutions that are in general locally determinate and in applications often unique. We shall consider one such application in the next section.

Now we establish that an equilibrium in truthful strategies implements an efficient action.

Proposition 4. Let a policy vector $\mathbf{a}^\circ$ and a vector of payment functions $\mathbf{C}^\circ$ that are truthful with respect to the utility levels $u_i^\circ = U^i(\mathbf{a}^\circ, C_i^\circ(\mathbf{a}^\circ))$ constitute a truthful equilibrium. Then there do not exist an action $\mathbf{a}^*$ and a payment vector $\mathbf{c}^*$ such that the following conditions hold: (i) feasibility: $\mathbf{a}^* \in \mathcal{A}; 0 \le c_i^* \le \overline{C}_i(\mathbf{a}^*)$ for all $i \in L$; and (ii) Pareto superiority:

$$G(\mathbf{a}^*, \mathbf{c}^*) \ge G[\mathbf{a}^\circ, \mathbf{C}^\circ(\mathbf{a}^\circ)],$$

$$U^i(\mathbf{a}^*, c_i^*) \ge U^i[\mathbf{a}^\circ, C_i^\circ(\mathbf{a}^\circ)] \text{ for all } i \in L,$$

with at least one strict inequality.

Explanation. Suppose that such an action $\mathbf{a}^*$ and payment vector $\mathbf{c}^*$ did exist. Since principal i must be at least as well off with $\mathbf{a}^*$ and c_i^* as in the equilibrium and since his equilibrium payment schedule is truthful, c_i^* can be no greater than the payment elicited by the action $\mathbf{a}^*$ in the equilibrium schedule; that is, $c_i^* \le C_i^T(\mathbf{a}^*, u_i^\circ)$. Therefore, the agent, who has a positive marginal utility of money, cannot strictly prefer $\mathbf{a}^*$ and $\mathbf{c}^*$ to the equilibrium values, because the combination of $\mathbf{a}^*$ and $\{C_i^T(\mathbf{a}^*, u_i^\circ)\}_{i \in L}$ was available and yet he chose $\mathbf{a}^\circ$ and $\mathbf{C}^\circ(\mathbf{a}^\circ)$. It follows that it must be some principal i who strictly prefers $\mathbf{a}^*$ and c_i^* to the equilibrium action and equilibrium payment. But then this principal has not obeyed requirement (iii) of proposition 1: he should have asked the agent to choose $\mathbf{a}^*$ by offering c_i^*. The agent would be happy to do this because he would also get the truthful contributions $C_j^T(\mathbf{a}^*, u_j^\circ)$, which are greater than or equal to c_j^* by the argument above, from all the other principals j. It follows that no such $(\mathbf{a}^*, \mathbf{c}^*)$ exists.

2.3 Quasi-Linear Preferences

The equilibrium above can be pinned down further when all players' preferences are linear in the payments. Specifically, the action is independent of the distribution in this case.

Corollary 1 to Proposition 4. Let the preference functions $(\{U^i\}_{i \in L}, G)$ have the quasi-linear form

$$U^i(\mathbf{a}, c_i) = \omega^i(\mathbf{a}) - \kappa_i c_i \quad \text{for all } i \in L$$

and

$$G(\mathbf{a}, \mathbf{c}) = \Gamma(\mathbf{a}) + \gamma \sum_{i \in L} c_i.$$

Consider a truthful equilibrium in which the action is $\mathbf{a}^\circ$ and all payments are in the interior: $0 < C_i^\circ(\mathbf{a}^\circ) < \bar{C}_i(\mathbf{a}^\circ)$. Then

$$\mathbf{a}^\circ = \underset{\mathbf{a} \in \mathscr{A}}{\operatorname{argmax}} \ \frac{\Gamma(\mathbf{a})}{\gamma} + \sum_{i \in L} \frac{\omega_i(\mathbf{a})}{\kappa_i}.$$

Explanation. With quasi-linear preferences, the equilibrium action maximizes a weighted sum of gross welfare levels of the principals and the agent. This result has been useful in applications to political economy, such as in Grossman and Helpman (1994). There, the agent is a government that sets a vector of tariff policies, and the principals are interest groups representing owners of sector-specific factors of production. The government's objective is assumed to be linear in the aggregate welfare of voters and the total of campaign contributions collected from special interests. The corollary predicts a structure of protection that maximizes a simple weighted sum of the welfare of voters and interest group members.

3 Application to Government Policy Making

As we noted in the Introduction, common agency arises frequently in the political processes that generate economic policies. The policy makers often can be viewed as an agent and some or all of their constituents as principals. Principals can "lobby" the policy makers by promising payments in return for policies, within some prescribed limits on available policies and feasible gifts. The payments may take the form of illicit bribes or, more typically, implicit (and therefore legal) offers of campaign support. In such settings, it may be natural to think of the government as having an objective function with social welfare and the total of contribution receipts as arguments. The government might care about social welfare for ethical reasons, or it may want to provide a high standard of living to enhance its reelection prospects, to keep the populace sufficiently happy to prevent riots, and so forth. Contributions likewise might enter the government's objective because they affect its reelection chances or merely as utility of the governing elites' private consumption. Accordingly, we suppose $G(\mathbf{a}, \mathbf{c}) = g(\mathbf{u}, c)$, where $\mathbf{u}$ is the vector of all the individuals' utilities and $c = \sum_{i=1}^{n} c_i$ is the aggregate contribution received by the government. We assume that g is strictly increasing and strictly quasi-concave in all its arguments.[4]

Let L be the set of individuals who can lobby the government for special favors. We leave L exogenous: some individuals may have personal

---

[4] A special case frequent in economic models is one in which the individual utilities are channeled through a social welfare function of the Bergson-Samuelson type:

$$w = W[u_1(\mathbf{a}, c_1), u_2(\mathbf{a}, c_2), \ldots, u_n(\mathbf{a}, c_n)]$$

and $G(\mathbf{a}, \mathbf{c}) = g(w, c)$. But the more general form $g(\mathbf{u}, c)$ will suffice for our purpose.

connections to the politicians, or some groups of individuals may be able to solve the free-rider problem of collective political action while others cannot.[5] Then $C_i(\mathbf{a}) \equiv 0$ for $i \notin L$. For $i \in L$, the upper limit on feasible contributions, $\bar{C}_i(\mathbf{a})$, is implicitly defined by $U^i[\mathbf{a}, \bar{C}_i(\mathbf{a})] = \underline{u}_i$, where $\underline{u}_i$ is the lowest or subsistence utility level for individual i.

Proposition 4 has strong implications for the outcome of this lobbying game.

Corollary 2 to Proposition 4. Let the agent's preferences be given by $G(\mathbf{a}, \mathbf{c}) = g(\mathbf{u}, c)$, where $c = \Sigma_{i=1}^{n} c_i$. Let a set $L \subset \{1, 2, \ldots, n\}$ of individuals offer payment schedules $\{C_i(\mathbf{a})\}_{i \in L}$, whereas $C_i(\mathbf{a}) \equiv 0$ for $i \notin L$. Finally, let a policy vector $\mathbf{a}^{\circ}$ and a vector of payment functions $\mathbf{C}^{\circ}$ that are truthful with respect to the utility levels $u_i^{\circ} = u_i[\mathbf{a}^{\circ}, C_i^{\circ}(\mathbf{a}^{\circ})]$ for $i \in L$ constitute a truthful equilibrium in which $u_i^{\circ} = u_i(\mathbf{a}^{\circ}, 0)$ for $i \notin L$. Then there exists no other policy vector $\mathbf{a}' \in \mathcal{A}$ such that $u_i(\mathbf{a}', c_i^{\circ}) \geq u_i^{\circ}$ for all $i \in \{1, 2, \ldots, n\}$, with strict inequality holding for some i.

Explanation. The corollary says that, even under the pressure of lobbying from a subset of organized special interests, a government that has some concern for social welfare will make Pareto-efficient choices from the set of feasible policies. With truthful payment schedules, the government has an incentive to collect its tributes efficiently. If the government's objective weighs positively the well-being of all members in society, then efficiency for the government and lobbies translates into Pareto efficiency for the polity as a whole.[6]

It is important to distinguish between efficiency in the sense of the earlier proposition 4 and that of its corollary 2. In the former, only the welfare of the active players in the game (the lobbies and the government) is considered. This leaves open the possibility that when there are other individuals in the background but they are not strategic players (principals in the lobbying game), inefficiencies in their welfares can remain. In corollary 2 to proposition 4, the government's objective function gives some weight to the welfare levels of such individuals, and therefore, for the given level of its receipts from the lobbies, it implements an action that is efficient for all individuals, whether lobbying or not.

The implications of our result can be seen most clearly in a simple and familiar economic application. We consider now a positive analogue to

---

[5] In reality, most lobbying is undertaken by such coalitions. If a group of individuals can arrange an optimal internal transfer scheme, it can be regarded as a Samuelsonian aggregated "individual" in our model.

[6] It also follows from proposition 4 that there exists no vector of policies $\mathbf{a}$ and contributions $\mathbf{c}$ that would leave the government and all lobbyers and nonlobbyers at least as well off as in the political equilibrium, and some individual or the government strictly better off. In this sense, the political outcome achieves second-best efficiency given the set of available policy instruments.

COMMON AGENCY AND COORDINATION

the normative theory of taxes and transfers à la Diamond and Mirrlees (1971). Our analysis extends theirs to situations in which the government cares not only about aggregate welfare but also about the campaign contributions it can amass.[7]

To simplify the exposition, we suppose that the economy is small and open. Let $\mathbf{p}^w$ denote the exogenous vector of world prices and $\mathbf{q}$ and $\mathbf{p}$ the price vectors faced by the domestic consumers and producers, respectively. Then $\mathbf{q} - \mathbf{p}^w$ is the implied vector of consumer tax rates (negative components are subsidies) and $\mathbf{p} - \mathbf{p}^w$ the implied vector of producer subsidy rates (negative components are taxes). The government's tax and subsidy policies are therefore equivalent to choosing $\mathbf{q}$ and $\mathbf{p}$. The government can also make lump-sum transfers or levy lump-sum taxes on any or all individuals; let $\mathbf{t}$, with components t_i, denote the vector of such transfers (negative components are taxes). We leave out any other government activities for simplicity.

There are several firms labeled $f \in M$ with profit functions $\psi^f(\mathbf{p})$. Individual i owns an exogenous share ω_{if} of firm f and therefore gets profit income $\pi^i(\mathbf{p}) = \Sigma_{f \in M} \omega_{if} \psi^f(\mathbf{p})$. Let c_i denote the lobbying payment of individual i to the government, for $i \in L$. Set $c_i \equiv 0$ for $i \notin L$. Then individual i's income is $I_i \equiv \pi^i(\mathbf{p}) + t_i - c_i$, and we can write the resulting indirect utility function as $u_i = V^i(\mathbf{q}, I_i)$. We assume that each V^i is strictly increasing and strictly concave in I_i. These lump-sum incomes I_i do not have to be nonnegative because individuals have additional incomes from sales of factor services. There is some other lower bound to the I_i.[8] However, we assume an "Inada condition" that the marginal utility of income $V_I^i(\mathbf{q}, I_i)$ goes to infinity as this lower bound is approached; therefore, the bound is never hit and we ignore it in what follows.

We should emphasize that the payments made by the lobbies do not enter into the government's tax and transfer budget. This budget reflects the "public" or policy part of the government's activities. The lobbies' payments go into a separate "private" or political kitty. They might be used by the governing party for its reelection campaign or by a governing dictator for his own consumption.

We can now regard the government as choosing $\mathbf{a} = (\mathbf{q}, \mathbf{p}, \mathbf{t})$ to maximize $g(\mathbf{u}, c)$ subject to the two (public and political) budget constraints. This puts the problem in the framework of our model of government policy making. Corollary 2 to proposition 4 tells us that the equilibrium action achieves a Pareto-efficient outcome in an auxiliary problem in which the lobbies' payments are held fixed at their equilibrium levels. In the auxiliary problem, the government's choice is the standard nor-

---

[7] The model is laid out and analyzed in greater detail in our working paper (Dixit et al. [1996]).
[8] This limit may depend on the price vector $\mathbf{q}$ and is defined by the condition $V^i(\mathbf{q}, I_i) = \underline{u}_i$, where $\underline{u}_i$ is the lowest or subsistence utility level.

mative optimal tax and transfer problem, where we know that if lump-sum transfers are available, distorting commodity taxes and subsidies will not be used. Therefore, we have shown that the political equilibrium will also preserve $\mathbf{q} = \mathbf{p} = \mathbf{p}^w$ and use only the lump-sum transfers $\mathbf{t}$ for the two purposes of eliciting contributions from the lobbies and of meeting the government's concern for the welfare of the non-lobbying individuals.

Before the reader forms the belief that we have established the universal efficiency of the political process of tax policy, we should warn that the story is not yet complete. It remains to examine the distribution of gains between the lobbies and the government in the political equilibrium; that analysis may cast doubt on the efficient equilibrium as a description of political reality.

Condition (ii) of proposition 3 helps us to calculate the individuals' utility levels $u°$ and the government's receipts from the lobbies. The condition says that the government's utility in equilibrium should equal what it would get by responding optimally to the equilibrium payment schedules of all the lobbies except one that pays nothing. The equations this generates are to be solved simultaneously.

Using our efficiency result, we set $\mathbf{p} = \mathbf{q} = \mathbf{p}^\omega$ and omit these arguments from the various functions. Let $U^i(I_i) = V^i(\mathbf{p}^\omega, I_i)$. Define $\pi_i = \pi^i(\mathbf{p}^\omega)$, and think of them as the individuals' endowments. Finally, let $\pi \equiv \Sigma_{i \in N} \pi_i$ for the total endowment in the economy, and assume that it is positive. Then the nonlobbyers' incomes are $\pi_i + t_i$, and the lobbies' truthful contribution schedules are $C_i(t_i, u_i°) = \max[\pi_i + t_i - E^i(u_i°), 0]$, where the expenditure functions E^i are inverses to the utility functions U^i.

We shall find that when there are two or more lobbies, any one of them has no economic power in its agency relationship with the government. Indeed, the effect is exactly as though the government could rob the official budget directly for its political kitty, without having to rely on any lobbies or their contributions at all. If the government is given this much power, the only reason it would give anything to any group is that it cares directly about social welfare as well as about its own consumption. In other words, such a "partially benevolent dictator" government would solve the following maximization problem.

Problem A. $\max_{I, c} g(U^1(I_1), \ldots, U^n(I_n), c)$ subject to $c \geq 0$ and $\Sigma_{i \in N} I_i + c \leq \pi$.

Given our assumptions, namely that all the functions $U^i(I_i)$ are strictly increasing and strictly concave and that the function $g(\mathbf{u}, c)$ is strictly increasing and quasi-concave, this problem has a unique solution. Because we have assumed the Inada condition that the marginal utility of each individual goes to infinity as the utility goes to its subsistence level, we do not need to impose any lower bounds on the I_i.

We state the equivalence between the political equilibrium and the choice of this partially benevolent dictator in the following result.

Proposition 5. Assume that the set L has at least two members. Then the unique solution of problem A yields a truthful equilibrium. Moreover, if all the functions $U^i(\cdot)$ and $g(\cdot)$ are differentiable, then any truthful equilibrium solves problem A (and is therefore unique).

Explanation. The government's power in the agency relationship derives from the fact that if any one lobby were to withdraw from its activity, the government would get exactly the same total contribution from its dealings with the others. It would simply cut the transfer to the deviant lobby by an amount equal to that lobby's contribution and redirect the funds to some other lobbies. Since these others all have truthful payment schedules, the government would receive back the entire amount of the redirected transfers as additional contributions from them. Therefore, all the lobbies are perfect substitutes in the eyes of the government as sources of funding, and so no one of them can bring harm to the government by withholding its tribute. The government implicitly wields the credible threat of cutting any one lobby out of the deal at no cost to itself.[9]

An alternative way to think of this is that truthful schedules set up a Bertrand-like competition among the lobbies. In the resulting equilibrium, they outbid each other for every dollar of government transfer, to the point at which everyone is bidding the full dollar.

The lobbies fare no better than they would if they were nonlobbyers but some others were active in lobbying. This is a terrible outcome for the lobbies, and each one could achieve the same result *unilaterally* by renouncing its lobbying activities. However, such unilateral renunciation by *all* lobbies would not be an equilibrium because starting from such a position, each one would want to lobby; that is the essence of a prisoners' dilemma!

Note that our result requires that there be at least two lobbies: were one to deviate, the government could find a substitute with which to "work a deal." If there is only one lobby, then were that lobby to deviate, the government could not bestow its transfer on another contributor and get it back dollar for dollar. The best the government could do would be to spread its transfer around to maximize social welfare, which cannot be better or else it would already be doing so in the equilibrium. In short, a single lobby captures all the surplus inherent in its relationship

---

[9] This is not an explicit threat in the game-theoretic sense because the government makes no prior move to set up its contingent response; the right response happens to be its ex post optimal action.

with the government.[10] But as soon as there are two or more lobbies, each one loses all power and the government captures the entire surplus in the form of contributions.

We can also see that the existence of lump-sum transfers is essential for this argument. If all the available redistributive instruments were distortionary, then to compensate fully for the contributions lost when one lobby deviates, the government must increase the levels of the instruments favoring the other lobbies. This causes greater and greater marginal distortion and so is costly to the government. The extra cost is the power that each potential deviator has in its dealings with the government, and the equivalent variation of this extra distortion equals the amount of surplus the lobby can extract in equilibrium. This is illustrated by Grossman and Helpman (1994) for tariffs and by Dixit (1996) for production subsidies.

Thus, while our result that more efficient instruments are used in equilibrium when they are available supports the argument of Becker (1983), the distributional implications of the two models are totally different. In Becker's paper (pp. 385–86), the replacement of a less efficient by a more efficient instrument generally allows the lobbies to achieve the same or better results using less resources in exerting political pressure. Therefore, they unanimously favor the more efficient instrument. In our model, the government's choice of action achieves efficiency because the government attaches some weight to social welfare. The lobbying groups actually fare poorly in their competition when more efficient instruments are used. Each of these groups gets only the utility it would get if it were not lobbying, but some other group or groups were lobbying, which is even worse than what it gets if no one lobbies at all.

Finally, compare two alternative policy regimes, one with nondistorting lump-sum taxes or transfers and the other with distorting transaction-based taxes or subsidies. The political equilibrium in the former has more total output, which should translate into higher market incomes for everyone. But in this regime, the government gets all the surplus that can be extracted by taxing the unorganized groups in society. In the other regime, all groups generally get lower market incomes, but the organized interests capture some of the surplus from their political activity. It is conceivable that on balance the organized interests fare better in the latter regime, so they would unanimously endorse a constitutional rule restricting the government to inefficient redistributive policies. Thus our model suggests a new way by which distorting policies might emerge

---

[10] The single lobby derives its power from its assumed ability to make take-it-or-leave-it offers. If the lobby and the government instead were to negotiate over the size of the tribute, then each would share in the surplus from their bilateral relationship.

as a political equilibrium.[11] This seems an interesting question for future research.

[11]Hammond (1979) argues that individualized lump-sum trannsfers are infeasible for informational reasons. See also Coate and Morris (1995) for an informational reason and Dixit and Londregan (1995) for a commitment reason why the political process uses inefficient instruments.

References

Becker, Gary S. (1983). A theory of compensation among pressure groups for political influence. *Quarterly Journal of Economics* 98 (August): 371–400.

Bernheim, B. Douglas, and Whinston, Michael D. (1986). Menu auctions, resource allocation, and economic influence. *Quarterly Journal of Economics* 101 (February): 1–31.

Coate, Stephen, and Morris, Stephen (1995). On the form of transfers to special interests. *Journal of Political Economy* 103 (December): 1210–1235.

Diamond, Peter A., and Mirrlees, James A. (1971). Optimal taxation and public production. 2 pts. *American Economic Review* 61 (March): 8–27; (June): 261–278.

Dixit, Avinash K. (1996). Special-interest lobbying and endogenous commodity taxation. *Eastern Economic Journal* 22 (fall): 375–388.

Dixit, Avinash K., Grossman, Gene M., and Helpman, Elhanan (1996). Common agency and coordination: General theory and application to tax policy. Discussion paper no. 1436. Centre for Economic Policy Research.

Dixit, Avinash K., and Londregan, John B. (1995). Redistributive politics and economic efficiency. *American Political Science Review* 89 (December): 856–866.

Grossman, Gene M., and Helpman, Elhanan (1994). Protection for sale. *American Economic Review* 84 (September): 833–850.

Hammond, Peter J. (1979). Straightforward individual incentive compatibility in large economies. *Review of Economic Studies* 46 (April): 263–282.

*Two*_____

Electoral Competition and
Special Interest Politics

1 Introduction

Special interest groups appear to wield considerable influence over
public policy in many representative democracies. The trade policies of
many industrialized countries favor vested interests in the clothing,
textile, and heavy industries. Their agricultural policies give various forms

By Gene M. Grossman and Elhanan Helpman. Originally published in *Review of Economic
Studies* 63 (April 1996): 265–286. Copyright © 1996 by *Review of Economic Studies*. Reprinted
with permission. We thank Tim Besley, Avinash Dixit, Ian Jewitt, Torsten Persson, and two
anonymous referees for helpful comments and suggestions, and the National Science Foundation and the US-Israel Binational Science Foundation for financial support. Grossman also
thanks the John S. Guggenheim Memorial Foundation, the Sumitomo Bank Fund, the Daiwa
Bank Fund, and the Center of International Studies at Princeton University. Part of this work
was carried out while the authors were visiting Innocenzo Gasparini Institute for Economic
Research (IGIER) in Milan, Italy, and the European University Institute in Florence, Italy.
Needless to say, these were very hospitable environments.

of income support to farmers. Health and safety measures show the imprimatur of the local insurance industry on the one hand, and of powerful labor unions on the other. And manufacturers have had much to say about a myriad of environmental and regulatory policies. It seems difficult to argue that the political process serves only the interests of the median voter.

Interest groups pursue their quest for political advantage by a number of different means. They gather information that supports their positions and make it available to powerful politicians. They take their arguments to the public in an effort to win voter sympathy. Sometimes they undertake disruptive activities, which are intended to coerce rather than persuade. And, of course, they contribute to political parties and to individual candidates' campaigns.

This paper focuses on interest groups' use of campaign contributions as a vehicle for influencing public policy. Contributions may take the form of cash transfers or gifts in kind. In any event, we assume that the contributions can be used by the candidates to persuade and cajole a group of undecided voters. Our aim is to characterize the policies that emerge when rival groups vie for the politicians' favor while the politicians themselves compete for voter support.

The literature on campaign giving identifies two motives that interest groups might have when they contribute to politicians or to political parties. Contributors with an *electoral motive* intend to promote the electoral prospects of preferred candidates. Those with an *influence motive* aim to influence the politicians' policy pronouncements. Our model allows interest groups to entertain either or both of these reasons for giving, but our analysis of the equilibrium emphasizes the second. We believe that special interests do often try to use their campaign gifts to influence politicians' positions and we find support for this view in the empirical evidence presented by Kau and Rubin (1982), Fremdreis and Waterman (1985), Tosini and Tower (1987), and others.

Our setting is one in which two political parties compete for seats in a legislative body. To attract votes, the parties announce policy platforms and engage in political advertising and other costly forms of campaigning. The platforms may include commitments on two types of policy issues. The first are issues about which the party has strong preferences or predetermined positions. The preferences may reflect the party's ideology or the positions may be inherited from the past if, for example, the party feels it must keep earlier promises in order to preserve its reputation. In any event, we take this component of a party's program as fixed. We focus instead on the determination of what we shall term *pliable policies*. These are policies about which the parties have no explicit preferences and so are willing to tailor their positions to further their election prospects.[1]

Our interest groups are collections of individuals who share a common interest in the pliable policies. These organized groups can offer contributions to one or both of the political parties. Their gifts may be granted unconditionally or they may be tied to the positions adopted by the recipients. Unconditional gifts are used to satisfy an electoral motive for giving, while contingent gifts are designed to influence decisions. We assume that the groups are able to communicate the sense of their conditional offers, even if they cannot spell out the details in a legally binding contract.

If the interest groups choose to offer contingent contributions, they will confront the parties with a fundamental trade-off. By setting a platform that serves the general interest, a party can attract votes from the portion of the electorate that is well-informed about the issues. But by choosing policies that cater to the special interests it may be able to elicit greater contributions that then can be used to influence the voting of less-informed or impressionable voters. We assume that the parties resolve this trade-off with the aim of maximizing their representation in the legislature. An equilibrium consists of a pair of platforms and a set of contribution schedules such that no group or party can better its lot given the anticipated actions of the others. The equilibrium platforms and associated contributions together determine the election outcome, which in turn determines the likelihood that each party's platform will be enacted.

The remainder of the paper is organized as follows. In the next section, we discuss the relationship of our paper to several others in the literature. Section 3 describes the details of the model. In Section 4, we examine a special case in which there is only a single, organized interest group while Section 5 treats the general case with competition among groups. The last section contains a summary of our findings.

2 Related Literature

There is, of course, a vast literature on policy determination in representative democracies. Our goal in this section is to explain the relationship

---

[1] Admittedly, the distinction between the pliable policies and others is not always clear cut. In the long run, all of a party's positions are presumably subject to change. But candidates and parties are willing to change their positions on some issues more freely than others. The set of pliable policy issues might include allocation of "pork-barrel" spending, attitudes on gun control and some environmental questions, and positions on a variety of economic policies.

of our paper to some others that have a similar focus. We make no claims to comprehensive coverage.

Our paper has antecedents in the literature on probabilistic voting.[2] Enelow and Hinich (1982), for example, developed a "spatial" model in which voters' utilities comprise two additively separable components. One component relates to the policy issue under consideration while the other reflects exogenous characteristics of the candidates. The politicians are assumed unable to observe individual tastes with regard to the exogenous characteristics. In consequence, they remain uncertain about how any individual will vote, even if they know how he or she will be affected by the policy in question.[3]

Lindbeck and Weibull (1987) and Dixit and Londregan (1994) adopted a similar probabilistic-voting approach to study policies that redistribute income to narrow groups of voters. They assumed that the various groups differ in their predisposition to the parties and identified characteristics of a group that make it a good candidate to receive political largesse. Although these authors focused on the determinants of the political success of special interests, there is an important difference between their work and ours. Specifically, they did not allow interest groups to compete actively for favors whereas we are primarily interested in how compaign contributions can be used as a tool for such competition.

We treat campaign contributions here in much the same way as in Grossman and Helpman (1994). There we built on Bernheim and Whinston (1986), who described influence-seeking as an example of a "menu auction" game. In a menu auction, each of several *principals* who will be affected by an action offers a bid to an *agent* who will take that action. These bids take the form of schedules that associate a payment to the agent with each feasible option. Once the agent chooses an action, all of the principals pay the bids stipulated by their schedules. Bernheim and Whinston defined an equilibrium in a menu auction as a set of contribution schedules such that each one is a best response to all of the others, and an action by the agent that maximizes her utility given the schedules that confront her.

Our 1994 paper provided an application of this view of influence-seeking. We focused on the determination of import and export taxes and subsidies in a small, open economy. We took the government to be

---

[2] We consider this label to be something of a misnomer. In our model, and in many others in the literature, every individual votes deterministically. It is only that the politicians do not know individuals' preferences on some issues, which causes them to be uncertain about how a particular ballot will be cast.

[3] See also Coughlin (1984, 1986) and Wittman (1983), and Mueller (1989, ch. 11) for a survey.

a common agent for a group of special interest groups, each representing the owners of some industry-specific factor. The policy makers, who were already in power, were assumed to set trade policy to maximize a weighted sum of total campaign contributions and aggregate (or average) welfare. In this model, the incumbent government did not face any explicit competition from rival candidates nor did we provide any rigorous justification for its assumed objective.

Austen-Smith (1987) and Baron (1994) addressed very similar issues to the ones that interest us here. Both of these authors studied policy determination in a two-party model of electoral competition. And both were interested in the effects of campaign contributions by special interest groups. Austen-Smith assumed that the parties use campaign funds to alleviate (risk-averse) voters' uncertainty about candidates' policy positions. Baron, like us, allowed campaign spending to have a direct effect on the voting behavior of a group of uninformed voters. A more important distinction between their papers and ours concerns the motive that groups are assumed to have for giving to the parties. In both Austen-Smith and Baron the lobbies take platforms as given and offer gifts to their favorites with an eye toward affecting the probabilities of election.[4,5] Here, we do not restrict interest groups to such an electoral motive, but also afford them an opportunity to influence the parties' platforms.

3 The Model

We examine a jurisdiction with two political parties, an exogenous number of special interest groups, and a fixed continuum of voters. Our description begins with the voters.

3.1 The Voters

Like Baron (1994), we distinguish the behavior of two classes of voters, the *informed* and the *uninformed*. Informed voters are those

---

[4] Magee *et al.* (1989) make a similar assumption in the context of their models of trade policy formation.

[5] This is Baron's assumption in the last part of his paper, where he allows for several competing interest groups and considers the determination of "collective" policies. In the first part of his paper, dealing with "particularistic" policies, the contributions are simply an exogenous fraction of the net benefits captured by the interest group. Although Baron refers to this as a bargaining solution, he does not specify any explicit bargaining process and his "solution" fails to account for the surplus to the political party relative to the fallback option.

An advantage that we see of our model compared to Baron's—beyond the one we stress in the text—is that it is capable of handling both particularistic policies (with a single interest group) and collective policies (with multiple interest groups) within the same analytical framework.

who know and understand the parties' positions on both the pliable policies and other issues. The welfare of these voters will be affected by the policies that are ultimately enacted and perhaps by other (exogenous) attributes of the candidates and the parties. For example, the voters' welfare may depend on personal characteristics of the candidates, such as their competence or charisma, or voters may derive some pleasure from supporting the party to which they have developed an historical attachment. Informed voters cast their ballots for whichever party offers higher utility, considering both their pliable positions and their exogenous programs and characteristics. In the model developed here, this is a dominant strategy for these voters. The uninformed voters, by contrast, do not know or are unable to evaluate the parties' positions on (at least) the pliable issues. These voters may have initial leanings toward one party or the other, but at least some of them can be swayed by the messages they receive in the course of the campaign. Let a denote the fraction of these uninformed (perhaps "impressionable" is a better word) voters in the total voting population.

Consider then a typical informed voter with the label i. This individual derives utility $u^i(\mathbf{p}^A)$ from the vector $\mathbf{p}^A$ of pliable policies endorsed by party A, and utility $u^i(\mathbf{p}^B)$ from the vector $\mathbf{p}^B$ of such policies endorsed by party B. with $u^i(\cdot)$ continuous and differentiable. She votes for the candidates from party A if and only if $u^i(\mathbf{p}^A) - u^i(\mathbf{p}^B) \geqq \beta^i$, where β^i measures her assessment of the superiority (or inferiority, if negative) of party B's fixed policy positions and other exogenous characteristics relative to those of party A. We assume that the parties cannot observe the ex ante proclivities of any particular voter, although they presume these to be drawn from a known distribution $F(\beta)$. Moreover, we assume that the distribution of preferences on the fixed programs and other characteristics of the parties and candidates is statistically independent of the effects of the pliable policies on individuals' utilities. Then both parties will perceive a probability $F[u^i(\mathbf{p}^A) - u^i(\mathbf{p}^B)]$ that individual i will vote for the slate of candidates from party A. With a continuum of informed voters, the law of large numbers implies that the share of informed ballots cast for party A equals $(1/n_I) \int_{i \in I} F[u^i(\mathbf{p}^A) - u^i(\mathbf{p}^B)] \, di$, where I denotes the set of informed voters and n_I the total number (or measure) of such individuals.

An uninformed voter, too, may have a predisposition toward one party or the other. However, this leaning can be overcome with enough campaign rhetoric. In particular, if party A spends more on its campaign than party B, some of those who were initially inclined toward party B will vote instead for party A. We denote by $H(\cdot)$ the fraction of the uninformed voters that votes for party A and assume that it depends on the difference in the parties' total campaign budgets.[6]

We assume that seats in the parliament are allocated by proportional representation. Then the fraction of the legislature controlled by party A matches the fraction of the total votes garnered by this party. Letting s denote this fraction, we have

$$s = \frac{1-\alpha}{n_I} \int_{i \in I} F[u^i(\mathbf{p}^A) - u^i(\mathbf{p}^B)]\, di + \alpha H(C^A - C^B), \qquad (1)$$

where C^K is the total campaign spending undertaken by party K, $K = A, B$.

3.2 The Parties and the Government

Each party seeks to maximize its representation in the legislature (or any monotonically increasing function thereof). The parties may see this as their objective for any of several reasons. For example, political parties often reward their core members with jobs in and around the government. A party may seek to maximize its patronage and may recognize a monotonic relationship between the number of political jobs it controls and the number of its seats in the legislature. Alternatively, a party may wish to implement its ideological agenda, and may see a positive relationship between the prospects of successfully doing so and the size of its legislative contingent. Of course, with two parties and proportional representation, the objective of maximizing seats is equivalent to that of maximizing (expected) plurality in the election. This is a commonly assumed objective in the literature on electoral competition.[7]

With this objective, parties A and B choose their platforms of pliable policies in order to maximize s and $1 - s$, respectively. They do so recognizing that their policy endorsements will affect their popularity among the informed voters. At the same time, the platforms are chosen

---

[6] It is perhaps more common in the literature to assume that the ratio of campaign expenditures affects the allocation of votes. See, for example, Baron (1989, 1994) and Snyder (1989). In our view, a specification in terms of absolute differences is more reasonable, because a larger budget allows a campaign to reach a wider segment of the population. This view could be formalized in a model of advertising similar to the one in Grossman and Shapiro (1984), where the fraction of the target population that hears a given message is assumed to vary with the amount that is spent on the advertising campaign. If each message that an uninformed voter hears makes him more likely to vote for the party issuing the announcement, then the number of uninformed voters who cast their ballots for party A will depend on the difference in the sizes of the two budgets.

[7] See, for example, Enelow and Hinich (1982), Denzau and Kats (1977), and Coughlin and Nitzan (1981). The different campaign objectives that candidates might hold are discussed and compared in Aranson, Hinich and Ordeshook (1974).

with an eye toward the organized interest groups, who may vary their support according to the positions that are taken. The parties know that any contributions they collect can be used to finance campaign activities.

After the election is over, the legislature convenes to set policy. We do not model the policy-setting process in any detail. Rather, we assume that each party attempts to implement its announced platform and that a party's probability of success increases monotonically with the size of its legislative delegation. In other words, the legislature adopts the vector of pliable policies $\mathbf{p}^A$ with probability $\varphi(s)$ and the vector $\mathbf{p}^B$ with probability $1 - \varphi(s)$, where $\varphi(\frac{1}{2}) = \frac{1}{2}$ and $\varphi'(s) > 0$. The function $\varphi(s)$ may, for example, increase sharply just above $s = \frac{1}{2}$, if having a slight majority of the seats in the parliament greatly enhances a party's prospects for successfully implementing its program.

While we believe that it is reasonable to suppose that parties aim to maximize their representation in the legislature and that parties in the majority sometimes fail to implement their programs, the appendix treats a more "pure" case. There we examine policy determination when the legislature operates according to strict majority rule and when parties seek to maximize their probability of winning a majority. To conduct this alternative analysis, we must assume that the number of voters is large but finite and that members of special interest groups constitute a negligible share of the voting population. With these assumptions and a further one of equal party popularity (i.e., the parties would each capture 50% of the vote if they happened to adopt identical positions on the pliable policies and to spend identical amounts on their campaigns), the equilibrium policies are the same as the ones derived in the main text.[8]

3.3 The Special Interests

Special interest groups are collections of voters who share a common interest in the pliable policies. The members of an interest group may differ in their views on the fixed programs and other characteristics of the candidates, and, in the privacy of the polling booth, they behave just like any other voters. Nonetheless, these individuals may have an incentive to cooperate with one another, if by doing so they can influence the parties' policy platforms.

As Olson (1965) has discussed, the mere fact that individuals share a common interest in some policy or policies is not enough to ensure that

---

[8] Lindbeck and Weibull (1987) come to a similar conclusion in their study of electoral competition without interest groups or campaign spending. Our analysis of the case in which parties maximize their probability of winning is modeled after theirs.

they will engage in collective political action. The temptation always exists for each to free ride on the costly political efforts of the others. But some interest groups do overcome these free-rider problems and manage to coordinate their lobbying activities. We take the number and identities of the organized special interests as given (while recognizing that it would be interesting to know how the policy environment serves to galvanize certain interests and not others), and examine how these groups influence the policy-setting process.

Interest groups may have two motivations for making campaign contributions in our model. First, they may hope to influence the outcome of the election. An interest group may gain if it can enhance the prospects of the party whose positions on the pliable policies are more similar to its own. Second, the interest groups may hope to influence the parties' platforms; that is, to push the candidates to support policies that better serve the group's interests. Some of the members of an interest group may object to spending on the first of these objectives, if their ideological attitudes differ from those of the party that is being supported. But all members of a group will agree on the desirability of pushing the two parties toward the group's collective *desideratum* on the pliable policy issues. Moreover, as we shall see, the second motive remains operative even when the individual interest groups are relatively small, so that each has little ability to affect the election outcome.

We denote by $W_j(\mathbf{p})$ the aggregate utility that members of interest group j derive from the vector of pliable policies $\mathbf{p}$. It is possible that the members of interest group j care directly about only one element of $\mathbf{p}$, say p_j, and that the other elements of $\mathbf{p}$ affect these individuals only indirectly (e.g., as taxpayers who must pay for the benefits provided to other groups), just as they do the general public. Alternatively, the interest group may have a direct interest in several components of $\mathbf{p}$, and several different interest groups may have a stake in the same policy component. If the members of a group share identical preferences concerning the issues where politicians are willing to be flexible, then $W_j(\mathbf{p})$ is simply the number of members of interest group j times the utility component of the representative one. In any event, we assume that the members of an interest group cooperate fully in their collective action, and so seek to maximize their expected joint welfare from the pliable policies net of campaign contributions. Letting C_j^K represent the contribution of interest group j to party K, we write the objective function for this group as

$$V_j = \varphi(s) W_j(\mathbf{p}^A) + [1 - \varphi(s)] W_j(\mathbf{p}^B) - C_j^A - C_j^B. \qquad (2)$$

If an interest group hopes to influence a party's policy endorsement, it must make sure that the party sees a connection between its platform and the size of the contribution that will be forthcoming. The group need not announce an explicit *quid pro quo*; indeed, the public might frown upon politicians who openly peddle their political influence. Rather, the interest group need only convey an understanding that its contribution will vary with the positions that is taken. We would argue that politicians understand this connection quite well; for example, in the United States, proponents of gun control do not expect to receive donations from the National Rifle Association.

We allow the interest groups considerable freedom in designing their contribution schedules, $C_j^K(\mathbf{p}^K)$. We assume only that the schedules are continuous, differentiable when positive, and everywhere nonnegative. The latter means that interest groups can offer resources to the parties or withhold them but cannot levy taxes on politicians. A group can, of course, choose to make its contribution independent of policy; in this way it can bolster the chances of its favorite party without causing it to lose any (additional) informed votes. A group also might choose to offer its support to only one of the two political parties.

3.4 Political Equilibrium

We seek a subgame-perfect Nash equilibrium of a two-stage, noncooperative, political game. In the first stage, the various interest groups independently and simultaneously announce their contribution schedules, one to each of the two parties. In the second stage, the parties choose their policy platforms. After the platforms are set, the contributions are paid and the campaigns are waged. Then the election takes place and finally the legislature meets to implement one of the party's platforms. We assume that all expectations about subsequent events are accurate and that all promises are honored.[9]

More formally, we propose the following definition:

DEFINITION 1. An equilibrium consists of a pair of feasible policy vectors $(\mathbf{p}^{Ao}, \mathbf{p}^{Bo})$ and a set of contribution schedules $\{C_j^{Ao}(\mathbf{p}^A), C_j^{Bo}(\mathbf{p}^B)\}$, one for each lobby j, such that

(i) $\mathbf{p}^{Ao}$ maximizes s given $\mathbf{p}^{Bo}$, $\{C_j^{Ao}(\mathbf{p}^A)\}$ and $\{C_j^{Bo}(\mathbf{p}^B)\}$;
(ii) $\mathbf{p}^{Bo}$ maximizes $1 - s$ given $\mathbf{p}^{Ao}$, $\{C_j^{Ao}(\mathbf{p}^A)\}$ and $\{C_j^{Bo}(\mathbf{p}^B)\}$;
(iii) each $C_j^K(\cdot)$ is continuous and differentiable when positive, with $C_j^K(\mathbf{p}^K) \geqq 0$ for all $\mathbf{p}^K$; and

---

[9] In our one-shot game, the interest groups have an incentive to renege on their contribution offers once the platforms are announced. Similarly, the politicians have no incentive to pursue their announced positions on the pliable policies once the campaign contributions have been paid up. The keeping of promises could be motivated in a repeated game, where agents would be punished for failure to live up to their commitments.

(iv) for each lobby j, there do not exist feasible contribution schedules $\tilde{C}_j^A(\mathbf{p}^A)$ and $\tilde{C}_j^B(\mathbf{p}^B)$, such that

$$\varphi(\tilde{s})\,W_j(\tilde{\mathbf{p}}^A) + [1 - \varphi(\tilde{s})]\,W_j(\tilde{\mathbf{p}}^B) - \tilde{C}_j^A(\tilde{\mathbf{p}}^A) - \tilde{C}_j^B(\tilde{\mathbf{p}}^B)$$

$$> \varphi(s)\,W_j(\mathbf{p}^{Ao}) + [1 - \varphi(s)]\,W_j(\tilde{\mathbf{p}}^{Bo}) - C_j^{Ao}(\mathbf{p}^{Ao}) - C_j^{Bo}(\mathbf{p}^{Bo})$$

where $\tilde{\mathbf{p}}^A$ maximizes and $\tilde{\mathbf{p}}^B$ minimizes

$$\frac{1 - \alpha}{n_I} \int_{i \in I} F[u^i(\mathbf{p}^A) - u^i(\mathbf{p}^B)]\, di$$

$$+ \alpha H[\textstyle\sum_{k \neq j} C_k^{Ao}(\mathbf{p}^A) + \tilde{C}_j^A(\mathbf{p}^A) - \sum_{k \neq j} C_k^{Bo}(\mathbf{p}^B) - \tilde{C}_j^B(\mathbf{p}^B)]$$

and $\quad \tilde{s} = \dfrac{1 - \alpha}{n_I} \int_{i \in I} F[u^i(\tilde{\mathbf{p}}^A) - u^i(\tilde{\mathbf{p}}^B)]\, di$

$$+ \alpha H[\textstyle\sum_{k \neq j} C_k^{Ao}(\tilde{\mathbf{p}}^A) + \tilde{C}_j^A(\tilde{\mathbf{p}}^A) - \sum_{k \neq j} C_k^{Bo}(\tilde{\mathbf{p}}^B) - \tilde{C}_j^B(\tilde{\mathbf{p}}^B)].$$

Here, conditions (i) and (ii) express the Nash equilibrium among parties in the policy announcement phase, while condition (iii) ensures that no lobby can beneficially deviate during the initial stage of the game.

Implicit in definition 1 is the assumption that each party can observe the contribution schedules offered to the other. This assumption can be justified with the observation that the "schedules" here are intended as metaphors, rather than as literal descriptions of explicit contracts. In practice, offers of political support are conveyed as much by the public posture of a lobby as by any private communications it may have with the politicians. Accordingly, the *quid pro quo* for campaign support may come to be common knowledge among the parties.[10]

---

[10] If, instead, we were to allow the contribution schedules to be communicated privately to the parties, then each party would be forced to condition its policy choices on its *beliefs* about the offers that had been made to its rival. As O'Brien and Shaffer (1992) have argued in a related context, such a game has many subgame-perfect Nash equilibria, as there is little to discipline the out-of-equilibrium beliefs of the parties. Still, there would be two reasons to focus on the equilibria that satisfy our definition 1. First, even with unobservable contribution schedules, these equilibria are the only ones that can arise when $F(\cdot)$ and $H(\cdot)$ are linear functions, as we shall assume in the next subsection and thereafter. More on this point in a moment. Second, the equilibria described by definition 1 are immune to joint-welfare-increasing bilateral renegotiation between a lobby and a party and thus satisfy the conditions for a "contract equilibrium" proposed by Crémer and Riordan (1987). See O'Brien and Shaffer (1992) for a discussion of why such equilibria might be focal in the set of equilibria that can arise when contracts between a principal and a particular agent are unobservable to other agents.

3.5 Functional Forms

To simplify the analysis, we adopt particular functional forms for the distribution function, $F(\cdot)$, and for the effectiveness-of-campaign-spending function, $H(\cdot)$. We assume that informed voters' relative preferences for the immutable characteristics and program of party B are distributed uniformly in the range

$$\left(-\frac{1}{2f}-\frac{b}{f}, \frac{1}{2f}-\frac{b}{f}\right),$$

where $f > 0$ is a parameter measuring the diversity of ex ante views about the parties. Then

$$F[u^i(\mathbf{p}^A) - u^i(\mathbf{p}^B)] = \tfrac{1}{2} + b + f[u^i(\mathbf{p}^A) - u^i(\mathbf{p}^B)]$$
$$\text{for } u^i(\mathbf{p}^A) - u^i(\mathbf{p}^B) \in \left(-\frac{1}{2f}-\frac{b}{f}, \frac{1}{2f}-\frac{b}{f}\right).$$

We also take $H(\cdot)$ to be linear and of the form $H(C^A - C^B) = \tfrac{1}{2} + b + h(C^A - C^B)$, where $h > 0$ is a parameter reflecting the productivity of campaign spending. With this specification, if the two parties happen to endorse the same pliable policies and if they happen to spend the same amounts on their campaigns, then party A will capture a fraction $\tfrac{1}{2} + b$ of the votes. The parameter b can be interpreted as the ex ante voter bias in favor of party A. We might expect $b > 0$ if party A is the incumbent party and $b < 0$ if party B is the incumbent party. Such an incumbency advantage could reflect name recognition and perhaps the feeling that "the devil you know is better than the devil you don't." Also, b might differ from zero because one party's candidates are seen as more competent or because its ideological agenda has greater public appeal. When $b = 0$, we will say that the parties are *equally popular*.

One consequence of linearity (among others) is that the objective function for each party becomes additively separable in the variables describing its own policy platform and level of campaign spending, and those of its rival. With separability, each party can make its decisions about what contribution offers to accept and what platform to adopt independently of its knowledge or beliefs about the incentives facing the other. Accordingly, the equilibria that arise when contribution schedules are observable to both parties coincide with those that can arise when the schedules are communicated privately, in the linear case.

4 Equilibrium with One Lobby

We begin the analysis with the case in which there is only a single, organized lobby. In this setting we are able to expose most clearly the incentives facing a lobby and to set the stage for the more complicated situation that arises when several groups compete for favors. The single-lobby case also may be of independent interest, inasmuch as it sheds light on the determination of what Baron (1994) refers to as *particularistic policies*. These are policies whose benefits can be denied to those who do not contribute to the lobbying effort and whose costs are spread so thinly in the population that they do not inspire groups to organize in opposition. Baron cites as examples the special provisions in legislation that favor particular firms or industries and the interventions that legislators sometimes make with the bureaucracy on behalf of their supporters.

When only a single interest group curries politicians' favors, its problem can be treated as one of direct control. That is, we can view the lobby as if it could implement any pair of (pliable) policy platforms it desires, provided that its contribution offers are sufficiently large as to be acceptable to the parties. Each party always has the option of declining the lobby's offer, in which case it would choose the platform that attracted the greatest number of informed voters. To prevent this from happening, the lobby's contribution must be among those that satisfy a *participation constraint*.

How large must the contribution to party A be in order to induce it to endorse some policy $\mathbf{p}^A$? Recall the relationship between the parties' platforms and campaign budgets and the election outcome, in the light of our linearity assumptions for $F(\cdot)$ and $H(\cdot)$. We have $s = b + \frac{1}{2} + (1 - \alpha)f \times [W(\mathbf{p}^A) - W(\mathbf{p}^B)] + \alpha h(C_j^A - C_j^B)$, where $W(\mathbf{p}) \equiv (1/n_I) \int_{i \in I} u^i(\mathbf{p})\, di$ is the average welfare of informed voters when the vector of pliable policies is $\mathbf{p}$. If the party were to refuse to be swayed by the lobby's offer, it would support the policies that best served the average informed voter. This policy vector, which we denote by $\mathbf{p}^*$, satisfies $\nabla W(\mathbf{p}^*) = 0$.[11] So the lobby must guarantee the party at least as many seats as it would capture by endorsing $\mathbf{p}^*$. Evidently, it must offer to party A a contribution of at least $[(1 - \alpha)f/\alpha h][W(\mathbf{p}^*) - W(\mathbf{p}^A)]$. Notice that the size of the minimum payment does not depend on the policy position anticipated from party B.

Similarly, the lobby must offer party B a contribution of at least $[(1 - \alpha)f/\alpha h][W(\mathbf{p}^*) - W(\mathbf{p}^B)]$ to induce it to adopt the platform $\mathbf{p}^B$. The lobby's problem, then, is to choose $\mathbf{p}^A$ and $\mathbf{p}^B$ to maximize (2), subject to the constraints that

$$C_j^K \geqq \frac{(1 - \alpha)f}{\alpha h}[W(\mathbf{p}^*) - W(\mathbf{p}^K)] \text{ for } K = A, B. \qquad (3)$$

[11] If the informed voters are a representative sample of the total population of voters, in the sense that the distribution of utility functions among informed and uninformed voters is the same, then the policy $\mathbf{p}^*$ is the one that maximizes a Benthamite social welfare function.

The constraints stipulate the minimum sizes of the campaign contributions as functions of the platforms that the group chooses to induce.

4.1 Contributions with Only an Influence Motive

Let us suppose, for the moment that the lobby decides to give the two parties exactly what is needed to induce them to support the platforms $\mathbf{p}^A$ and $\mathbf{p}^B$ but nothing more. With these influence-motivated contributions, party A captures a fraction $\frac{1}{2} + b$ of the seats, while party B captures the remaining fraction $\frac{1}{2} - b$, *no matter what the policy vectors* $\mathbf{p}^A$ *and* $\mathbf{p}^B$ *happen to be.* The lobby's problem becomes one of choosing the two platforms to maximize its expected utility, given $\varphi^A = \varphi(b + \frac{1}{2})$ and $\varphi^B = 1 - \varphi(b + \frac{1}{2})$, and contributions that satisfy (3) with equality. We have, then, the following proposition that describes equilibrium policies when the lobby eschews the electoral motive for political giving.

Proposition 1. If the contributions from a sole lobby satisfy both participation constraints in (3) with equality, the equilibrium policy platforms satisfy

$$\mathbf{p}^K = \operatorname*{argmax}_{\mathbf{p}} \left[\varphi^K W_j(\mathbf{p}) + \frac{(1 - \alpha)f}{\alpha h} W(\mathbf{p}) \right] for\ K = A, B, \qquad (4)$$

where $\varphi^A = \varphi(b + \frac{1}{2})$ and $\varphi^B = 1 = \varphi(b + \frac{1}{2})$.

Evidently, the influence-seeking lobby induces both parties to behave as if they were maximizing weighted sums of the collective welfare of interest group members and the average welfare of informed voters.

It may help to think about some specific examples in order to understand exactly what this formula means. Consider, for instance, the classical problem of an industry that generates a negative externality. If the externality is linked to the scale of production, then a per-unit output tax equal to the marginal damage best serves the interests of the average voter. But suppose that the industry's lobby links its campaign contributions to the size of the industry tax or subsidy. Then the equilibrium platforms will be ones that maximize weighted sums of average welfare (i.e., consumer surplus plus profits plus tax revenue) and industry profits. These platforms may involve a tax or a subsidy, and will certainly be more generous to the industry than the "optimal" Pigouvian tax.[12] Or consider an economy that produces a single output from fixed supplies of capital and labor and where utility is linear in consumption. The welfare of the average voter is maximized by a flexible wage policy that ensures full

---

[12] Let d be the marginal damage caused by a unit of the industry's output and let t^K be the per-unit tax advocated by party K. Then in political equilibrium, $t^K = d - [(\varphi^K \alpha h)/(1 - \alpha)f](x/x')$, where x is industry output and x' is the slope of the industry supply curve.

employment of the L workers. But if a union representing the workers offers donations to the parties that are contingent on their endorsing a minimum wage policy, then the equilibrium platforms will contain such proposals as long as the elasticity of labor demand is not too high.[13]

Another illustration of equation (4) draws on the political-science literature. Consider the familiar spatial voting model, where a scalar policy variable p is to be chosen from among points on the real line. Suppose that voter i has bliss point p_i and utility from policy p given by $u^i = -(p - p_i)^2$. Let voters' bliss points be uniformly distributed on $[0, 1]$ and let informed voters comprise a representative sample of the whole. The distribution of voters' ex ante preferences is, as before, independent of the distribution of benefits from the pliable policy. Finally, let there be a single, organized interest group, representing all voters with bliss points in the range $[m, n]$. Then proposition 1 implies that, when the lobby contributes only to influence policy choices, the equilibrium platforms satisfy

$$p^K = \frac{1}{2}\left[\frac{\delta + \varphi^K(n - m)(n + m)}{\delta + \varphi^K(n - m)}\right] \quad \text{for } K = A, B.$$

where $\delta \equiv (1 - \alpha)f/\alpha h$. Notice that $p^K \to \tfrac{1}{2}$ (the bliss point of the median and average voter) as $\delta \to \infty$, while $p^K \to (n + m)/2$ (the bliss point of the median and average interest group member) as $\delta \to 0$. Also, $p^K > \tfrac{1}{2}$ when $(n + m)/2 > \tfrac{1}{2}$ and $p^K < \tfrac{1}{2}$ when $(n + m)/2 < \tfrac{1}{2}$; i.e., the platforms always lie between the bliss point of the median interest-group member and that of the median voter. Finally, the larger is φ^K, the farther is p^K from $\tfrac{1}{2}$ and the closer it is to $(n + m)/2$.

Returning to the more general interpretation of the model, we next establish a proposition that compares the campaign platforms of the two parties and the contributions received by each one, again for situations in which the lobby pursues only an influence motive for giving. Suppose, for concreteness, that party A is the more popular party; (i.e., $b > 0$). Then we have:

Proposition 2. If $b > 0$ and the contributions from a sole lobby satisfy the participation constraints in (3) with equality, then $W_j(\mathbf{p}^A) > W_j(\mathbf{p}^B)$, $W(\mathbf{p}^A) < W(\mathbf{p}^B)$, and $C^A > C^B$.

---

[13] Let $F(K, L)$ be the aggregate production function. The minimum wage $\hat{w}^K$ supported by party K maximizes $\varphi^K \hat{w} L + (1 - \alpha)f/\alpha h F(K, L)$, subject to the constraints that $L \leq L$ and $F_L(K, L) = \hat{w}$. The solution has a minimum wage above the market-clearing wage provided that

$$\varepsilon < \frac{\alpha h \varphi^K}{\alpha h \varphi^K + (1 - \alpha)f}$$

where $\varepsilon \equiv -F_L/LF_{LL}$ is the elasticity of labor demand.

The proposition follows straightforwardly from (3) and (4).[14] Notice first that $b > 0$ implies $\varphi(b + \frac{1}{2}) > 1 - \varphi(b + \frac{1}{2})$. Therefore, it is the more popular party that applies greater weight to the welfare of the special interest group in setting its flexible policy positions. In other words, the lobby induces the party whose candidates and fixed program have greater public appeal to choose a platform of pliable policies that is closer to the lobby's ideal.[15] But then this party's platform must be further from the ideal of the average (informed) vector. The latter fact, together with (3), implies that the lobby contributes more to the party with the better election prospects. The last observation is in keeping with Snyder's (1990) view of political contributions as investments in contingent claims (the claims pay off only if the recipients end up in a position to influence policy), a view that he supports with evidence on campaign gifts to candidates for the U.S. House of Representatives.

The following proposition indicates how the platforms that arise in an equilibrium with influence-motivated contributions respond to the parameters describing the political environment.[16]

Proposition 3. If the contributions from a sole lobby satisfy the participation constraints in (3) with equality, then $W_j(\mathbf{p}^K)$ is smaller and $W(\mathbf{p}^K)$ is larger the larger is $\delta \equiv (1 - \alpha)f/\alpha h$.

---

[14] Proof: From (4) we have $\varphi^K W_j(\mathbf{p}^K) + \delta W(\mathbf{p}^K) > \varphi^K W_j(\mathbf{p}^L) + \delta W(\mathbf{p}^L)$ for $L \neq K$; $K, L = A, B$ and $\delta \equiv (1 - a)f/ah$. These inequalities imply: (i) $(\varphi^A - \varphi^B) W_j(\mathbf{p}^A) > (\varphi^A - \varphi^B) W_j(\mathbf{p}^B)$ and (ii) $\delta[W(\mathbf{p}^K) - W(\mathbf{p}^L)] > \varphi^K[W_j(\mathbf{p}^L) - W_j(\mathbf{p}^K)]$. For $\varphi^A > \varphi^B$, condition (i) implies $W_j(\mathbf{p}^A) > W_j(\mathbf{p}^B)$, which combined with (ii) for $K = B$, implies $W(\mathbf{p}^B) > W(\mathbf{p}^A)$. Finally, when (3) holds as an equality for $K = A$ and $K = B$, $W(\mathbf{p}^B) > W(\mathbf{p}^A)$ implies $C^A > C^B$.

[15] This result is at odds with one derived by Baron (1994). Baron establishes that, in his model, a candidate with an incumbency advantage "can afford to be more independent of interest groups," whereas the challenger with worse election prospects caters more to special interests. When discussing particularistic policy positions, Baron assumes that the interest groups contribute a fixed portion of the benefits they derive from politicians' favors. He models incumbency advantage alternatively as a bias in the voting pattern of uninformed voters (only) and as the ability of a candidate to deliver greater benefits to interest groups for a given burden to the electorate. When it is the former, the incumbent anyway captures more of the votes of the uninformed for a given amount of campaign spending and so devotes more effort on the margin to attracting the informed voters. When it is the latter, the incumbent anyway attracts greater campaign contributions for a given policy stance, and so again attempts to appeal more to the informed voters on the margin. In our model, the popularity advantage applies equally to the behavior of informed and uninformed voters, neither candidate can reward the interest group without at the same time harming the general public, and the interest group chooses how much to contribute to the parties. In such circumstances, an interest group will wish to invest more in the party that is more likely to be in a position to set policy and so will exert a greater influence on its platform.

[16] The proof of this proposition is similar to the proof of proposition 2.

Both parties cater more to the special interest group the greater is the susceptibility of uninformed voters to campaign spending and the larger is the fraction of these individuals in the total voter population (i.e., the larger are h and α, respectively), because the lobby gives larger gifts to each party the more productive are its funds in buying votes. On the other hand, the platforms more fully reflect the interests of the average informed voter the smaller is the diversity of preferences over the ideological issue. When the range of the β's is small (i.e., f is large), there are more voters at the margin of indifference between the two parties, and so an endorsement of a platform that neglects the public interest is more costly to the parties.[17]

As a final observation, we note the similarity between the form of the equilibrium platforms described by (4) and the equilibrium policies that emerged from the model in Grossman and Helpman (1994). There (in the context of tariff formation) we assumed that a single incumbent policy maker has as her objective the maximization of a weighted sum of campaign contributions and average voter welfare. We showed that the equilibrium policies satisfy an equation with the same form as (4). We now find that—at least when there is one organized lobby which pursues only an influence motive for campaign giving—the government-as-agent framework represents a proper reduced form of a model with electoral competition.

4.2 When Is an Electoral Motive Operative?

We have so far assumed that the interest group would wish to make the participation constraints bind for both political parties. In other words, the group offers each party only what it takes to win its support for the desired platform. Let us examine now when this will be the case.

The first-order conditions for the maximization of V_j with respect to C_j^A and C_j^B, subject to the participation constraints (3), imply

$$\varphi'(s)\alpha h[W_j(\mathbf{p}^A) - W_j(\mathbf{p}^B)] = 1 - \lambda^A; \qquad (5)$$

$$\varphi'(s)\alpha h[W_j(\mathbf{p}^B) - W_j(\mathbf{p}^A)] = 1 - \lambda^B; \qquad (6)$$

where λ^K is the Lagrange multiplier on the participation constraint applicable to party K. It is clear that λ^K must be positive for at least one K (i.e., the participation constraint must bind for at least one party), because the left-hand sides of (5) and (6) have opposite signs. In other words, it never pays for the lobby to give more than is necessary to both parties. More-

---

[17] Dixit and Londregan (1994) find similarly that transfer policies tend to favor groups of voters that have "central" views on ideological issues and thus many members on the margin of indifference between the two candidates.

over, if the lobby does give more than is required to one of the parties, it must be the one that endorses its more-preferred platform; for example, (5) can be satisfied with $\lambda^A = 0$ only if $W_j(\mathbf{p}^A) > W_j(\mathbf{p}^B)$. The party with a nonbinding participation constraint receives more contributions in total than its rival (i.e., $C^A > C^B$ in the case just described) and adopts a platform of pliable policies that is less mindful of the welfare of the average voter.[18]

Indeed, only the party that is ex ante more popular is a candidate to receive extra campaign support. To see this, suppose that the other was receiving the larger contribution. Then the lobby could switch the labels on its offers (i.e., offering to party A what it had intended to offer to B. and *vice versa*) and at the same time reduce its (new) offer to the more popular party in such a way as to preserve the original probability distribution over policy outcomes. This would reduce its total contribution bill, which clearly would be profitable for the lobby. We have thus established

Proposition 4. Let party A be the more popular party (i.e., $b > 0$). Then (a) the participation constraint (3) is satisfied with equality for party B; and (b) if the participation constraint (3) is satisfied as a strict inequality for party A, then $W_j(\mathbf{p}^A) > W_j(\mathbf{p}^B)$, $W(\mathbf{p}^A) < W(\mathbf{p}^B)$, and $C^A > C^B$.

Notice that propositions 2 and 4 imply that the more popular party amasses greater campaign funding and adopts a platform more favorable to the special interest group and less considerate of the average voter irrespective of whether the interest group chooses to satisfy the participation constraint with equality or not.

If the lobby does give to the more popular party in excess of what is needed to gain its acquiescence, the motivation would be to help that party capture additional seats in the legislature. By doing so, the lobby could increase the probability that its preferred platform would be implemented. Suppose that party A is the more popular party, and suppose that the lobby contemplates giving this party a bit more than is needed to induce the party to choose the policy $\mathbf{p}^A$. The expected marginal benefit from the first dollar of "extra" contribution is $\varphi'(s)\alpha h[W_j(\mathbf{p}^A) - W_j(\mathbf{p}^B)]$, which reflects the group's preference for A's platform and its marginal effect on the probability that this platform will be implemented. The marginal cost of the extra contribution is of course equal to one. Thus, we have

---

[18] If (3) holds as an equality for party B, for example, then its platform satisfies (4), but with $\varphi^B = -b + \frac{1}{2} - (1-\alpha)fW(\mathbf{p}^A) - \alpha hC^A + (1-\alpha)fW(\mathbf{p}^*)$. Then $\varphi^B W_j(\mathbf{p}^B) + \delta W(\mathbf{p}^B) > \varphi^B W_j(\mathbf{p}^A) + \delta W(\mathbf{p}^A)$, where $\delta \equiv \alpha f/(1-\alpha)h$. This, together with $W_j(\mathbf{p}^A) > W_j(\mathbf{p}^B)$, implies $W(\mathbf{p}^A) < W(\mathbf{p}^B)$. Moreover, if (3) holds as an equality for party B and as an inequality for party A, we have $C^A > C^B + \delta[W(\mathbf{p}^B) - W(\mathbf{p}^A)]$, which together with $W(\mathbf{p}^A) < W(\mathbf{p}^B)$ implies $C^A > C^B$.

Proposition 5. If $b > 0$ and $\varphi'(s)\alpha h[W_j(\mathbf{p}^A) - W_j(\mathbf{p}^B)] > 1$, where $\mathbf{p}^K$ satisfies (4) for $K = A, B$, then the participation constraint in (3) will hold as a strict inequality for party A.

Evidently, the lobby finds an electoral motive to contribute to party A (beyond the influence motive that always exists) only if the lobby would fare very differently under the alternative platforms, if campaign spending is relatively productive in buying votes (α and h are large), and if increased representation in the legislature greatly enhances a party's prospects for implementing its program ($\varphi'(s)$ is large). The size of the difference $W_j(\mathbf{p}^A) - W_j(\mathbf{p}^B)$ reflects two considerations. First, it reflects the extent of the informed voters' predisposition to party A. The smaller the bias b, the closer together will be the two policy vectors in (4), and the less likely it will be that the lobby perceives a benefit from helping party A to win more seats. Second, it reflects the absolute size of the lobby's stake in the policy issues.

5 Equilibrium with Several Lobbies

Now we seek a subgame-perfect Nash equilibrium when several interest groups vie for influence over the parties' platforms. Again we are free to treat the lobbies as if they were facing problems of direct control, but this time we must incorporate into their constraints the anticipated actions of the rival organizations. Consider for example the problem confronting the interest group l. This group behaves as if it were designing the platforms $\mathbf{p}_l^A$ and $\mathbf{p}_l^B$, but it takes as given the contribution schedules offered by the other lobbies. It makes the choice to maximize its own welfare, subject to the constraint that the offers must be large enough to induce the parties to comply. Of course, in equilibrium, all of the lobbies' "choices" must be mutually consistent; i.e., they all must designate the same platforms, which are the ones that the two parties announce.

More formally, let $C_{-l}^K(\mathbf{p}^K) \equiv \sum_{j \neq l} C_j^K(\mathbf{p}^K)$ be the aggregate contribution schedule offered to party K by all lobbies other than l. Then lobby l chooses $\mathbf{p}_l^A$, $\mathbf{p}_l^B$, C_l^A, and C_l^B to maximize its expected welfare in (2), subject to the constraints that

$$C_l^K \geq \max_{\mathbf{p}} \left[\frac{1-\alpha}{\alpha h} fW(\mathbf{p}) + C_{-l}^K(\mathbf{p}) \right] - \left[\frac{1-\alpha}{\alpha h} fW(\mathbf{p}_l^K) + C_{-l}^K(\mathbf{p}_l^K) \right]$$
$$\text{for } K = A, B. \quad (7)$$

The (participation) constraints ensure that each party prefers to endorse its prescribed platform than to decline the offer from lobby l and choose an alternative platform. For future reference, we denote by $\mathbf{p}_{-l}^K$ the policy vector that maximizes $(1 - \alpha)fW(\mathbf{p}) + \alpha h C_{-l}^K(\mathbf{p})$. This is the best that party K could do if it were to ignore the offer from lobby l.

Let us provisionally assume that lobby l opts to make its participation constraints bind with equality. When lobby l pays these minimally acceptable contributions, it anticipates that party A will capture a fraction

$$\tfrac{1}{2} + b + (1 - \alpha)f[W(\mathbf{p}^A_{-l}) - W(\mathbf{p}^B_{-l})] + \alpha h[C^A_{-l}(\mathbf{p}^A_{-l}) - C^B_{-l}(\mathbf{p}^B_{-l})]$$

of the seats. This fraction is a constant (say $\bar{s}_l$) from the lobby's point of view. It follows that the platforms that maximize the group's expected welfare satisfy the first-order conditions

$$\varphi(\bar{s}_l)\boldsymbol{\nabla} W_l(\mathbf{p}^A_l) + \frac{1 - \alpha}{\alpha h}\, f \boldsymbol{\nabla} W(\mathbf{p}^A_l) + \boldsymbol{\nabla} C^A_{-l}(\mathbf{p}^A_l) = 0 \qquad (8)$$

and

$$[1 - \varphi(\bar{s}_l)]\boldsymbol{\nabla} W_l(\mathbf{p}^B_l) + \frac{1 - \alpha}{\alpha h}\, f \boldsymbol{\nabla} W(\mathbf{p}^B_l) + \boldsymbol{\nabla} C^B_{-l}(\mathbf{p}^B_l) = 0. \qquad (9)$$

Now look at the problem from the politicians' perspective. When confronted with the full set of contribution schedules, the political parties set their platforms to maximize their shares of the vote. The first-order conditions for these maximizations imply

$$(1 - \alpha)f\,W(\mathbf{p}^K) + \alpha h \boldsymbol{\nabla} C^K(\mathbf{p}^A) = 0 \quad \text{for } K = A, B, \qquad (10)$$

where $C^K(\mathbf{p}^K) \equiv \sum_j C^K_j(\mathbf{p}^K)$ is the aggregate contribution schedule confronting party K. In other words, the parties balance the marginal loss of informed votes caused by their deviating from $\mathbf{p}^*$ against the additional uninformed votes they capture by spending the extra donations from the interest groups.

In the equilibrium, the platforms anticipated by each lobby must be the same as those actually announced by the parties; i.e., $\mathbf{p}^K_l = \mathbf{p}^K$ for all l and for $K = A, B$. Therefore, we can combine (8), (9), and (10) to derive

$$\varphi(\bar{s}_l)\boldsymbol{\nabla} W_l(\mathbf{p}^A) = \boldsymbol{\nabla} C^A_l(\mathbf{p}^A), \qquad (11)$$

$$[1 - \varphi(\bar{s}_l)]\boldsymbol{\nabla} W_l(\mathbf{p}^B) = \boldsymbol{\nabla} C^B_l(\mathbf{p}^B). \qquad (12)$$

These equations reveal an important property of the equilibrium contribution schedules; namely, these schedules must be locally "truthful" in the neighborhood of the equilibrium platforms. In other words, when a lobby treats the make-up of the legislature as a given, it designs its bids so that the shape of each schedule accurately reflects the expected benefit it would derive from a small change in the party's platform around the equilibrium.[19] Lemma 1 states this requirement more precisely.

---

[19] See Grossman and Helpman (1994) for further discussion of local truthfulness and its relation to "global truthfulness," as defined by Bernheim and Whinston (1986).

Lemma 1. If all lobbies set contribution schedules that are everywhere continuous and differentiable where positive, and if all lobbies satisfy the participation constraints (7) with equality, then the contribution schedules $C_l^K(\cdot)$ for lobby l must be locally truthful (i.e., satisfy (11) and (12)) when evaluated at the equilibrium policies $\mathbf{p}^A$ and $\mathbf{p}^B$.

In a subgame-perfect equilibrium, all lobbies must anticipate the same election outcome. So $\bar{s}_l = s^o$ for all l. Using this fact, (11) and (12) can be combined with (10), to yield conditions that the equilibrium platforms must satisfy when all lobbies opt to have both participation constraints bind. These are

$$\varphi(s^o)\sum_j \nabla W_j(\mathbf{p}^{Ao}) + \frac{(1 - \alpha)}{\alpha h} f\nabla W(\mathbf{p}^{Ao}) = 0; \tag{13}$$

$$[1 - \varphi(s^o)]\sum_j \nabla W_j(\mathbf{p}^{Bo}) + \frac{(1 - \alpha)f}{\alpha h} f\nabla W(\mathbf{p}^{Bo}) = 0. \tag{14}$$

These conditions imply:

Proposition 6. When all lobbies satisfy the participation constraints (7) with equality, each party's equilibrium platform satisfies the necessary conditions for maximizing a weighted sum of the aggregate welfare of all interest group members and the average welfare of informed voters.

Conditions (13) and (14) provide a partial answer to the following question: Which interest groups are most successful in influencing government policy? The answer, we find, is that all organized interest groups are equally successful, in the sense that their members receive equal weight in the parties' political calculus. The net effect of private campaign financing is to push policy in a direction that is favorable to the average member of an interest group and away from the policy that would best serve the interests of the average (informed) voter. Of course, the final platform choices will not be equally close to the bliss points of all of the lobbies; this depends on how similar a lobby's preferences are to those of the average voter and how the other interest groups line up on the issues of concern to it.

The conditions that characterize the equilibrium platforms have another interesting implication. The political system works best, of course, when all voters are informed about the issues ($\alpha = 0$). Then the interest groups are ineffectual and both parties choose the platform that maximizes aggregate welfare. But the same outcome is achieved in a very different set of circumstances. Suppose that every voter is a member of exactly one interest group and that the informed voters constitute a representative sample of the electorate. Then, no matter how large the fraction of uninformed voters nor how susceptible these voters may be to campaign rhetoric, the equilibrium policies again will be the ones that best serve the voters' (collective) interests.

Notice that (13) and (14) do not uniquely determine the equilibrium platforms, even when $W(\cdot)$ and $W_l(\cdot)$ are concave functions. Besides $\mathbf{p}^{Ao}$ and $\mathbf{p}^{Bo}$, the (expected) composition of the legislature (s^o) appears in these expressions. The equilibrium seat count depends, in turn, on the total amounts of contributions collected by the parties. It is true, as in the case of a single lobby, that an individual interest group prefers to concentrate its giving on the party that it expects will be in a better position to implement its platform. And it is also true that the party expected to capture a legislative majority caters more to the special interests. But there is a potential here for self-fulfilling prophesies that does not exist when a single lobby plays the contribution game. The self-fulfilling prophesies reflect a type of coordination failure among the lobbies.[20]

Suppose, for example, that party A happens to be the more popular party ($b > 0$), but that each lobby expects that party B will capture the majority of the seats. These expectations are based on the belief that the other lobbies will give more generously to party B than to party A. Then each lobby will be well justified in concentrating its efforts on influencing B's platform and, in the end, their expectations may be validated. Whereas an only lobby can always gain by ensuring that the more popular party wins the majority of the seats, a lobby that is one among many cannot necessarily do so. To reverse the fortunes of the two parties in a way that conserves resources, it may need the tacit cooperation of other lobbies.

The potential for multiplicity of equilibria can also be understood in another way. Recall that $s = \frac{1}{2} + b + (1 - \alpha)f[W(\mathbf{p}^A_{-l}) - W(\mathbf{p}^B_{-l})] + \alpha h[C^{Ao}_{-l}(\mathbf{p}^A_{-l}) - C^{Bo}_{-l}(\mathbf{p}^B_{-l})]$ when lobby l makes the minimal contributions needed to induce the platforms $\mathbf{p}^{Ao}$ and $\mathbf{p}^{Bo}$. Of course, if all lobbies give minimally, then this condition must hold for each one. The policies $\mathbf{p}^A_{-l}$ and $\mathbf{p}^B_{-l}$ are the ones that the parties would choose if they ignored the offer from lobby l. Notice that these policies depend on the shapes of the lobbies' contribution schedules *away from the equilibrium*. And while the equilibrium requirements place some restrictions on the global shapes of these schedules (for example,

$$(1 - \alpha)f[W(\mathbf{p}^A_{-l}) - W(\mathbf{p}^B_{-l})] + \alpha h[C^{Ao}_{-l}(\mathbf{p}^A_{-l}) - C^{Bo}_{-l}(\mathbf{p}^B_{-l})]$$

must be the same for all l) the requirements are not enough to pin down the equilibrium uniquely.

---

[20] Morton and Myerson (1992) find a similar result in a one-dimensional spatial-voting model, where parties sell "services" to special interest groups and use the proceeds to fund advertising that directly enhances the welfare of voters.

Still, some of the Nash equilibria may be more compelling than others. For example, if $b = 0$, the symmetric equilibrium—in which the lobbies treat the parties similarly and the election yields an evenly split legislature—may be focal. If $b > 0$, the lobbies would have no particular reason to expect the bulk of the contributions to go to party B. and in some cases they will have good reasons to expect the opposite. One such case arises when all lobbies are offering positive contributions to both parties, not only in the neighborhood of the equilibrium, but also around the various points that the parties would choose if one of the lobby groups were to be ignored. In this situation, the equilibrium with $s < \frac{1}{2}$ is Pareto dominated for the entire set of interest groups by another with $s > \frac{1}{2}$. The alternative equilibrium can be constructed as follows. Let each lobby offer to party B in the new equilibrium exactly what it offered to party A in the old. Let each construct its new offer to party A by subtracting a fixed amount from the (positive) offers to party B in the old equilibrium, plus an additional amount that increases with the distance from the initial $\mathbf{p^{Bo}}$. Finally, let the fixed reductions be chosen so that party A captures as many seats in the new equilibrium as party B did in the old, and let the additional reductions be chosen so that no party will decline the offer from some lobby in setting its platform.[21] The newly constructed contribution schedules are best responses to one another, and they induce each party to choose the platform in the new equilibrium that the other chose in the old. Finally, since each party wins as many seats in the new equilibrium as the other did in the old, the new equilibrium has exactly the same distribution of policy outcomes as the old. It follows that all interest groups gain.

More generally, anytime $b > 0$ and $s < \frac{1}{2}$, the lobbies are paying excessively to allow the less popular party to capture a majority of the seats. It is never in their collective interest to do so. But it may not always be possible to devise alternative contribution schedules that allow each to pay a smaller contribution while preserving the probability distribution over policy outcomes. If it is not possible to do so, then a Pareto improvement may not be available within the set of Nash equilibria. In such cases the

---

[21] That is, let $C_j^K(\mathbf{p})$ be the initial schedule offered by lobby j to party K and let $\tilde{C}_j^K(\mathbf{p})$ be the alternative. We propose $\tilde{C}_j^B(\mathbf{p}) = C_j^A(\mathbf{p})$ for all j and $\tilde{C}_j^A(\mathbf{p}) = C_j^B(\mathbf{p}) - z_j - Z_j(\mathbf{p} - \mathbf{p^B})$, where each $Z_j(\cdot)$ is a function that is everywhere nonnegative and that reaches a unique maximum at 0. Let the constants z_j be chosen so that $z_j \geqq 0$ and $\sum_j z_j = 2b/\alpha h$, and the functions $Z_j(\cdot)$ so that

$$(1 - \alpha)fW(\mathbf{p^B}) + \sum_j C_j^B(\mathbf{p^B}) > \max_\mathbf{p}\{(1 - \alpha)fW(\mathbf{p}) + \alpha h\sum_{j \neq l}[C_j^B(\mathbf{p}) - Z_j(\mathbf{p} - \mathbf{p^B})] - \alpha h z_l\}$$

for all l. This will be possible, provided that the $C_j^B(\mathbf{p_{-l}^B})$ in the initial equilibrium are large enough. In the event, party A chooses the platform $\tilde{\mathbf{p}}^A = \mathbf{p^B}$, party B chooses $\tilde{\mathbf{p}}^B = \mathbf{p^A}$ and lobby l gains z_l relative to the initial equilibrium.

realization of joint gains may require the enforcement of an explicitly cooperative arrangement, where some lobbies agree to some political actions that are not best responses to the others and where certain of the interest groups receive transfers as side payments under the agreement.[22]

Let us now examine whether some interest groups would opt to give to their favorite parties beyond what is needed to influence their platforms. We first establish the following proposition, indicating that at most one lobby group can perceive an electoral motive for contributing to a given party.

Proposition 7. For each political party $K = A, B$. there is at most one lobby (generically) that satisfies the participation constraint (7) as a strict inequality.

Suppose to the contrary that lobbies 1 and 2 each gave extra contributions to party A to bolster its election returns. Then, in equilibrium, the marginal benefit perceived by lobby j for contributing to this party would be $\varphi'(s)\alpha h[W_j(\mathbf{p}^A) - W_j(\mathbf{p}^B)]$, for $j = 1, 2$, while of course the marginal cost for each would be 1. Both lobbies could satisfy their first-order conditions for optimal giving only if $W_1(\mathbf{p}^A) - W_1(\mathbf{p}^B)$ happened to equal $W_2(\mathbf{p}^A) - W_2(\mathbf{p}^B)$; that is, if the two lobbies held exactly the same absolute preference for party A's pliable policies over those of party B. Electoral support beyond what is justified by the influence motive constitutes a public good for all interest groups preferring a given party's platform. As in many other contexts, it is only the player that has the most to gain that might contribute voluntarily toward the purchase of a public good.

The electoral motive might be operative for a lobby if it stands to gain greatly by having one party's platform implemented rather than the other's. But if all interest groups are "small," in a sense made precise in the next proposition, then none will see a marginal benefit of "excess" contributions equal to their marginal cost. In this case, all campaign giving is governed by an influence motive alone.

Proposition 8. Consider a constrained equilibrium, in which each lobby must satisfy (7) as an equality for each party. Let $(\mathbf{p}^A, \mathbf{p}^B, s)$ be the platforms and seat count in this constrained equilibrium. Then if $\varphi'(s)\alpha h|W_j(\mathbf{p}^A) - W_j(\mathbf{p}^B)| < 1$ for all j, the constrained equilibrium is also an unconstrained equilibrium in which none of the lobbies exercises an electoral motive for campaign giving.

The proposition is straightforward. Starting from an equilibrium where all participation constraints bind, lobby j perceives a marginal benefit of $\varphi'(s)\alpha h[W_j(\mathbf{p}^A) - W_j(\mathbf{p}^B)]$ from giving a little bit more to party A, and

---

[22] We suspect that any equilibrium that has the less popular candidate winning a majority of the seats will not be a coalition-proof equilibrium (see Bernheim *et al.* [1987]). But we have not been able to prove this for all types of equilibria.

$\varphi'(s)\alpha h[W_j(\mathbf{p^B}) - W_j(\mathbf{p^A})]$ from giving a little more to party B. If the inequality in the proposition is satisfied, it will not wish to give the extra amount to either party, in view of the marginal cost of the additional contribution of 1. The interpretation of this in terms of the sizes of the groups is as follows. Suppose we start with a given set of interest group members and then divide these individuals into a larger and larger number of (smaller) lobbies, using any allocation of individuals to groups at all. When the number of different groups is large enough, $W_j(\mathbf{p})$ will be small for every j, and so will the difference $|W_j(\mathbf{p^A}) - W_j(\mathbf{p^B})|$. In the event, the electoral motive for campaign giving vanishes, but the influence motive remains. Indeed, (13) and (14) continue to characterize the equilibrium platforms no matter how finely the groups are divided, so long as the participation constraints bind for each one.

6 Summary

Interest groups make campaign contributions either to influence election outcomes or to influence policies. We have developed a model of campaign finance in which special interests may have either or both of these motives for giving. In the model, the special interests tailor schedules that link campaign gifts to policy endorsements. The schedules are proposed to two political parties, who are vying for seats in a legislature. The parties have fixed stances on some issues but have yet to announce their positions on other "pliable" policies, about which they have no inherent preferences. Confronted with offers from the various interests, the parties announce their campaign platforms. They trade off the extra campaign contributions that may be forthcoming if they cater to the groups' demands against the votes that this may cost them among the well-informed segment of the electorate.

The paper analyzes the equilibrium of a two-stage game. In the first stage, the interest groups strategically design their contribution schedules to maximize their expected welfare net of political pay-outs. In the second stage, the parties choose platforms to maximize their representation in the legislature. In the voting booth, an informed voter casts her ballot for the party whose candidates and platform she prefers. In contrast, an uninformed (or, perhaps, impressionable) voter may respond to campaign rhetoric. The difference in policies and spending levels determines the election outcome, which in turn decides the probability that each party's platform will be implemented.

Our model predicts divergence in policy platforms. The party that is expected to win the majority of the seats garners greater attention from the special interests. As a result, it is induced to adopt a platform that gives more weight to their concerns. The underdog party also caters

somewhat to the special interests, but its equilibrium platform is closer
to the bliss point of the average informed voter. This finding may have
relevance for the debate over term limits. With the advantage that incumbency brings in terms of name recognition and reputation, incumbents
are overwhelming favorites in many elections. Our analysis suggests that
these candidates may convert their popularity into campaign war chests,
with detrimental effects on the welfare of the average voter. Term limits
would periodically restore a more even election and thus might dimin-
ish the influence of special interest groups.

When interest groups offer the parties contributions that are platform
contingent, they induce in them a preference ordering over the pliable
policies. In our model, these preferences take a particularly simple form.
Each party is induced to behave as if it were maximizing a weighted sum
of the welfare levels of two groups in the polity. The aggregate interest
of *informed voters* receives a weight that increases with the share of such
voters in the voting population and decreases with the diversity of their
opinions about the relative desirability of the parties' ideological positions. The aggregate interest of *members of organized interest groups* receives
a weight that increases with the susceptibility of uninformed voters to
campaign spending. The weight implicitly given to the interest group
members also varies with the number of seats a party is expected to win,
which accounts for the above-mentioned difference in the parties' platforms. It is interesting to note that many political-economy models ascribe
weighted social welfare functions to politicians making policy choices.
Our model provides some underpinnings for this common specification.

If interest groups can communicate platform-contingent contribution
offers, they will always perceive an influence motive for giving to each
party whose platform might eventually become policy. But the groups may
or may not perceive an incentive to give to their favorite party beyond
what is needed to exert the desired degree of influence. We have shown
that the electoral motive for giving—which features prominently in many
previous models of campaign contributions—can operate for at most
one interest group favoring each political party. This is because gifts that
bolster a party's election prospects benefit all interest groups that prefer
the party's platform. Only the interest group with the greatest relative
preference for the party is a candidate to contribute toward this public
good. We find, moreover, that campaign gifts with an electoral motive
may be the exception, rather than the rule. No group will give beyond
what is needed to compensate the party for altering its policy position
unless the group has an aggregate stake in policy that is relatively large
compared to the stake of the electorate as a whole.

Finally, what of the election outcome? Our model predicts a unique
equilibrium when only a single interest group is organized to offer con-

tributions to the parties. In this equilibrium, the party that is more popular ex ante captures a majority of the seats in the elected legislature. The interest group contributes more to the more popular party and at least compensates this party for choosing the less-popular, pliable policies. Thus, the contributions ensure that the more popular party captures at least as many seats as it would in the absence of any influence-seeking.

However, once there are several interest groups that actively compete for influence, our model allows scope for self-fulfilling prophesies. Each group's giving depends on its expectations about the others. If a lobby expects the others to compete vigorously for a certain party's favor, then it too will have an incentive to focus its efforts on that party. Then, if all happen to concentrate on the party whose candidates and fixed program have less popular appeal, the result may be a legislature in which this party captures a majority. In the aggregate, the lobbies may pay handsomely to overcome voters' resistance. Still, each may be stuck with this outcome unless they reach a cooperative solution through the use of side payments.

APPENDIX

Strict Majority Rule

We assumed in the main text that political parties seek to maximize their representation in the legislature and that a party holding a majority of seats may fail to implement its policy program. While quite reasonable as descriptions of the political process, these assumptions are admittedly somewhat ad hoc. In this appendix, we take a more "purist" approach, by assuming that parties maximize their chances of winning a majority and that the legislature operates by strict majority rule. We concentrate on the symmetric equilibrium that may emerge when the two parties are equally popular. Equal popularity implies $F(0) = \frac{1}{2}$ and $H(0) = \frac{1}{2}$, and, with the previously encountered linearity assumptions on $F(\cdot)$ and $H(\cdot)$, $b = 0$.

We now suppose that interest group members comprise a negligible fraction of the voting population and that voters' preferences for the fixed program of party B are statistically independent. Also, the total number of voters, n, is large but finite. Then, the number of votes for party A can be approximated by a normal distribution, with mean $\sum_{i \in I} F(\Delta^i) + \alpha n H(\Delta^C)$ and variance $\sum_{i \in I} F(\Delta^i)[1 - F(\Delta^i)] + \alpha n H(\Delta^C)[1 - H(\Delta^C)]$, where $\Delta^i \equiv u_i(\mathbf{p}^A) - u^i(\mathbf{p}^B)$ and $\Delta^C \equiv C^A - C^B$.[23] Party A wins the election with (approximate) probability

---

[23] The approximation follows from the Liapunov central limit theorem, which requires also that the variance term becomes unbounded as n grows large. For a discussion of the applicability of this theorem in the context of a probabilistic voting model, see Lindbeck and Weibull (1987).

$$\pi(\mathbf{p}^A,\mathbf{p}^B,\Delta^C) = N\left(\frac{\sum_{i \in I}F(\Delta^i) + \alpha n H(\Delta^C) - \frac{n}{2}}{\sqrt{\sum_{i \in I}F(\Delta^i)[1 - F(\Delta^i)] + \alpha n H(\Delta^C)[1 - H(\Delta^C)]}}\right) \quad (15)$$

where $N(\cdot)$ represents the standardized normal distribution function.

Each interest group designs its contribution schedule to maximize the aggregate expected utility of its members. Recognizing that with probability $\pi(\cdot)$ the legislature will implement the policy vector $\mathbf{p}^A$ and with probability $1 - \pi(\cdot)$ it will implement the vector $\mathbf{p}^B$, lobby l chooses $C_l^A(\mathbf{p}^A)$ and $C_l^B(\mathbf{p}^B)$ to maximize $\pi(\cdot)W(p^A) + [1 - \pi(\cdot)]W(\mathbf{p}^B) - C_l^A(\mathbf{p}^A) - C_l^B(\mathbf{p}^B)$, taking as given the contribution schedules proffered by the other lobbies. The parties subsequently set $\mathbf{p}^A$ and $\mathbf{p}^B$ to maximize π and $1 - \pi$, respectively.

As before, we can treat each lobbies' problem as one of direct control. Lobby l chooses $\mathbf{p}_l^A$, $\mathbf{p}_l^B$, C_l^A, and C_l^B to maximize its expected utility, taking $C_{-l}^A(\mathbf{p}^A)$ and $C_{-l}^B(\mathbf{p}^B)$ as given. It also recognizes the participation constraints, which require that each party achieve at least as great a probability of winning when setting the policy designated by lobby l as it could be choosing an alternative policy and receiving nothing from the lobby. That is, the lobby must respect the inequality

$$\pi[\mathbf{p}_l^A, \mathbf{p}_l^B, C_{-l}^A(\mathbf{p}_l^A) + C_l^A - C_{-l}^B(\mathbf{p}^B) - C_l^B] \geqq$$
$$\max_{\mathbf{p}} \pi[\mathbf{p}, \mathbf{p}_l^B, C_{-l}^A(\mathbf{p}) - C_{-l}^B(\mathbf{p}^B) - C_l^B]$$

and a similar condition for party B. We focus on symmetric equilibria, wherein $C_{-l}^A(\cdot) = C_{-l}^B(\cdot)$, lobby l chooses the same platform and contribution for each party, and the participation constraints bind.

Let $\mathbf{p}_l^o$ be the platform designated by lobby l. The first-order condition for maximizing the lobbies' expected utility with respect to the choice of $\mathbf{p}_l^A$ implies

$$\tfrac{1}{2}\boldsymbol{\nabla} W_l(\mathbf{p}_l^o) + \frac{(1 - \alpha)f}{\alpha h}\boldsymbol{\nabla} W(\mathbf{p}_l^o) + \boldsymbol{\nabla} C_{-l}^o(\mathbf{p}_l^o) = 0, \quad (16)$$

where we have made use of the fact that $\pi(\mathbf{p}_l^o, \mathbf{p}_l^o, 0) = \frac{1}{2}$ at the symmetric equilibrium.[24]

Party A chooses its equilibrium platform, $\mathbf{p}^{Ao}$, to maximize $\pi[\mathbf{p}^A, \mathbf{p}^{Bo}, C^{Ao}(\mathbf{p}^A) - C^{Bo}(\mathbf{p}^{Bo})]$. Again making use of the symmetry conditions, $\mathbf{p}^{Ao} = \mathbf{p}^{Bo} = \mathbf{p}^o$ and $C^{Ao}(\cdot) = C^{Bo}(\cdot) = C^o(\cdot)$, this implies

$$(1 - \alpha)f\boldsymbol{\nabla} W(\mathbf{p}^o) + \alpha h\boldsymbol{\nabla} C^o(\mathbf{p}^o) = 0. \quad (17)$$

Consistency requires $\mathbf{p}_l^o = \mathbf{p}^o$ for all l. Thus, (16) and (17) imply

$$\tfrac{1}{2}\sum\boldsymbol{\nabla} W_l(\mathbf{p}^o) = \boldsymbol{\nabla} C_l^o(\mathbf{p}^o) \quad (18)$$

[24] In deriving (16) we have used the first-order condition with respect to C_l^A to substitute out the Lagrange multiplier on the participation constraint. We have also made extensive use of the symmetry conditions, $\mathbf{p}_l^{Ao} = \mathbf{p}_l^{Bo} = \mathbf{p}_l^o$ and $C_l^A = C_l^B = C_l^o$.

which is another "local truthfulness" result. Finally, combining (17) and (18) we find

$$\frac{1}{2} \sum_j \nabla W_j(\mathbf{p}^o) + \frac{(1-\alpha)f}{\alpha h} \nabla W(\mathbf{p}^o) = 0 \qquad (19)$$

The platform $\mathbf{p}^o$ that satisfies (19) is the same as the platform $\mathbf{p}^{Ao}$ that satisfies (13) and the platform $\mathbf{p}^{Bo}$ that satisfies (14), when $s^o = \frac{1}{2}$. We see that, with equal popularity, the platform that emerges in a symmetric equilibrium when the legislature operates by strict majority rule and parties maximize their chances of winning a majority is the same as the platform that emerges in symmetric equilibrium when parties maximize their representation in the legislature and a minority platform has some chance of being implemented.[25]

[25] This result mimics a similar finding by Lindbeck and Weibull (1987), who assumed that all voters are informed voters and that campaign contributions play no role in the election.

References

Aranson, P., Hinich, M. and Ordeshook, P. (1974). Election goals and strategies: equivalent and nonequivalent strategies. *American Political Science Review* 68: 135–152.

Austen-Smith, D. (1987). Interest groups, campaign contributions, and probabilistic voting. *Public Choice* 54: 123–139.

Baron, D. P. (1989). Service-induced campaign contributions and the electoral equilibrium. *Quarterly Journal of Economics* 104: 45–72.

Baron, D. P. (1994). Electoral competition with informed and uninformed voters. *American Political Science Review* 88: 33–47.

Bernheim, B. D., Peleg, B., and Whinston, M. (1987). Coalition-proof Nash equilibria, I: Concepts. *Journal of Economic Theory* 42: 1–12.

Bernheim, B. D., and Whinston, M. (1986). Menu auctions, resource allocation, and economic influence. *Quarterly Journal of Economics* 101: 1–31.

Coughlin, P. (1984). Expectations about voter choices. *Public Choice* 44: 49–59.

Coughlin, P. (1986). Elections and income redistribution. *Public Choice* 50: 27–99.

Coughlin, P., and Nitzan, S. I. (1981). Electoral outcomes with probabilistic voting and Nash social welfare maxima. *Journal of Public Economics* 15: 113–122.

Crémer, J., and Riordan, Michael H. (1987). On governing multilateral transactions with bilateral contracts. *RAND Journal of Economics* 18: 436–451.

Denzau, A. T., and Kats, A. (1977). Expected plurality voting equilibrium and social choice functions. *Review of Economic Studies* 44: 227–233.

Dixit, A. and Londregan, J. (1994). The determinants of success of special interests in redistributive politics (mimeo: Princeton University).

Enelow, J. M., and Hinich, M. (1982). Nonspatial candidate characteristics and electoral competition. *Journal of Politics* 44: 115–130.

Fremdreis, J. P., and Waterman, R. W. (1985). PAC Contributions and legislative behavior: Senate voting on trucking deregulation. *Social Science Quarterly* 66: 401–412.

Grossman, G. M., and Helpman, E. (1994). Protection for sale. *American Economic Review* 84: 833–850.

Grossman, G. M., and Shapiro, C. (1984). Informative advertising with differentiated products. *Review of Economic Studies* 51: 63–81.

Kau, J. B., and Rubin, P. H. (1982). *Congressmen, Constituents, and Contributors* (Boston: Martinus Nijhoff Publishing).

Lindbeck, A., and Weibull, J. W. (1987). Balanced-budget redistribution as the outcome of political competition. *Public Choice* 54: 273–297.

Magee, S. P., Brock, W. A., and Young, L. (1989). *Black Hole Tariffs and Endogenous Policy Theory* (Cambridge, U.K.: Cambridge University Press).

Morton, R., and Myerson, R. (1992). Campaign spending with impressionable voters (CMSEMS Working Paper No. 1023: Northwestern University).

Mueller, D. C. (1989). *Public Choice II* (Cambridge, U.K.: Cambridge University Press).

O'Brien, D. P., and Shaffer, G. (1992). Vertical control with bilateral contracts. *RAND Journal of Economics* 23: 299–308.

Olson, M. (1965). *The Logic of Collective Action* (Cambridge, MA: Harvard University Press).

Snyder, J. M. (1989). Election goals and the allocation of campaign resources. *Econometrica* 57: 637–660.

Snyder, J. M. (1990). Campaign contributions as investments: The U.S. House of Representatives 1980–1986. *Journal of Political Economy* 98: 1195–1227.

Tosini, S. C., and Tower, E. (1987). The textile bill of 1985: The determinants of congressional voting patterns. *Public Choice* 54: 19–25.

Wittman, D. (1983). Candidate motivation: A synthesis of alternative theories. *American Political Science Review* 77: 142–157.

Three

Competing for Endorsements

In most elections the leaders of organized interest groups publicly announce their support for one candidate or slate of candidates or another. Why are these political endorsements made? And what role do they play in the election process and in the determination of policy?

We see public endorsements as a means of communication between the well-informed leaders of special interest groups and the lesser informed rank-and-file members. The members of an interest group may

By Gene M. Grossman and Elhanan Helpman. Originally published in *American Economic Review* 89 (June 1999): 501–524. Copyright © 1999 by the American Economic Association. Reprinted with permission. We thank David Austen-Smith, Elchanan Ben Porath, Avinash Dixit, Jacob Glazer, Faruk Gul, Eliana Laferra, Giovanni Maggi, Adi Pauzner, Ariel Rubinstein, Jean Tirole, and three anonymous referees for helpful discussions and comments, and the National Science Foundation and the U.S.-Israel Binational Science Foundation for financial support.

not fully understand how a particular policy proposal will affect their well-being or where the various candidates stand on the issues. Moreover, it may be costly for these individuals to acquire all of the information they need to vote "correctly." Indeed, the cost of gathering information can easily exceed the private gains they might expect to achieve with their single votes. Then the individuals may look for readily available cues to guide them in the polling booth. In this context, endorsements by group leaders may convey useful information to like-minded voters, and perhaps to others.

The available evidence on voting behavior supports this view. For example, in 1988, voters in California were called upon to decide a number of complex issues concerning reform of the insurance industry. Based on the results of an exit poll, Arthur Lupia (1994) concludes that voters who were uninformed about the technical issues but who could correctly identify the position of the insurance industry on an initiative were more likely to vote like other similar, but better-informed, voters than those who could not identify the industry's position. This finding suggests that at least some voters used industry endorsements to help them overcome their lack of information about the issues. Similarly, James H. Kuklinski et al. (1982) found that relatively uninformed voters looked to reference groups more than others in deciding how to vote in the 1976 California primary, an election that turned on a complex initiative to reduce construction of nuclear power plants in the state. Endorsements by labor unions have been found to affect voting behavior by union members in a number of different studies, including those by Arthur Kornhauser et al. (1956), Philip E. Converse and A. Angus Campbell (1968), and Michael H. LeRoy (1990).

If groups of voters use endorsements as cues—as the evidence suggests—then candidates and parties may well have incentives to compete for these endorsements. Such competition would have the candidates announcing platforms that appeal to the leaders of the various groups. Interest groups do seem to demand such announcements as conditions for their endorsements; the National Organization of Women taps only candidates who commit to fight for an Equal Rights Amendment and who support unrestricted abortion rights (Linda Berg, [1996]), while the National Rifle Association (NRA) insists that candidates issue public statements and respond to an NRA questionnaire in a way that reveals a sympathetic position on firearms and related issues (National Rifle Association of America, [1996]). And while there can be no hard evidence that politicians take positions specifically to capture endorsements, numerous anecdotes suggest that this might be the case. Jimmy Carter, for example, allowed the National Education Association to write the education plank in his party's national platform in 1980; Harrison Donnelly (1980) indicates that this was the payoff for the group's endorsement of Carter in his nomination battle with Edward Kennedy. Similarly, Jo Freeman (1988) reports that Walter Mondale ceded "sign-off" authority on platform language concerning women's issues to the National Organization of Women in 1984 in exchange for that group's endorsement of him in the Democratic primaries.[1] Both George Bush and Bob Dole changed their positions on abortion in the race for the Republican nomination in 1992, in apparent attempts to win the endorsement of the Christian Coalition. Most recently, the AFL-CIO made opposition to fast-track trade legislation a litmus test for its support of congresspersons seeking reelection in 1998 (Jack W. Germond and Jules Witcover, [1997]); this apparently influenced the positions taken by some Democrats in the House of Representatives (Gebe Martinez, [1997]).

To what extent (if any) do policy outcomes favor special interests relative to the general interest as a result of the endorsement process? To answer this question, we require a coherent theoretical framework in which voters, politicians, and interest groups interact. Our goal in this paper is to provide such a framework and use it to examine the effects of political endorsements on policy outcomes.

In conducting an analysis of endorsements, it is important to recognize that announcements of support are a coarse language for communication. An endorsement provides only a binary comparison between candidates in a situation where voters might need a more detailed report to cast their votes optimally. The coarse nature of the endorsement may explain why it can be communicated relatively cheaply; the identity of the backed individual or party can be relayed in a simple message requiring little input from the recipient to be "heard." But the members of an interest group may share only certain policy preferences with their associates, while holding personal views on a host of other issues. For example, the members of a labor union may be united in their feelings about the minimum wage and trade liberalization, but differ in their opinions about abortion and gun control. Then it would not be enough for the union members to know the identity of the candidate or party preferred by their leader; they would wish as well to know the intensity of that preference. Only then could these voters weigh their concerns over labor matters against their interests in other policy dimensions. In short, the coarseness of the message space confronts the recipients with a signal-extraction problem. Our paper employs concepts used in analyzing games of asymmetric information to shed light on this problem.

---

[1] The Donnelly (1980) and Freeman (1988) articles are cited by Ronald B. Rapoport et al. (1991, p. 194), who conclude that "endorsements were actively sought by the candidates, and groups received tangible rewards in the form of platform commitments."

In this paper we develop a simple model of a two-party election with interest-group endorsements. We consider an election that will determine two policies. The parties are assumed to have *fixed* and invariant positions on one of the issues, reflecting perhaps their different ideologies. On the other issue, the positions are *pliable*. The parties announce platforms on this issue with an eye toward maximizing their vote counts. On both the fixed (ideological) and pliable issues, the policy outcome is taken to be a compromise between the respective positions, with weights that reflect the parties' shares of the popular vote.

All voters know the positions of the parties on the ideological issue and their own preferences regarding this issue. They also know the stated positions on the pliable policy issue. However, they do not fully comprehend how the various levels of this policy instrument would affect them personally. For example, voters might know that one party favors a minimum wage of $4.25 per hour while the other favors a wage of $5 per hour, yet they may be unsure about how the minimum wage impinges on their own expected income. We model this imperfect information as uncertainty in the minds of voters as to their own ideal point in the (pliable) policy space.

Certain of the voters are members of an organized interest group. This group comprises voters who share similar interests with respect to the pliable policy issue. When the members learn the positions of the two parties and hear which has been endorsed by their leader, they gain information about where their interests might lie. This new information allows these voters to update their beliefs about their expected ideal point. Using their updated beliefs, the group members assess the pliable platforms of the two parties and weigh the differences against their own personal feelings about the parties' ideological stances.

The remainder of the paper is organized as follows. In the next section we describe the few previous papers that have focused on political endorsements and indicate the place of our work in this literature. Section 2 gives the details of our model and examines the benchmark case of no endorsements (or, equivalently, endorsements that are totally uninformative). In Section 3, we derive a neutrality result. Suppose there is only one interest group and the members of this group have interests that are perfectly complementary to the rest of the voting population. Then, if the group leader's endorsement is heard by all voters and they all draw similar inferences from it, the policy positions and election outcome are the same as in the benchmark case. This result suggests conditions under which endorsements may have electoral impacts: when they are not (perfectly) observed by nonmembers of the interest group or when the interests of group members are not (perfectly) complementary to those of the outsiders. In Section 4, we describe an equilibrium that can arise under either of these circumstances, assuming the existence of a single interest group whose leader follows either a simple endorsement rule or behaves strategically. This equilibrium is further examined in Section 5, where we evaluate its efficiency properties and compare the group members' welfare to what they would obtain were they perfectly informed. The final section contains a summary of the findings and discusses how they extend to situations with multiple interest groups.

1 The Literature on Political Endorsements

Much of the literature on the role of interest groups in electoral competition and policy determination has focused on campaign contributions. David P. Baron (1994), for example, studied an election in which interest groups contribute resources to the parties whose positions they prefer, and parties use these gifts to fund spending aimed at a group of impressionable voters. Our own previous work (1994, 1996b) has examined how contributors might use their giving to directly influence the positions adopted by policy makers and political parties.

While there is no denying the importance of campaign contributions in American politics and elsewhere, the literature's thorough investigation of them has perhaps diverted analytical attention from other tools that groups can and do use in their efforts to influence political outcomes. Political endorsements, for example, although prominent in many elections, have received scant attention in the literature.

Richard McKelvey and Peter Ordeshook (1985) were the first to identify group endorsements as a potential source of information for imperfectly informed voters. In their model, a subset of voters does not know the positions of two candidates in a policy space represented by the real line. These voters acquire information by observing the outcomes of a sequence of "polls" taken prior to the election. Endorsements are assumed to provide additional information; they allow voters to identify the candidate whose position is further to the left or the right.

The endorsement process is left implicit in the paper by McKelvey and Ordeshook, but is treated explicitly by Bernard Grofman and Barbara Norrander (1990). In their model, two candidates have fixed positions on the real line. These positions are obscure to the single voter. The voter takes his cues from two knowledgeable "endorsers" whose preferences are known to him. Each endorser is assumed to support her favorite candidate, either invariably, or in the event that the candidate's position lies within some maximum distance from her own ideal point. The voter updates his beliefs based on his observation of these (nonstrategic) endorsements.

Lupia (1992) and Charles M. Cameron and Joon Pyo Jung (1995) consider the role of endorsements in referendum voting. In each case there is a status quo point on the real line and an "agenda setter" who can propose an alternative. The setter has preferences over policy outcomes and designs a proposal to maximize her welfare, knowing that the initiative will displace the status quo only if it garners majority support. The voters do not observe the proposal directly (e.g., they do not understand the details of the referendum initiative), but they do know the utility function of its proponent. Lupia introduces a nonstrategic endorser who informs voters whether the proposal is to the left or the right of the status quo. In contrast, Cameron and Jung allow the endorser to behave strategically. Their endorser, who has preferences like anyone else, chooses whether to support the proposal or not in order to further her own self-interest. The voters know the endorser's preferences and use the information implicit in her decision to update their beliefs.

Several features distinguish our paper from these earlier ones. First, we allow two political parties to compete for endorsements. That is, the parties consider how their positions will affect the endorsers' pronouncements and factor this in when choosing their platforms. Of course, this is not possible in Grofman and Norrander's model, where the candidates' positions are fixed exogenously. The agenda setter studied by Lupia and by Cameron and Jung does anticipate the actions of the endorser(s), but the status quo policy is taken as given in their setting. Second, we consider an election with multiple policy dimensions, only some of which are of concern to the endorsers. This is important, as we noted in the introduction, because it forces the voters to assess the likely quantitative significance of the endorsement, and not just its qualitative significance. Our paper treats both the case of an endorser who follows a mechanical rule, as in Grofman and Norrander and in Lupia, and one who is a strategic agent, as in Cameron and Jung. In short, ours is the first paper that seeks to reconcile the simultaneous and complex interactions between multiple office-seeking politicians, self-interested endorsers, and welfare-maximizing voters.

Our paper follows the previous literature by isolating endorsements from the other actions that interest groups might undertake to influence political outcomes. In particular, our model allows no role for campaign contributions. While it is true that contributions and endorsements often come hand in hand, these tools seem aimed at different audiences. The intent of contributors may be to purchase influence directly or to signal to politicians a group's keen concern about a particular issue (see Richard Ball, [1995]). Indeed, groups often attempt to conceal their contributions from the public to the extent possible. Endorsements, on the other hand, are public announcements explicitly intended to convey information to voters. In any event, it seems a natural first step to try to understand the role of endorsements in isolation, before addressing their effectiveness in more complicated settings where several tools are being used at once. Ultimately, of course, we would like to understand what instruments different groups will use in different political environments, and how the various tools interact.

2 The Model and a Benchmark

We study the competition between two political parties for seats in a legislature. The legislature will be called on to set two policies. On one issue the positions of the two parties are assumed to be *fixed*. These positions might reflect, for example, the parties' political ideologies or their stated goals on an issue of long-standing deliberation. It may be difficult for the parties to change such committed positions in the course of a single campaign. In contrast, the parties' positions on the second issue are perfectly *pliable*. The politicians have no particular preferences concerning the outcome in this dimension and view their platforms as tactical choices in the electoral competition. Our analysis focuses on the determination of the pliable policy.

After the election, the levels of the two policies are set. The outcome of this will depend inter alia on the rules and institutions of the governing body and the nature of the negotiating process. Rather than modeling these in any detail, we simply assume that a compromise agreement is reached, one that gives more weight to a party's platform the greater its share of the popular vote. In particular, let q^A and q^B denote the positions of the parties on the fixed policy issue and normalize these positions so that $q^A = 0$ and $q^B = 1$. Let p^A and p^B be their positions on the pliable issue, where p^j is any real number between 0 and 1. We assume

$$p = \psi(s)p^A + [1 - \psi(s)]p^B, \tag{1}$$

and

$$q = 1 - \psi(s), \tag{2}$$

where p and q are the policy outcomes in the pliable and fixed dimension, s is the fraction of votes captured by party A, and $\psi(s)$ is the weight attached to this party's position in forming the policy compromise. We also assume that $\psi'(s) \geq 0$ for all s and that $\psi(s) = 1 - \psi(1 - s)$; the latter means that the parties have equal ability to bargain over policies given the number of votes.

The objective of each party is to maximize its vote share. This objective might reflect a party's desire for a fixed policy outcome close to its ideological ideal, or the parties might seek to maximize patronage while believing that the spoils of office expand with the size of their delegation. In any event, the parties' pronouncements on the pliable policy are their sole tools of electoral competition.

Voters are numerous and distinguished by their preferences over the two policy outcomes. For any policy vector (p, q) the utility of a voter with taste parameters (π, β) is given by

$$u(p, q) = -a(p - \pi)^2 + \beta q. \tag{3}$$

Here, $\pi \in [0, 1]$ identifies the voter's ideal point in the pliable policy space and β indicates her relative preference (positive or negative) for the fixed policy position of party B.

We assume that all voters know their tastes for the fixed policy and know how to evaluate the possible policy outcomes. This issue might be ideologically charged or one of long-standing contention—as we have already noted—and so voters may have discussed it thoroughly or witnessed many reports on it in the media. Voters are less well informed about the pliable issue. In particular, because this is a new or complicated issue, voters do not recognize the relationship between the level of the policy instrument and their own well-being. We model a voter's imperfect understanding of the policy issue as uncertainty about the location of her ideal point π.

Voters fall into one of two categories. A fraction n of the voters belong to a special interest group. These voters, whom we refer to as *insiders*, know that they share similar goals for the pliable policy. In particular, an insider is aware that her group comprises a set of voters whose ideal pliable policy is π_I.[2] The typical insider holds the prior belief that her group's ideal point has been drawn from some distribution with a support of $[0, 1]$. We denote by $F(\pi_I)$ the cumulative distribution function associated with these beliefs, and impose on it the following restrictions.

ASSUMPTION 1. The cumulative distribution function $F(\pi_I)$ of prior beliefs about π_I is log-concave for all $\pi_I \in [0, 1]$, and its density function $f(\pi_I)$ is positive and symmetric around ½.

The assumption of log-concavity [i.e., that $\log F(\pi_I)$ is a concave function of π_I] is a relatively weak restriction satisfied by the uniform and triangular distributions and many others.

Although the interest-group members hold identical preferences with respect to the pliable policy issue, this does not mean that they all feel similarly about the two political parties. We suppose, in fact, that insiders

---

[2] In an earlier version of this paper (Grossman and Helpman, [1996a]), we supposed that insiders' interests regarding the pliable issue are not identical, but rather the group comprises a set of voters whose ideal pliable policy is uniformly distributed over some range. This alternative specification gives nearly identical results.

hold disparate views on the fixed policy issue, much like the voting population at large. For each possible value of π for for an insider, the conditional distribution of β is uniform on the interval $[-1/2k - b/k, 1/2k - b/k]$, $k > 0$ and $|b| < \frac{1}{2}$. Here k is the density of the conditional distribution and so $1/k$ measures the diversity of opinions. The parameter b indicates the average preference among insiders for the fixed position of party A.

The remaining fraction $1 - n$ of voters do not belong to any interest group. Later, we will distinguish situations where these *outsiders* believe that there is a relationship between their own interests in the pliable policy and that of the insiders from cases where they believe no such relationship exists. For now, we only assume that an outsider holds the prior belief that her ideal point has been drawn from some symmetric distribution with mean $\frac{1}{2}$ and support $[0, 1]$. Among these voters, too, the distribution of β conditional on π is uniform on $[-1/2k - b/k, 1/2k - b/k]$.

Each voter recognizes that the policy outcome will be a compromise between the positions of the two parties. A ballot cast for party A will augment slightly the weight attached to its platform in forming the compromise. An individual votes for party A if and only if, given her beliefs at the time of the election, she perceives that the implied change in policy would raise her expected utility. More formally, let Ω denote the information available to a voter at the time of the election and let $\mathcal{E}$ represent the expectation operator. Then the voter casts her ballot for party A if and only if $d\mathcal{E}[u(p, q|\Omega)]/ds \geq 0$. Using (1), (2), and (3), we can restate the voting rule as[3]

$$\text{vote for party } A \text{ if and only if} \qquad (4)$$

$$\beta \leq 2a(p - \mathcal{E}[\pi|\Omega])(p^B - p^A).$$

The voter compares the anticipated compromise on the pliable issue to her expected ideal point, basing the expectation on her beliefs at the time of the election. If the former is larger (smaller), then she votes for the party with the lower (higher) position on the pliable issue, unless her relative preference for the other party's fixed policy position is great. This specification presumes that each voter correctly forecasts the compromise outcomes for p and q; i.e., that voters' expectations are rational.

We allow for the possibility that insiders and outsiders have access to different information sets; e.g., insiders will have observed the endorsement issued by their group's leader while outsiders may not have done

---

[3] Since very few voters will be indifferent between voting for party A and voting for party B, it does not matter whether we assume that all of these voters vote for A or that each such voter selects randomly.

so. Then, to calculate the fraction of votes captured by each party, we need to compute separately the fractions among each voter category and take a weighted average of the two. Using (4) and the assumed distribution of β, we find that party A captures a fraction

$$s = \tfrac{1}{2} + b + 2ka(p - n\mathcal{E}_I[\pi|\Omega_I] \tag{5}$$
$$- (1 - n)\mathcal{E}_O[\pi|\Omega_O])(p^B - p^A)$$

of the votes, where $\mathcal{E}_I(\cdot)$ and $\mathcal{E}_O(\cdot)$ are the expected values of π among insiders and outsiders, respectively, and Ω_I and Ω_O are the information sets available to these two types of voters.[4]

We seek to characterize a perfect Bayesian equilibrium (PBE) of a game with the following sequence of stages. First, nature chooses π_I from the distribution $F(\pi_I)$ on $[0, 1]$. This "choice" is revealed to the political parties and the leader of the interest group but not to the individual voters.[5] Second, the parties simultaneously announce their positions on the pliable issue. Third, the interest group's leader endorses one of the parties. Fourth, the voters update their beliefs about their personal desiderata based on their new information and cast their ballots. Finally, the election determines the vote shares and the policies are set in accordance with the compromise rule.

In seeking to maximize their vote shares, the parties need to evaluate not only the direct effects of their announcements, as reflected in the last parenthetical term in (5) and implicitly in p, but also the indirect effects that result from any induced impact on the behavior of the endorser and the consequent changes in voters' perceptions. This is a complicated calculation requiring an understanding of the leader's endorsement rule (or strategy) and the process by which voters form their expectations about π. But before we even specify these elements, there are several observations we can make about an electoral equilibrium. First, party A can ensure itself that s is no less than $\frac{1}{2} + b$ by mimicking the pliable position of party B. Similarly, party B can ensure itself that s is no greater than $\frac{1}{2} + b$ by copying the position of party A. In a Nash equilibrium we must have s no greater and no less than $\frac{1}{2} + b$; therefore, the equilibrium composition of the legislature reflects only the ex ante preferences of the voters. Now (5) implies that either the two pliable platforms are the same or that

---

[4] In computing (5) we assume that the diversity of views on the fixed policy issue is wide enough (i.e., the density k is small enough) so that for every possible value of π and every pair of pliable policies that might emerge in equilibrium, there is at least one insider and one outsider who votes for party A, and one from each category who votes for party B.

[5] In other words, the politicians and the group leader learn the members' true preferences, even as these preferences remain obscure to the members themselves. This assumption is meant to capture the politicians' and leader's superior understanding of the technical details of the policy issue.

the pliable compromise exactly matches the expected π in the aggregate population. We have thus established the following proposition.

Proposition 1. In any electoral equilibrium, (i) $s = \frac{1}{2} + b$, (ii) $p = \psi(\frac{1}{2} + b)p^A + [1 - \psi(\frac{1}{2} + b)]p^B$, and (iii) either $p^A = p^B$ or $p = n\mathcal{E}_I[\pi|\Omega_I] + (1 - n)\mathcal{E}_O[\pi|\Omega_O]$.

We conclude this section by considering a benchmark case. Suppose the interest-group leader makes no endorsement whatsoever or one that is perceived by voters to be totally uninformative. As an example of the latter, voters might believe that the leader will endorse each party with probability $\frac{1}{2}$ regardless of π_I and of the parties' positions. With an uninformative endorsement, the *ex post* information sets Ω_I and Ω_O are the same. It is reasonable to suppose, in this case, that insiders and outsiders will head to the polls with similar expectations about their own interests on the pliable issue. This is because the prior distribution for both types has the same mean value of π, and both types update their priors based on the same new information (namely, the policy positions).

It is straightforward to construct a plausible PBE for this benchmark case. Suppose that all voters retain their prior beliefs about π no matter what platforms they observe; that is, without an informative endorsement to serve as a cue, $\mathcal{E}_I[\pi|\Omega_I] = \mathcal{E}_O[\pi|\Omega_O] = \frac{1}{2}$. With these expectations, the parties' maximization of their vote shares implies that there is a unique electoral equilibrium in which $s = \frac{1}{2} + b$ and both parties locate at the center of the pliable policy space. We describe this equilibrium more formally in the following proposition.

Proposition 2. Suppose there is no endorsement or one that is perceived to be uninformative. Then there exists a PBE in which: (i) $\mathcal{E}_I[\pi|\Omega_I] = \mathcal{E}_O[\pi|\Omega_O] = \frac{1}{2}$ for all possible information sets Ω_I and Ω_O; and (ii) $p^A(\pi_I) = p^B(\pi_I) = \frac{1}{2}$ for all $\pi_I \in [0, 1]$.

It is easy to verify that this is a PBE. With $\mathcal{E}_I[\pi|\Omega_I] = \mathcal{E}_O[\pi|\Omega_O] = \frac{1}{2}$, the voting rule in (4) implies that $s = \frac{1}{2} + b + 2ak(p - \frac{1}{2})(p^B - p^A)$. This vote function generates a unique Nash equilibrium in which each party announces a pliable position of $\frac{1}{2}$. Moreover, the updating of beliefs satisfies Bayes' rule, because when the voters observe $p^A = p^B = \frac{1}{2}$ they obtain no information that would cause their posterior expectations to diverge from their priors. We will use this Hotelling-like equilibrium as a benchmark against which to assess the potential role of (informative) political endorsements.[6]

---

[6] The equilibrium described in proposition 2 is not the only PBE in our game. The parties might use their pliable positions to signal to voters the value of π_I and the insiders might draw (consistent) inferences from these signals. However, signalling by parties is not the focus of this paper, so we choose to ignore this possibility in order to highlight the possible informational role of endorsements.

3 A Neutrality Result

In this section we describe a situation in which interest-group endorsements are informative but not effective. This will set the stage for the next
section, where we identify conditions under which endorsements can
have real effects on political outcomes.

Suppose that outsiders perceive their interests on the pliable policy to
be exactly complementary to those of insiders; i.e., they believe that
"what's good for them is bad for us." In an economic model, such complementarity would apply to a purely redistributive policy; gains for one
group of voters would come at the expense of the others. In our spatial
model we can represent strict complementarity of interests by imposing
a relationship between the realization of π_I for insiders and the realization of the mean value of π among outsiders. In particular, let π_O be the
mean of π among outsiders, and let the processes generating π_I and π_O
be such that the *population mean* is constant and fixed at $\frac{1}{2}$; i.e.,

$$n\pi_I + (1 - n)\pi_O = \tfrac{1}{2} \tag{6}$$

$$\text{for all } \pi_I \in [0, 1].$$

Under this assumption, the outsiders will understand that any movement
of the pliable policy away from the center of the policy space that benefits insiders will, on average, be harmful to themselves. In this setting,
information about π_I, such as might be conveyed by an endorsement,
allows outsiders to update their beliefs about their own ideal policy much
as the insiders update theirs.[7]

If the endorsement is observed by all voters, all will share the same
information set $\Omega_I = \Omega_O = \Omega$. Insiders will use the endorsement to
infer something about their likely ideal point; i.e., they will form expec-
tations $\mathcal{E}_I[\pi_I|\Omega]$. Meanwhile, outsiders will be forming their own indi-
vidual expectations about their personal ideal points, $\mathcal{E}_O[\pi|\Omega]$. In view
of voters' understanding of the complementarity of interests as
expressed in (6), it is plausible to suppose that the voters' beliefs will
satisfy $n\mathcal{E}_I[\pi_I|\Omega] + (1 - n)\mathcal{E}_O[\pi_O|\Omega] = \frac{1}{2}$. This would be true, for
example, if every voter drew the same inference about π_I from her
observation of p^A, p^B, and the identity of the party that has been
endorsed. In the event, we have the same circumstances of electoral
competition as when the endorsement is uninformative. The average
(expected) ideal point among all voters will be $\frac{1}{2}$. And so the parties
will seek to maximize and minimize $s = \frac{1}{2} + b + 2ka(p - \frac{1}{2})(p^B - p^A)$
with their choices of p^A and p^B, respectively. In a Nash equilibrium,
both parties locate in the center of the pliable policy space. All of this

---

[7] From the evidence presented in Lupia (1994), it appears that respondents to the exit poll
recognized that the industry's preferences over a reform proposition were likely to be contrary to their own.

is true no matter what the true value of π_I happens to be. We have established the following proposition.

Proposition 3. Let the distribution of π for outsiders conditional on the value of π_I satisfy (6) and let the endorsement be observable to all voters. Then if all voters use the same mapping to update their beliefs about π_I based on their observations, a PBE must have $p^A(\pi_I) = p^B(\pi_I) = \frac{1}{2}$ for all $\pi_I \in [0, 1]$ regardless of the endorsement rule or strategy.

Intuitively, the parties will have no reason to compete for the endorsement if they know that the goodwill they can generate among members of the interest group will be matched by an equal or greater loss of goodwill among the remaining voters. It will always pay for a party to move to the center, even if this means losing the interest-group's endorsement as a result.

Of course, proposition 3 also suggests conditions under which an endorsement may not be so benign. First, the interests of the outsiders on the pliable issue may not be perfectly complementary to those of the insiders. At an extreme, the interests of the two types of voters may be completely independent; i.e., the conditional distribution of π among outsiders might be the same for every value of π_I. Second, the endorsement might be heard by a greater proportion of insiders than of outsiders. Again, an extreme case would arise if the endorsement could be conveyed privately to the group's membership. We will adopt one or the other of these extreme assumptions in the next section to explore the potential policy effects of endorsements.

4 Effective Endorsements

In this section we describe equilibria with effective endorsements. Our aim is to provide a joint characterization of the rule used by the endorser, the reasoning used by voters to interpret the endorser's message, and the policies adopted by the political parties in view of the endorsement rule and the voters' beliefs. Since these interactions are complex, our analysis proceeds in stages. First, we suppose that the group leader uses a mechanical endorsement rule. Such a rule dictates the endorsement for every pair of policy positions and every possible value of π_I. We restrict the class of rules to what we term *dividing-line rules* and show that the same set of beliefs and pliable policies are equilibria for *every* endorsement rule in this class. Next we allow the leader to behave strategically. In the event, the leader issues an endorsement that maximizes aggregate welfare of the interest group, in light of her understanding of how any message will be interpreted. Now the equilibrium endorsement rule is jointly determined with beliefs and policy positions: the leader does her best for the group given the pliable policies and the structure of beliefs, while beliefs depend on the rule the voters suspect is being used. Consistency requires that the rule perceived by the voters coincides with the rule that the strategic endorser actually wishes to use. We show that such a consistent rule exists and that it belongs to the class of dividing-line rules. For this reason, equilibrium policies and beliefs with a strategic endorser are identical to those with a mechanical endorser who uses an arbitrary dividing-line rule.

4.1 Mechanical Endorsements

We start with the case of a mechanical endorser who uses a dividing-line rule. Before defining this class of rules, we need some additional notation. Let E denote the recipient of the endorsement; either $E = A$ or $E = B$. Let $E_{\min}$ identify the party whose pliable position is smaller; i.e., $E_{\min} \equiv \text{argmin}_{A, B} \{p^A, p^B\}$. Similarly, $E_{\max} \equiv \text{argmax}_{A, B} \{p^A, p^B\}$. Finally, let $g(p^A, p^B)$ be any continuous function with the property that $\min\{p^A, p^B\} \leq g(p^A, p^B) \leq \max\{p^A, p^B\}$ for all p^A and p^B. Our definition of a dividing-line rule is as follows.

DEFINITION (DIVIDING-LINE RULE). If $p^A \neq p^B$ and either $g(p^A, p^B) < \pi_I$ or $g(p^A, p^B) = \pi_I = \max\{p^A, p^B\}$, then $E = E_{\max}$. If $p^A \neq p^B$ and either $g(p^A, p^B) > \pi_I$ or $g(p^A, p^B) = \pi_I = \min\{p^A, p^B\}$, then $E = E_{\min}$. Finally, if $p^A = p^B$ or if $\min\{p^A, p^B\} < g(p^A, p^B) = \pi_I < \max\{p^A, p^B\}$, then $E = A$ with probability one-half and $E = B$ with probability one-half.

Intuitively, the function $g(\cdot)$ determines a dividing line between the announced positions of the two parties. If the ideal point π_I of group members lies above the dividing line, then the endorser taps the party whose pliable policy position is higher. If the ideal point falls below the dividing line, then the endorser names the party whose pliable position is lower. If π_I falls right on the dividing line and (exactly) one of the parties has announced the group's ideal position, then this party is endorsed. Otherwise, each party receives the endorsement with probability one-half.

The function $g(p^A, p^B) = (p^A + p^B)/2$ provides a good example of a dividing-line rule. This rule sets the dividing line midway between the pliable positions of the two parties and so identifies the party whose pliable position is closer to the interest group's ideal.

We will now describe a PBE that applies for *all* rules in this class. Assume first that the interests of the outsiders happen to be orthogonal to those of the interest-group members; i.e., the conditional distribution of π for any outsider is independent of nature's choice of π_I. Then, obviously, the endorsement gives the outsiders no useful information. Insiders, meanwhile, will use the information conveyed by the endorsement to update their beliefs about their interests on the pliable issue.

The description of an equilibrium must specify not only the positions adopted by the parties, but also how voters update their beliefs in response to the events they witness. The updating of beliefs by insiders

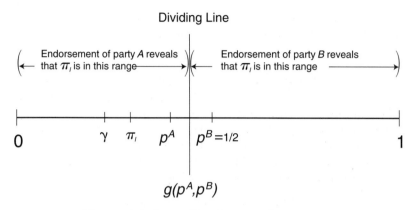

$$g(p^A, p^B)$$

Figure 1. Information from endorsement

can be best understood with the aid of Figure 1. The figure shows two possible policy positions for the two political parties. We have placed party B at the center of the policy spectrum ($p^B = \frac{1}{2}$) to facilitate later discussion. Suppose party A has announced some position $p^A < \frac{1}{2}$, as shown. Between the two policies is the dividing line $g(p^A, p^B)$. If the interest-group leader knows that the group's ideal point π_I lies to the left of $g(p^A, p^B)$, she will endorse party A. Seeing this endorsement, the insiders will be able to rule out the possibility that $\pi_I > g(p^A, p^B)$. This information allows the insiders to form a new expectation about π_I, one that gives no weight to the possibility that $\pi_I > g(p^A, p^B)$. Similarly, if π_I happens to fall to the right of the dividing line, the endorser would tap party B and group members, inferring that $\pi_I \geq g(p^A, p^B)$, would form their expectations of π_I based on a posterior distribution that puts no weight on the possibility that $\pi_I < g(p^A, p^B)$.

The insiders use Bayes' rule for updating their beliefs. When an endorsement reveals that π_I must be less than some number z, their posterior distribution has density $f(\pi_I)/F(z)$ for $\pi_I \in [0, z]$ and density 0 for $\pi_I \in (z, 1]$. They can calculate an expected value of π_I based on the knowledge that $\pi_I \leq z$, which we denote by $M(z)$;

$$M(z) \equiv \frac{1}{F(z)} \int_0^z x f(x)\, dx. \tag{7}$$

Outsiders, meanwhile, retain their prior belief that their own ideal point is (on average) at $\frac{1}{2}$. Thus, the expected value of π in the population at large becomes $nM(z) + (1 - n)/2$ when the insiders learn that $\pi_I \leq z$. This allows us, finally, to define a variable γ, which is the cutoff point such that, if insiders knew their ideal point to lie to the left of γ and updated using Bayes' rule, then the resulting expected value of π in the population at large also would be γ. More formally, γ solves

$$\gamma = nM(\gamma) + (1 - n)\tfrac{1}{2}. \tag{8}$$

It can be seen that (8) gives a unique value for $\gamma < \tfrac{1}{2}$ and that γ is inversely related to the size of the special interest group.[8] We will see that γ plays an important role in the characterization of an equilibrium.

Before proceeding further, we shall make a technical assumption limiting the size of the interest group. This assumption is sufficient for our characterization of the equilibrium, but in most cases it is stronger than what is actually needed. We assume the following.

ASSUMPTION 2. $n \leq \min\{[\psi(\tfrac{1}{2} + b)/M], [1 - \psi(\tfrac{1}{2} + b)/M], \tfrac{1}{2}\}$, where $M \equiv \max_{x \in [0,1]} M'(x)$. We note that $M = \tfrac{1}{2}$ when priors are uniform, $M = \tfrac{2}{3}$ when they are triangular, and that M always is a finite number.

We are now ready to describe a PBE in which political endorsements play a role in policy determination. In this equilibrium, the parties compete for the interest group's endorsement by shifting their positions on the pliable issue (relative to the benchmark outcome) in the direction beneficial to the group's members. Our statement of the proposition in the text indicates only the platforms and policy outcomes that are observed in the equilibrium. The technically minded reader may consult the Appendix for a fuller statement of the proposition that provides the details of the supporting beliefs.

Proposition 4. Let the conditional distribution of π for outsiders be independent of π_I and let the endorsement be observable to all voters. Suppose that the endorsement obeys a dividing-line rule and that assumptions 1 and 2 are satisfied. Then there exists a PBE in which

(i) $p^A(\pi_I) = p^B(\pi_I) = p(\pi_I)$

$$= \begin{cases} \gamma & \text{for } 0 \leq \pi_I \leq \gamma; \\ \pi_I & \text{for } \gamma < \pi_I < 1 - \gamma \\ 1 - \gamma & \text{for } 1 - \gamma \leq \pi_I \leq 1 \end{cases}$$

(ii) $q = 1 - \psi(\tfrac{1}{2} + b)$.

---

[8] Let $Q(\gamma)$ denote the right-hand side of (8). There must be at least one root of $\gamma = Q(\gamma)$ for $\gamma \in (0, \tfrac{1}{2})$, because $Q(0) > 0$, $Q(\tfrac{1}{2}) < \tfrac{1}{2}$, and $Q(\cdot)$ is continuous. Moreover, $Q'(\gamma) = n(1 - n)f(\gamma)[\tfrac{1}{2} - M(\gamma)]/F(\gamma)$ at points where $\gamma = Q(\gamma)$. Since $M'(\gamma) > 0$, it follows from the log-concavity of $F(\cdot)$ that $Q''(\gamma) < 0$ at such values of γ, and thus $Q'(\gamma)$ is smaller the larger is γ. Therefore, the solution for γ must be unique.

The proposition is proved in the appendix. Here we discuss its meaning and provide intuition.

In the equilibrium described by proposition 4, the parties compete vigorously for the endorsement, but only "up to a point." If the interest-group members truly are moderates—that is, if they hold an ideal policy position not too far from ½—then the parties converge on exactly this position, and the policy outcome fulfills the group's ideal. However, if the group members are more extreme in their preferences, the parties will not go all the way to satisfying their wishes. In fact, the parties do not announce positions less than γ (or greater than $1 - \gamma$), no matter how extreme the group's tastes. The pliable policy outcome is at γ whenever $\pi_I \leq \gamma$, and at $1 - \gamma$ whenever $\pi_I \geq 1 - \gamma$, and thus is not responsive to π_I in these ranges. The larger is the interest group, the smaller is γ, and so the larger is the range of values of π_I for which the group attains its ideal.

To understand the basis for this equilibrium, let us begin at the benchmark. Suppose both parties were contemplating positions at the center of the policy spectrum, and now let party A entertain a possible deviation to the position marked p^A in Figure 1. This deviation would win party A the endorsement of the interest group. The group's members would update their beliefs, now recognizing that $\pi_I \leq g(p^A, \frac{1}{2})$, and would calculate an updated expected value of π_I equal to $M[g(p^A, \frac{1}{2})]$. For p^A sufficiently close to ½, this expected value of π_I would be less than p^A. But with $\mathcal{E}_I(\pi_I) < p^A < p^B$, the voting rule (4) implies that party A captures more than the fraction $\frac{1}{2} + b$ of the group members' votes. The deviation wins party A votes among the insiders, because by capturing the leader's endorsement the party induces the group members to believe that its pliable position better serves their interests. At the same time, the deviation costs party A votes among outsiders, because these voters retain their belief that their ideal pliable policy has an expected value of ½. However, the vote gain among insiders outweighs the loss among outsiders, at least for deviations close enough to $p^B = \frac{1}{2}$. For p^A close to ½, party A loses only a "few" votes among outsiders, because the parties' pliable positions are close to one another, and both are close to the outsiders' (expected) ideal. The vote gain among insiders is an order of magnitude larger, because although they too see the two platforms as similar, they see both as relatively distant from their (updated) ideal point at $\mathcal{E}_I(\pi_I)$. In other words, the perceived utility difference between the two pliable platforms is substantially larger for insiders than for outsiders, and so more of them will be inclined to shift their votes to the party whose pliable policy they prefer.

Now two things can happen, according to the proposition. First, for moderate values of π_I, both parties will depart from the benchmark to announce positions exactly at π_I. Second, for more extreme values of π_I, the parties will announce positions at γ (or, symmetrically, at $1 - \gamma$, if $\pi_I > \frac{1}{2}$) and evidently neither will have an incentive to deviate further. Let us consider each possibility in turn.

With a moderate value of π_I such as that depicted in Figure 1, suppose party A anticipates that its rival will announce a pliable position of $p^B = \pi_I$. What then are the incentives facing this party? If it also were to adopt π_I as its pliable position, then whatever the (random) endorsement by the group leader, party A would capture the fraction $\frac{1}{2} + b$ of the votes of both insiders and outsiders. This is shown in Figure 2, which plots the vote counts for party A among each group and in toto as functions of the position taken by party A (assuming $p^B = \pi_I$). Another possibility is that party A might opt for a position $p^A < \pi_I$. Clearly, it would then win less than the fraction $\frac{1}{2} + b$ of the outsiders' $1 - n$ votes. These voters perceive an expected ideal of $\frac{1}{2}$, and so they prefer the pliable platform of party B to that of party A when $p^A < p^B < \frac{1}{2}$. Moreover, the announcement by party A of a platform $p^A < \pi_I$ when $p^B = \pi_I$ would cause the group leader to endorse party B. The group members would infer that $\pi_I \geq g(p^A, \pi_I)$ and would calculate a new expectation of π_I greater than p^B. Then, since $\mathcal{E}_I(\pi_I) > p^B > p^A$, party A would capture fewer than the fraction $\frac{1}{2} + b$ of their votes. In short, the announcement by party A of a platform $p^A < \pi_I$ yields fewer than the fraction $\frac{1}{2} + b$ of the votes of both insiders and outsiders and so is dominated by the announcement of $p^A = \pi_I$.

A more interesting possibility is that party A might locate its policy slightly above π_I, closer to the center of the policy space. This would make

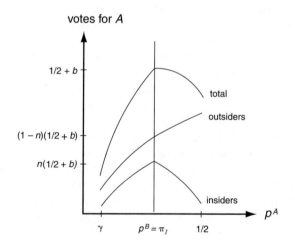

Figure 2. Vote counts

the party *more* attractive than its rival to outsiders (with their expected ideal points at $\frac{1}{2}$), and so party A would capture more than the fraction $\frac{1}{2} + b$ of their votes, as depicted in the figure. But the party again would sacrifice the endorsement of the interest group. With the leader endorsing party B, and $p^A > p^B$, insiders would interpret the endorsement to mean $\pi_I \leq g(p^A, \pi_I)$. They would calculate $E_I[\pi_I | \pi_I \leq g(p^A, \pi_I) = M[g(p^A, \pi_I)] < p^B$. Thus, the move would cost party A votes among insiders, relative to the alternative of locating exactly at π_I. Herein lies the trade-off confronting party A.

So which is bigger, the gain in votes among outsiders or the loss in votes among insiders? Equation (5) tells us that, with $p^A > p^B$, the aggregate vote share for party A exceeds $\frac{1}{2} + b$ if and only if the anticipated policy compromise p is below the population mean expected value of π. With p^A and p^B both close to π_I, the anticipated compromise also is close to π_I. But the population mean expected value of π must be greater than π_I, in view of the definition of γ and the fact that $\pi_I > \gamma$. It follows that party A attracts more total votes by locating at π_I than by locating slightly to the right of π_I; the gain in outsider votes from deviating slightly to the right does not compensate the loss in insider votes.[9] The best response to $p^B = \pi_I$ is for party A to announce π_I, and both parties converge on the interest group's ideal pliable position.

Now consider the case where the interest group's preferences are more extreme; i.e., $\pi_I < \gamma$. Then, if party B were located at π_I, party A could improve its vote count (relative to locating at π_I as well) by locating just to the right of its rival. This move would cost the party the interest group's endorsement, but the ensuing loss of insider votes would be more than compensated by the gain in outsider votes. The definition of γ ensures that this is so, because with $\pi_I < \gamma$, the updating of beliefs that attends the endorsement of party B leaves the population mean expected value of π less than π_I. But with $p^A > p^B$ and both close to π_I, this implies by (5) a vote share for party A in excess of $\frac{1}{2} + b$. Both parties will have an incentive to move from π_I toward the center, when π_I is extreme.

How far will they move? If party B is located anywhere to the left of γ, the above argument establishes that party A can capture more than $\frac{1}{2} + b$ of the seats by locating just to its right. Proposition 1 rules this out as a possible equilibrium outcome. Similarly, if party B is located to the right of γ, party A can capture more than $\frac{1}{2} + b$ of the seats by locating just to its left. This situation too cannot arise in equilibrium. The only remaining possibility is that party B locates exactly at γ, in which case it is a best

---

[9] The argument against deviations to points far to the right of π_I is somewhat more technical and requires that $nM < \psi(\frac{1}{2} + b)$, as stipulated by assumption 2. The argument is provided in the appendix.

response for party A to follow suit. This concludes our discussion of the equilibrium when the interests of outsiders are orthogonal to those of the interest-group members.

It is worth emphasizing that the political equilibrium described in proposition 4 is robust to the particulars of the endorsement rule; the same platforms and policies can emerge for all rules in the broad class of dividing-line rules.

Let us return briefly to the case where the interests of the outsiders are perfectly complementary to those of the insiders. Suppose now that the outsiders do *not* observe the group leader's endorsement. The main point to be made is that a PBE very similar to the one described in proposition 4 exists in this case as well. In this equilibrium, the platforms are the same as those specified in proposition 4, as are the updated beliefs of insiders. Only the beliefs of the outsiders are different.[10]

4.2 Strategic Endorsements

In the preceding section we restricted the leader to follow a simple mechanical rule. But what if the leader is a player in the game and is perhaps tempted to behave strategically?

The reader might be wondering why the interest-group leader would have any incentive to behave strategically vis-à-vis the members of the group. After all, the leader presumably has the best interests of the members at heart. An incentive for strategic behavior arises nonetheless from the members' disparate views on the fixed policy issue. No matter what his policy objectives, the leader may wish that all members of his group would vote for the same party, so as to push the compromise policy as close to his target outcome as possible. But the group members, if well informed, would not vote as a bloc. Rather, those with a strong affinity for the ideological position of party A would vote for that party notwithstanding the negative effect of their votes on the aggregate well-being of the group. Similarly, those with a strong preference for the fixed position of party B would vote unfailingly for that party. The leader then may behave strategically in an attempt to induce as many individuals as possible to cast their ballots in the collective interest.

We suppose here that the leader of the interest group is concerned only with the pliable policy outcome.[11] The leader seeks to maximize

$$U = -a(p - \pi_I)^2, \tag{9}$$

[10] Our working paper, Grossman and Helpman (1996a), describes the supporting beliefs.

[11] Our conclusions in this section are not sensitive to this assumption. We could alternatively have the leader maximizing the aggregate welfare of group members, including the utility they derive from the fixed policy outcome.

which is the utility that each member derives from the realization of the pliable policy. With this objective, the leader chooses whom to endorse with an eye toward minimizing the distance between the anticipated policy outcome and the group's ideal point. In order to decide whom to endorse, the leader must gauge how his backing will be interpreted by the group's members. At the same time, the members' interpretation presumably depends on the incentives they judge for their leader.

There is a surprisingly simple solution to this inference problem. We can show that there always exists a particular dividing-line rule with desirable consistency properties. Namely, if group members suspect their leader of following this particular rule, they can (consistently) update their beliefs in the manner specified by proposition 4. And if the leader anticipates this updating procedure, the indicated rule indeed maximizes $U(\cdot)$ in (9). This means that the parties can (consistently) forecast this rule and set their platforms in its full anticipation. In other words, the platforms and policies described in proposition 4 remain PBE outcomes when the group leader behaves strategically.

The appendix contains a proof of the following proposition.

Proposition 5. Let the conditional distribution of π for outsiders be independent of π_I and let the endorsement be observable to all voters. Suppose that the interest-group leader issues his endorsement to maximize (9) and that assumptions 1 and 2 are satisfied. Then there exists a PBE with a dividing-line rule $g(\cdot)$ such that

 (i)   voters expect the leader to use the dividing-line rule $g(\cdot)$;
 (ii) $g(\cdot)$ is optimal for the interest-group leader given voters' beliefs;
 (iii) voters' beliefs and parties' platforms are exactly as in proposition 4.

Here we will try to explain why the result is true.

Suppose that members of the interest group suspect their leader of using some particular dividing-line rule, say the one described by the function $g^\circ(p^A, p^B)$. Suppose further that, upon hearing the policy stances and the leader's endorsement, these individuals update their beliefs about π_I as we have described before. In particular, an endorsement of the party with the uppermost pliable policy leads members to rule out the possibility that $\pi_I \leq g^\circ(p^A, p^B)$, while an endorsement of the party with the lowermost pliable policy leads members to rule out $\pi_I \geq g^\circ(p^A, p^B)$. Beyond that, the updating applies Bayes' rule. Then, for each pair of platforms p^A and p^B an insider seeing an endorsement of one party or the other will form an expectation $E_I[\pi_I|p^A, p^B, E]$, which she will use in deciding what lever to pull in the voting booth.

Having specified how an endorsement will be interpreted, we know how each insider will vote when the platforms are p^A and p^B and when the leader has announced support for one party or the other. Suppose that outsiders retain their prior beliefs that their expected ideal position is ½ whenever the pliable platforms of the two parties diverge. Then the leader can calculate the votes that each party would garner were he to endorse party A upon hearing the platforms p^A and p^B, and also the votes that each would receive were he instead to tap party B. Since he can calculate the vote tallies that ensue from his actions, the leader also can calculate the policy compromises that would attend an endorsement of either party. One of these outcomes gives higher welfare according to the objective function $U(\cdot)$ in (9). This is the endorsement that the strategic leader will make when the platforms are p^A and p^B.

We argue now that the endorsement procedure just described is itself a dividing-line rule. For any two possible policy outcomes, the utility function $U(\cdot)$ in (9) is maximized by the choice of the policy that is closer to π_I. So, if the endorsement of party A would lead to a compromise outcome of, say, $\tilde{p}^A$, whereas the endorsement of party B would lead to an outcome of $\tilde{p}^B > \tilde{p}^A$, then the leader would endorse party A if and only if π_I fell below the midpoint between $\tilde{p}^A$ and $\tilde{p}^B$. But notice that this midpoint is itself between the platforms p^A and p^B, since each of the two compromises $\tilde{p}^A$ and $\tilde{p}^B$ lies between the two platforms. We conclude that, for each platform pair p^A and p^B, the leader's endorsement reflects a comparison of the ideal point π_I and a point between the two platforms. But that is precisely what characterizes a dividing-line rule.

We have argued that when members anticipate an arbitrary endorsement rule $g°(\cdot)$, the maximizing leader opts for a particular dividing-line rule, say $\tilde{g}(\cdot)$. Each suspected endorsement rule gives rise to some specific optimal endorsement rule. But there is, as yet, no guarantee of consistency between the two. But what if there existed a dividing-line rule that, when anticipated by members, gave rise to optimizing behavior by the leader of exactly the same form? Then such a rule would have the desired consistency property. Technically speaking, we need a fixed point in the mapping from $g°$ to $\tilde{g}$.

The proof of proposition 5 establishes the existence of such a fixed point by construction. For each pair of platforms, let the insiders suspect a "dividing point" specific to that pair. If this point were equal to the lesser of the two platforms, the optimal dividing point for the leader—which we have argued always lies between p^A and p^B—would be above the suspected dividing point. If the suspected dividing point were equal to the greater of the two platforms, the optimal dividing point would be below the suspected point. Since the optimal point can be shown to be a continuous function of the suspected point, there must be a value for which the two are equal. Repeating this procedure for every possible platform pair generates the desired dividing-line rule, $g(p^A, p^B)$.

As endorsers, strategic leaders do no better for their charges than mechanical leaders. Once the members take into account their leader's incentives, the leader loses his ability to manipulate the group. What remains is only the information that can be conveyed in a simple, binary message.

We have established that endorsements by special interest groups can affect policy outcomes. When the interests of group members are not perfectly complementary to those of outsiders, the parties will compete for an endorsement knowing that its value outweighs the cost of alienating some marginal supporters. Similarly, when outsiders do not observe the leader's pronouncement, the parties may have incentives to pander to the group's interests at the expense of unwitting outsiders. In either case, the parties grant a relatively centrist group its first-best pliable platform while tilting somewhat in the direction of a group with more extreme desires.

5 Welfare

We devote this section to analyzing the normative properties of the equilibrium described by propositions 4 and 5. Since proposition 4 contains the details of the equilibrium policies, we shall refer to it for comparison purposes. It should be clear, however, that the same applies to comparisons with proposition 5, which describes equilibria for a strategic endorser.

Conditional on the value of π_I the utility of a representative group member is given by

$$u_I(p, q|\pi_I) = -a(p - \pi_I)^2 + \beta q. \qquad (10)$$

An outsider has a conditional distribution for π that is independent of π_I under the conditions of proposition 4. Letting $\varphi(\pi)$ represent the density of this conditional distribution, an outsider's expected utility equals

$$u_O(p, q|\pi_I) = -a \int_0^1 (p - \pi)^2 \varphi(\pi) \, d\pi + \beta q \qquad (11)$$

$$= -a(p - \tfrac{1}{2})^2 - a \operatorname{var}(\pi_O) + \beta q.$$

where $\operatorname{var}(\pi_O)$ is the variance of π in this group of voters. Aggregate expected welfare is a weighted average of u_I and u_O, with the population sizes n and $1 - n$ serving as weights.

We compare the equilibrium described by proposition 4 with the benchmark equilibrium of proposition 2. In the benchmark setting, the pliable policy falls in the center of the policy space, whereas with competition for an endorsement, $p > \frac{1}{2}$ when $\pi_I > \frac{1}{2}$ and $p < \frac{1}{2}$ when $\pi_I < \frac{1}{2}$. In both equilibria, the fixed policy outcome is $q = 1 - \psi(\frac{1}{2} + b)$, because $s = \frac{1}{2} + b$ in either case. It follows immediately from (10) and (11) that, no matter what the value of π_I, group members fare better, and outsiders worse, in the equilibrium with endorsements than in the benchmark situation.

The overall efficiency implications of the competition for an endorsement are less obvious. On the one hand, an endorsement conveys useful information to a group of uninformed voters and allows their true interests to be reflected in the political process. On the other hand, the competition for the endorsement might lead to an overrepresentation of these interests at the expense of some others.

The equilibrium of proposition 4 does entail a loss of aggregate welfare compared to the benchmark outcome whenever $\pi_I \in [\gamma, 1 - \gamma]$. When group members have moderate tastes in this range, the equilibrium in proposition 4 caters fully to their interests. Then the n members each gain $a(\frac{1}{2} - \pi_I)^2$ in expected utility relative to the benchmark outcome with $p = \frac{1}{2}$. Meanwhile, the $1 - n$ nonmembers who prefer a central pliable policy (on average) suffer an expected utility loss of $a(\pi_I - \frac{1}{2})^2$ apiece. Since $n < 1 - n$ (see assumption 2), the competition for the endorsement generates political inefficiency in the indicated range.

However, the endorsement process can enhance political efficiency when the group members' true tastes are more extreme. When $\pi_I \notin [\gamma, 1 - \gamma]$ the parties stop short of fully satisfying the group's true wishes. Then the policy outcome $p = \gamma$ reflects a balancing of the members' interests and the (average) interests of the others. We find, in fact, that there exists a critical value γ_c, $\gamma_c \in (0, \gamma)$, such that aggregate welfare is higher in the equilibrium of proposition 4 than in the benchmark equilibrium whenever π_I is less than γ_c or greater than $1 - \gamma_c$.[12]

---

[12] To find this critical value γ_c observe that (10) and (11) imply that for $\pi_I \leq \gamma$ aggregate welfare is higher in the equilibrium of proposition 4 than in the benchmark equilibrium if and only if

$$n[(\tfrac{1}{2} - \pi_I)^2 - (\gamma - \pi_I)^2] > (1 - n)(\tfrac{1}{2} - \gamma)^2. \tag{12}$$

For ideal points π_I close to γ this condition is violated, because $n < 1 - n$. Therefore, the benchmark equilibrium is preferable for such values of π_I. But the left-hand side of (12) is declining in π_I (because $\gamma < \frac{1}{2}$). Moreover, the fact that the right-hand side of (8) is increasing in γ and obtains the value $(1 - n)/2$ at $\gamma = 0$ implies that the γ which solves (8) is greater than $(1 - n)/2$ and therefore greater than $\frac{1}{2} - n$. But $\gamma > \frac{1}{2} - n$ in turn implies that the inequality (12) is satisfied for $\pi_I = 0$. Therefore, there must exist a γ_c between zero and γ such that (12) holds for all $0 \leq \pi_I < \gamma_c$. By symmetry, it also holds for all $1 - \gamma_c < \pi_I \leq 1$.

Proposition 6. Let the conditional distribution of π for outsiders be independent of π_I and let assumptions 1 and 2 be satisfied. Then for all values of π_I, the utility of insiders is higher and the expected utility of outsiders is lower in the equilibrium described by proposition 4 than in the benchmark equilibrium. Aggregate welfare is higher in the equilibrium described by proposition 4 if and only if $0 \leq \pi_I < \gamma_c$ or $1 - \gamma_c < \pi_I \leq 1$.

It is also interesting to compare how group members fare in the equilibrium described by proposition 4 relative to the utility they would achieve in a hypothetical setting in which they were fully informed. In the latter scenario each group member would vote using the rule indicated by (4), except that the true value of π would stand in the place of its expected value. Assuming that outsiders had interests independent of the group members' interests and that $\mathcal{E}_0(\pi|\Omega_0) = \frac{1}{2}$, the parties' vote shares would vary with their announced platforms according to

$$s = \tfrac{1}{2} + b + 2ka\left(p - n\pi_I - \frac{1-n}{2}\right)(p^B - p^A).$$

Then the parties would set identical platforms of

$$p^A(\pi_I) = p^B(\pi_I) = n\pi_I + \frac{1-n}{2}$$

in the hypothetical PBE, and each would capture its "normal" share of the seats.

We can now compare the utility of a group member in the hypothetical equilibrium that has $p = n\pi_I + (1-n)/2$ and $q = 1 - \psi(\frac{1}{2} + b)$ with the realization of $u_I(p, q|\pi_I)$ that obtains when p and q take on the values prescribed by proposition 4. For all $\pi_I \in [\gamma, 1 - \gamma]$ the group enjoys its ideal pliable policy in the equilibrium of proposition 4. Thus, for values of π_I in this range, the members clearly fare better when they know only the endorsement than they do when they are fully informed. If the members ever benefit from having full information, it must be for relatively extreme values of π_I. In fact, it is straightforward to show, using (10), that the group fares better with full information if and only if its ideal pliable policy falls in the range between 0 and $M(\gamma)$ or between $1 - M(\gamma)$ and 1.[13]

Why might group members benefit from remaining partially in the dark about their own policy interests? The answer has to do with the inferences they can draw from observing an endorsement and the effect

---

[13] For $\pi_I \leq \gamma$ the group fares better in the full-information equilibrium if and only if $(\gamma - \pi_I)^2 > [n\pi_I + (1-n)/2 - \pi_I]^2 = (1-n)^2(\frac{1}{2} - \pi_I)^2$, which is satisfied if and only if $\pi_I < M(\gamma)$ [see (8)]. A similar argument establishes that for $\pi_I \geq 1 - \gamma$ it fares better in the full-information equilibrium if and only if $\pi_I > 1 - M(\gamma)$.

that these inferences have on their voting behavior. When an individual knows the true value of her ideal pliable policy, she votes for party A if and only if her personal value of β is less than $2a(p - \pi)(p^B - p^A)$. But when a group member learns only the identity of the endorsee she typically can infer only that her (expected) ideal point lies to one side of a dividing line or the other. If her ideal point is truly a central one, then the endorsement obscures this fact and leaves the insider thinking that she might be rather extreme. That is, it can happen that $E_I[\pi_I | p^A, p^B, E] > \pi_I > \frac{1}{2}$ or that $E_I[\pi_I | p^A, p^B, E] < \pi_I < \frac{1}{2}$, when π_I is relatively close to the center. In the event, the voter is more ready to switch her allegiance from one party to the other for a given change in a pliable policy stance than she would be if her true interests were clear to her. The parties recognize this greater policy sensitivity among the interest group's voters and so are more ready to make concessions in order to capture their votes.[14]

6 Conclusions

We have developed a model of political endorsements by special interest groups. In our model, the leader of a group endorses one party or another in a legislative election in order to communicate information about the group's interests to a set of like-minded but uninformed voters. The members use these cues to update their beliefs about what election outcomes might be good for them, and vote accordingly. In some cases, other voters—who do not share the same interests as the members—also learn from the endorsements and adjust their voting behavior as a result.

Parties will not always compete for interest groups' endorsements. In particular, endorsements are policy neutral when all voters hear them and

---

[14] We note that, from an *ex ante* standpoint, the group members always prefer to be fully informed than to be forced to rely on the endorsement as a cue. Group members view π_I as being drawn from a distribution $F(\pi_I)$ with support $[0, 1]$. We can use this distribution and the policy outcomes for each value of π_I to calculate their expected utility under each regime (full information and endorsement). Doing so, we find that expected utility is higher with full information. Of course, it may be costly for the members to become fully informed, which is why they might rely on the endorsement for information in the first place. Moreover, it can be shown that, even if the group's leader could transmit more detailed information than just an endorsement, such a leader would have an incentive to misreport π_I. Indeed, a leader seeking to maximize her group's welfare would always exaggerate her report of the group's ideal, claiming $\pi_I = 0$ when the group would benefit from additional votes for the party with the lowermost pliable position, and $\pi_I = 1$ otherwise. Unless there existed a mechanism to enforce truthful reporting by the leader, the members could not rely on their central organization to become fully informed. In fact, reasoning similar to that employed by Vincent Crawford and Joel Sobel (1982) can be used to show that the equilibrium described by proposition 4 remains an equilibrium in a "cheap-talk" game in which the interest-group leader is able to report costlessly the exact value of π_I (or any other information).

voters who are not members of any group have interests that are diametrically opposed to those of members. In these circumstances, any concession that the parties might make to an interest group would cost them more votes among nonmembers than it would win for them among the favored few. However, if the interests of group members are not perfectly complementary to those of outsiders, or if the endorsement by a group's leader is not readily observed by nonmembers, then parties indeed will find it worthwhile to compete for a group's backing. In such settings, the positions they take will favor the special interests at the expense of the unaffiliated voters.

Our model ascribes real effects to endorsements even though the parties' pliable platforms are the same in equilibrium and all equilibrium endorsements are random. These effects come from the competition for endorsements, not the endorsements themselves. In fact, even if the endorsements never are issued, the mere fact that they might be can influence political outcomes.

Endorsements can enhance political efficiency by allowing the true interests of a set of otherwise uninformed voters to be reflected in the parties' platforms. But the competition for an interest group's backing may lead to overrepresentation of its members' interests, in which case the endorsement process might lower aggregate welfare. The competition for an endorsement is most intense and the risk of inefficiency most severe when the group is small and its members relatively centrist. In fact, a group whose members are truly moderates might fare better in an equilibrium with political endorsements than they would in one in which they were fully informed. This is due to the coarse nature of the endorsement "language." The endorsement provides listeners with a binary comparison but does not reveal the intensity of the endorser's preference. Therefore, true moderates who hear their leader announcing a recommendation will not be able to rule out the possibility that they are really extreme. They will vote their expected interest, rather than their actual interest and so the parties may cater to them more aggressively.

In this paper we have examined situations where there is only a single interest group issuing endorsements. In actuality, many interest groups endorse candidates in the typical election. Of course, these groups often have distinct policy preferences and so use their own criteria for deciding which candidates to support. It is possible to extend our model to handle situations with multiple endorsers; see Grossman and Helpman (1998) for the details.

When endorsements are issued simultaneously by many groups, the calculus facing the parties changes in an important way. With only one group endorsing candidates, the parties need only consider that by pandering to the group's wishes they might alienate some of the unaffiliated voters. But with multiple groups in competition for influence, a party's bid for the support of one can cost it the endorsement of some others. Each party must judge which endorsements are most valuable, considering the sizes of the groups and to some extent the nature of their policy demands. In the equilibrium the parties locate toward the center of the pliable policy space, so that the endorsements they could win by shading their positions further to one side just balance the endorsements they would lose from groups with opposing interests plus any loss of votes among unaffiliated voters. It is interesting to observe, for example, that with two groups of equal size and opposing policy preferences (i.e., with ideal points on the opposite sides of one-half) the equilibrium policy is precisely in the center of the policy space. This is true even if the preferences of one group happen to be moderate while those of the other are quite extreme. In general, the equilibrium policy is displaced from the center in the direction favorable to the median interest-group member, and the intensity of groups' preferences for divergences from the center have only limited effect on the equilibrium outcome.

APPENDIX

Statement and Proof of Proposition 4

Let $\mu_I(\pi_I|p^A, p^B, E)$ be an insider's conditional probability distribution for π_I when the platforms p^A and p^B and the endorsement E is observed. The complete statement of proposition 4 follows.

Proposition 4. Let the conditional distribution of π for outsiders be independent of π_I and let the endorsement be observable to all voters. Suppose that the endorsement obeys a dividing-line rule and that assumptions 1 and 2 are satisfied. Then there exists a PBE in which

(i) $p^A(\pi_I) = p^B(\pi_I) = p(\pi_I) = \begin{cases} \gamma & \text{for } 0 \leq \pi_I \leq \gamma; \\ \pi_I & \text{for } \gamma < \pi_I < 1 - \gamma; \\ 1 - \gamma & \text{for } 1 - \gamma \leq \pi_I \leq 1; \end{cases}$

(ii) $q = 1 - \psi(\frac{1}{2} + b)$;

(iii) $E_0(\pi|\Omega_0) \equiv \frac{1}{2}$;

(iv) for all (p^A, p^B) such that $p^A \neq p^B$:

  (a) $\mu_I(\pi_I|p^A, p^B, E_{\min}[p^A, p^B]) = f(\pi_I)/F[g(p^A, p^B)]$ for $\pi_I \in [0, g(p^A, p^B)]$ and zero otherwise;

  (b) $\mu_I(\pi_I|p^A, p^B, E_{\max}[p^A, p^B]) = f(\pi_I)/\{1 - F[g(p^A, p^B)]\}$ for $\pi_I \in [g(p^A, p^B), 1]$ and zero otherwise;

(v) for $p^A = p^B \in [0, \gamma) \cup (1 - \gamma, 1]$ and $E = A$ or $E = B$, $\mu_I(\pi_I|p^A, p^B, E) = f(\pi_I)$ for $\pi_I \in [0, 1]$;

(vi)   for $p^A = p^B \in (\gamma, 1 - \gamma$ and $E = A$ or $E = B$, $\mu_I(\pi_I | p^A, p^B, E)$ has
       a mass point of measure one at $\pi_I = p^A = p^B$;
(vii) for $p^A = p^B = \gamma$ and $E = A$ or $E = B$, $\mu_I(\pi_I | p^A, p^B, E) = f(\pi_I)/F(\gamma)$
       for $\pi_I \in [0, \gamma]$ and zero otherwise;
(viii) for $p^A = p^B = 1 - \gamma$ and $E = A$ or $E = B$, $\mu_I(\pi_I | p^A, p^B, E) = f(\pi_I)/$
       $[1 - F(\gamma)]$ for $\pi_I \in [1 - \gamma, 1]$ and zero otherwise.

Proof. First observe that the updating of voters' beliefs is consistent
with Bayes' rule. Outsiders learn nothing new from the announced policies and the group's endorsement about the locations of their ideal
points. Part (iii) of the proposition ensures that their posterior beliefs
are the same as their priors. If $p^A \neq p^B$, the endorsement tells insiders on
which side of $g(p^A, p^B)$ the true π_I lies. The updating specified in part
(iv) is consistent with this new information. When $p^A = p^B \in (\gamma, 1 - \gamma)$,
insiders recognize that the announcements reveal the true value of π_I.
Part (vi) of the proposition reflects this recognition. When $p^A = p^B = \gamma$,
insiders realize that the true π_I must be in $[0, \gamma]$. Part (vii) of the proposition is consistent with this. Similarly, when $p^A = p^B = 1 - \gamma$, π_I must
fall in the range $[1 - \gamma, 1]$, and part (viii) reflects this. Finally, $p^A = p^B \notin$
$[\gamma, 1 - \gamma]$, the endorsement tells the insiders nothing new. Part (v) specifies that the insiders do not update their priors in this case.

Now consider the incentives facing the parties, when voters update
according to parts (iii) through (viii). Take first the case in which $\pi_I \leq \gamma$.
Suppose $p^B = \gamma$. If party A sets $p^A = \gamma$, then equation (5) implies that
$s = \frac{1}{2} + b$. If instead it sets $p^A > \gamma$, then $g(p^A, p^B) > \gamma \Rightarrow E = B$. Then
part (iv) of the proposition implies that $\mathcal{E}_I[\pi_I | p^A, \gamma, B] = M[g(p^A, \gamma)]$,
where $M(z) = \int_0^z xf(x) \, dx/F(z)$ [see (7)]. Then part (iii) and equation (5)
give

$$s = \tfrac{1}{2} + b + 2kaT(s, p^A, \gamma)(\gamma - p^A), \tag{A1}$$

where $T(s, p^A, p^B) \equiv \psi(s) p^A + [1 - \psi(s)]p^B - nM[g(p^A, p^B)] - (1 - n)/2$. The right-hand side of (A1) equals $\frac{1}{2} + b$ when $p^A = p^B = \gamma$ and
is declining in s for $p^A \neq p^B = \gamma$. So the s that solves (A1) exceeds $\frac{1}{2} + b$
if and only if $T(\frac{1}{2} + b, p^A, \gamma)(\gamma - p^A) > 0$. But note that

$$T(\tfrac{1}{2} + b, p^A, \gamma) \geq \psi(\tfrac{1}{2} + b)g(p^A, \gamma) + [1 - \psi(\tfrac{1}{2} + b)]\gamma - nM[g(p^A, \gamma)]$$

$$-\frac{1 - n}{2} \geq \psi(\tfrac{1}{2} + b)\gamma + [1 - \psi(\tfrac{1}{2} + b)]\gamma - nM(\gamma) - \frac{1 - n}{2} = 0 \tag{A2}$$

The first inequality follows from the fact that $p^A > \gamma$ and therefore $p^A \geq$
$g(p^A, \gamma)$. The second inequality follows from assumptions 1 and 2 and
the fact that $p^A > \gamma \Rightarrow g(p^A, \gamma) \geq g(\gamma, \gamma) = \gamma$. Observe that the right-

hand side of the first line is increasing in p^A for $p^A > \gamma$ if and only if $\psi(\frac{1}{2} + b) - nM'[g(p^A, \gamma)] > 0$. However,

$$\psi(\tfrac{1}{2} + b) - nM'[g(p^A, \gamma)] \geq \psi(\tfrac{1}{2} + b) - n\mathcal{M} \geq 0$$

by assumption 2 [recall that $\mathcal{M}$ is the largest value of $M'(\cdot)$ in the feasible range]. Finally, the last equality in (A2) stems from the definition of γ in (7). One of the inequalities must be strict, so $T(\frac{1}{2} + b, p^A, \gamma) > 0$. Therefore, $s < \frac{1}{2} + b$ when $p^A > \gamma$.

The final option available to party A is to set $p^A < \gamma$. Then $g(p^A, \gamma) \leq \gamma$. There are two subcases to consider. First, if $\pi_I \leq g(p^A, \gamma)$, then $E = A$ and part (iv) of the proposition implies $E_I[\pi_I | p^A, \gamma, A] + M[g(p^A, \gamma)]$. Then (A1) gives the vote share for party A, and $s > \frac{1}{2} + b$ if and only if $T(\frac{1}{2} + b, p^A, \gamma)(\gamma - p^A) > 0$. But now

$$T(\tfrac{1}{2} + b, p^A, \gamma) \leq \psi(\tfrac{1}{2} + b)g(p^A, \gamma) + [1 - \psi(\tfrac{1}{2} + b)]\gamma - nM[g(p^A, \gamma)]$$

$$-\frac{1-n}{2} \leq \psi(\tfrac{1}{2} + b)\gamma + [1 - \psi(\tfrac{1}{2} + b)]\gamma - nM(\gamma) - \frac{1-n}{2} = 0,$$

by analogous arguments to those used above. Again, one of the inequalities must be strict, so $s < \frac{1}{2} + b$, since $\gamma > p^A$.

The second subcase arises if $\pi_I > g(p^A, \gamma)$, in which case $E = B$. Then part (iv) of the proposition implies $E_I[\pi_I | p^A, \gamma, B] = N[g(p^A, \gamma)]$, where $N(z) = \int_z^1 x f(x)\,dx / [1 - F(z)]$. The share of votes for party A is given by

$$s = \tfrac{1}{2} + b + 2kaZ(s, p^A, \gamma)(\gamma - p^A), \tag{A3}$$

where $Z(s, p^A, p^B) \equiv \psi(s)\,p^A + [1 - \psi(s)]\,p^B - nN[g(p^A, p^B)] - (1 - n)/2$. The right-hand side of (A3) equals $\frac{1}{2} + b$ when $p^A = p^B = \gamma$ and is declining in s for $p^A \neq p^B = \gamma$. So the s that solves (A3) exceeds $\frac{1}{2} + b$ if and only if $Z(\frac{1}{2} + b, p^A, \gamma)(\gamma - p^A) > 0$; i.e., if and only if $Z(\frac{1}{2} + b, p^A, \gamma) > 0$. But

$$Z(\tfrac{1}{2} + b, p^A, \gamma) \leq \psi(\tfrac{1}{2} + b)g(p^A, \gamma) + [1 - \psi(\tfrac{1}{2} + b)]\gamma - nN[g(p^A, \gamma)]$$

$$-\frac{1-n}{2} \leq \psi(\tfrac{1}{2} + b)\gamma + [1 - \psi(\tfrac{1}{2} + b)]\gamma - nN(\gamma) - \frac{1-n}{2} = 0. \tag{A4}$$

The first inequality follows from the fact that $p^A < p^B = \gamma$ and therefore $p^A \leq g(p^A, \gamma)$. The second inequality follows from assumptions 1 and 2 and the fact that $p^A < \gamma \Rightarrow g(p^A, \gamma) \leq g(\gamma, \gamma) = \gamma$. Observe that the right-hand side of the first line is increasing in p^A for $p^A < \gamma$ if and only if $\psi(\frac{1}{2} + b) - nN'[g(p^A, \gamma)] > 0$. But from the definition of $N(\cdot)$ we have $N(z) = 1 - M(1 - z)$ for all $z \in [0, 1]$. $N(\cdot)$ is an increasing function and $N'(z) = M'(1 - z)$. Therefore,

$$\psi(\tfrac{1}{2} + b) - nN'[g(p^A, \gamma)] \geq \psi(\tfrac{1}{2} + b) - nM \geq 0$$

by assumption 2. The equality in (A4) stems from the definition of γ. Again, at least one inequality in (A4) must be strict. We conclude that $s < \tfrac{1}{2} + b$ in this case as well.

It follows that $p^A = \gamma$ is a best response to $p^B = \gamma$ when $\pi_I \leq \gamma$. Similar arguments can be used to establish that $p^B = \gamma$ is a best response to $p^A = \gamma$ for these values of π_I. Therefore, it is sequentially rational for the parties each to locate at γ when $\pi_I \leq \gamma$.

An exactly analogous argument establishes that it is sequentially rational for the parties to each locate at $1 - \gamma$ when $\pi_I \geq 1 - \gamma$.

It remains to consider the case in which $\pi_I \in (\gamma, 1 - \gamma)$. Suppose that $p^B = \pi_I$ and consider the incentives facing party A. If the party sets $p^A = \pi_I$, then $s = \tfrac{1}{2} + b$. If it sets $p^A > \pi_I$, then $p^A \geq g(p^A, \pi_I) \geq \pi_I > \gamma$ and $E = B$. Part (iv) of the proposition implies $E_I[\pi_I | p^A, \pi_I, B] = M[g(p^A, \pi_I)]$. Then part (iii) of the proposition and equation (5) imply

$$s = \tfrac{1}{2} + b + 2kaT(s, p^A, \pi_I)(\pi_I - p^A).$$

In this case, $s > \tfrac{1}{2} + b$ if and only if $T(\tfrac{1}{2} + b, p^A, \pi_I)(\pi_I - p^A) > 0$; i.e., if and only if $T(\tfrac{1}{2} + b, p^A, \pi_I) < 0$. But

$$T(\tfrac{1}{2} + b, p^A, \pi_I) \geq \psi(\tfrac{1}{2} + b)g(p^A, \pi_I) + [1 - \psi(\tfrac{1}{2} + b)]\pi_I - nM[g(p^A, \pi_I)]$$

$$-\frac{1-n}{2} \geq \psi(\tfrac{1}{2} + b)\gamma + [1 - \psi(\tfrac{1}{2} + b)]\gamma - nM(\gamma) - \frac{1-n}{2} = 0.$$

Therefore, $s < \tfrac{1}{2} + b$ when $p^A > \pi_I$, because one of the inequalities must be strict.

The final option available to party A is to set $p^A < \pi_I$. If it does so, then $p^A \leq g(p^A, \pi_I) \leq \pi_I < 1 - \gamma$ and $E = B$. Then

$$s = \tfrac{1}{2} + b + 2kaZ(s, p^A, \pi_I)(\pi_I - p^A),$$

and $s > \tfrac{1}{2} + b$ if and only if $Z(\tfrac{1}{2} + b, p^A, \pi_I) > 0$. But

$$Z(\tfrac{1}{2} + b, p^A, \pi_I) \leq \psi(\tfrac{1}{2} + b)g(p^A, \pi_I) + [1 - \psi(\tfrac{1}{2} + b)]\pi_I - nN[g(p^A, \pi_I)]$$

$$-\frac{1-n}{2} \leq \psi(\tfrac{1}{2} + b)(1 - \gamma) + [1 - \psi(\tfrac{1}{2} + b)](1 - \gamma) - nN(1 - \gamma) - \frac{1-n}{2} = 0.$$

The last equality follows from (8) and the fact that $M(\gamma) + N(1 - \gamma) = 1$. Therefore, $s < \tfrac{1}{2} + b$ when $p^A < \pi_I$, because one of the inequalities must be strict.

It follows that $p^A = \pi_I$ is a best response to $p^B = \pi_I$ when $\pi_I \in (\gamma, 1 - \gamma)$. Similar arguments can be used to establish that $p^B = \pi_I$ is a best response to $p^A = \pi_I$ for these values of π_I. Therefore, it is sequentially rational for the parties each to locate at π_I when $\pi_I \in (\gamma, 1 - \gamma)$.

Proof of Proposition 5

We proceed by construction. Suppose the members of the interest group suspect that their leader is using a dividing-line rule, with some particular function $g^\circ(p^A, p^B)$ giving the location of the dividing line. Suppose further that, upon hearing the policy stances and the leader's endorsement, these individuals update their beliefs about π_I as specified in proposition 4. This means that, if $p^A \neq p^B$ and $E = E_{\min}$, $\mathcal{E}_I[\pi_I | p^A, p^B, E_{\min}] = M[g^\circ(p^A, p^B)]$, while if $p^A \neq p^B$ and $E = E_{\max}$, $\mathcal{E}_I[\pi_I | p^A, p^B, E_{\max}] = N[g^\circ(p^A, p^B)]$, where $N(z) \equiv \int_z^1 x f(x) \, dx / [1 - F(z)]$. Also, when outsiders hear different pliable platforms announced by the two parties, they believe their ideal point to be symmetrically distributed about one-half. Then, applying the voting rule in (4), we have

$$s = \tfrac{1}{2} + b + 2ka\{p(s, p^A, p^B) - n\eta(p^A, p^B, E|g^\circ) - (1 - n)\tfrac{1}{2}\}(p^B - p^A), \quad (A5)$$

where $p(s, p^A, p^B) \equiv \psi(s)p^A + [1 - \psi(s)]p^B$ and

$$\eta(p^A, p^B, E|g^\circ) \equiv \left\{ \begin{array}{l} M[g^\circ(p^A, p^B)] \text{ for } E = E_{\min} \\ N[g^\circ(p^A, p^B)] \text{ for } E = E_{\max} \end{array} \right.$$

Equation (A5) defines an implicit mapping from the parties' platforms and the identity of the endorsee to the implied vote share for party A. This mapping depends on what dividing line $g^\circ(p^A, p^B)$ the members suspect their leader of using. We denote the mapping by $\tilde{s}(p^A, p^B, E|g^\circ)$.

The properties of $\tilde{s}(p^A, p^B, E|g^\circ)$ can be understood with the aid of Figure A.1. First note that $\tilde{s}(p^A, p^B, E|g^\circ) = \frac{1}{2} + b$ for all $p^A = p^B$, independent of g°. The curve SS in Figure A.1 depicts the qualitative properties of the right-hand side of (A5) for any pair of platforms that are not the same. This curve always slopes downward, as shown. Where it intersects the 45° line, we have the (unique) value of $\tilde{s}$. We know, moreover, that given the parties' positions p^A and p^B, the right-hand side of (A5) is larger for $E = A$ than it is for $E = B$. This ensures that, by endorsing a particular party, the group leader always furthers that party's electoral cause.

Once we know how the composition of the legislature responds to the platforms and the endorsement (given the dividing-line rule), we can compute how the pliable policy outcome responds to these variables as well. We define

$$\tilde{p}(p^A, p^B, E|g^\circ) \equiv \psi[\tilde{s}(p^A, p^B, E|g^\circ)]p^A + \{1 - \psi[\tilde{s}(p^A, p^B, E|g^\circ)]\}p^B$$

as the anticipated pliable compromise when the platforms are p^A and p^B, the leader endorses E, and the insiders use the dividing-line $g^\circ(p^A, p^B)$

domestic price equal to one. We denote by p_i the domestic price of good X_i in the home country, and π_i represents its offshore price.[5] With these preferences, each resident of the home country demands $d_i(p_i)$ units of good X_i, $i = 1, 2, \ldots, n$, where $d_i(\cdot)$ is the inverse of $u_i'(\cdot)$. The consumer devotes the remainder of his total spending of E to the numeraire good, thereby attaining the utility level

$$v(\mathbf{p}, E) = E + S(\mathbf{p}), \tag{2}$$

where $\mathbf{p} = (p_1, p_2, \ldots, p_n)$ is the vector of home prices of the non-numeraire goods and $S(\mathbf{p}) \equiv \sum_i u_i[d_i(p_i)] - \sum_i p_i d_i(p_i)$ is the consumer surplus enjoyed on these goods.

The numeraire good Z can be produced from labor alone, with constant returns to scale. We assume that the aggregate labor supply, l, is sufficiently large to ensure a positive output of this good. Then we can choose units so that the competitive wage rate equals one. Each of the other goods is manufactured from labor and a sector-specific input, also with constant returns to scale. The various specific inputs are available in inelastic supply. We denote by $\Pi_i(p_i)$ the aggregate rent accruing to the specific factor used in producing good X_i, and we note that the slope of this function gives the industry supply curve, that is,

$$X_i(p_i) = \Pi_i'(p_i). \tag{3}$$

The government has a limited set of policy instruments at its disposal. We allow it to tax or subsidize trade in any of the nonnumeraire goods and to collect revenues or distribute tax receipts using a (neutral) head tax or subsidy. In other words, the government must use trade policies to effect any income redistribution between groups in the economy. In reality, governments appear to have difficulty in using direct and transparent instruments to transfer income, so they resort to less direct means instead. Our model highlights the role of trade policy as a potential tool of income redistribution.

The ad valorem trade taxes or subsidies drive a wedge between domestic and offshore prices. We represent these policies by the parameters τ_i such that $p_i = \tau_i \pi_i$. Then $\tau_i > 1$ represents one plus the rate of tariff on an import good or one plus the rate of export subsidy on an export good. Similarly, $\tau_i < 1$ represents an import subsidy or an export tax. The vector of trade policies $\boldsymbol{\tau} = (\tau_1, \tau_2, \ldots, \tau_n)$ generates per capita government revenue of

$$r(\boldsymbol{\tau}, \boldsymbol{\pi}) = \sum_i (\tau_i - 1) \pi_i \left[d_i(\tau_i \pi_i) - \frac{1}{N} X_i(\tau_i \pi_i) \right], \tag{4}$$

[5] The offshore price need not be the same as the price prevailing in the foreign country, because the foreign country may impose trade taxes or subsidies of its own. We use p_i^* to denote the internal price in the foreign country.

maximizations in (21) and (21*). Combining these, we find that the equilibrium contribution schedules again are locally truthful and that the agreed-on policies must satisfy

$$a^* \sum_{i \in L} \boldsymbol{\nabla}_\tau W_i(\boldsymbol{\tau}^o, \boldsymbol{\tau}^{*o}) + a \sum_{i \in L^*} \boldsymbol{\nabla}_\tau W_i^*(\boldsymbol{\tau}^{*o}, \boldsymbol{\tau}^o)$$
$$+ \, a^* a [\boldsymbol{\nabla}_\tau W(\boldsymbol{\tau}^o, \boldsymbol{\tau}^{*o}) + \boldsymbol{\nabla}_\tau W^*(\boldsymbol{\tau}^{*o}, \boldsymbol{\tau}^o)] = 0 \qquad (22)$$

and

$$a^* \sum_{i \in L} \boldsymbol{\nabla}_{\tau^*} W_i(\boldsymbol{\tau}^o, \boldsymbol{\tau}^{*o}) + a \sum_{i \in L^*} \boldsymbol{\nabla}_{\tau^*} W_i^*(\boldsymbol{\tau}^{*o}, \boldsymbol{\tau}^o)$$
$$+ \, a^* a [\boldsymbol{\nabla}_{\tau^*} W(\boldsymbol{\tau}^o, \boldsymbol{\tau}^{*o}) + \boldsymbol{\nabla}_{\tau^*} W^*(\boldsymbol{\tau}^{*o}, \boldsymbol{\tau}^o)] = 0. \qquad (22^*)$$

It is straightforward to calculate the partial derivatives in (22) and (22*). Substituting these expressions, we obtain

$$a^*[I_{jL} X_j + a(\tau_j^o - 1)\pi_j M_j'](\pi_j + \tau_j^o \pi_{j1})$$
$$+ \, a[I_{jL}^* X_j^* + a^*(\tau_j^{*o} - 1)\pi_j M_j^{*\prime}]\tau_j^{*o} \pi_{j1} = 0 \quad \text{for } j \in L \qquad (23)$$

and

$$a[I_{jL}^* X_j^* + a^*(\tau_j^{*o} - 1)\pi_j M_j^{*\prime}](\pi_j + \tau_j^{*o} \pi_{j2})$$
$$+ \, a^*[I_{jL} X_j + a(\tau_j^o - 1)\pi_j M_j']\tau_j^o \pi_{j2} = 0 \quad \text{for } j \in L^*. \qquad (23^*)$$

Equations (23) and (23*) are two sets of equations that, if independent, might be used to solve for $\boldsymbol{\tau}^o$ and $\boldsymbol{\tau}^{*o}$. However, these equations are linearly dependent.[21] In other words, the equilibrium requirements that we have stated so far determine only the ratios $\tau_1^o/\tau_1^{*o}, \tau_2^o/\tau_2^{*o}, \dots,$ τ_n^o/τ_n^{*o}, but not $\boldsymbol{\tau}^o$ and $\boldsymbol{\tau}^{*o}$ separately. We shall explain the meaning of this finding presently, but first we derive from (23) and (23*) the following equation that implicitly gives the equilibrium policy ratio in industry i:

$$\tau_i^o - \tau_i^{*o} = \left(- \frac{I_{iL}}{a} \, \frac{X_i}{\pi_i M_i'} \right) - \left(- \frac{I_{iL}^*}{a^*} \, \frac{X_i^*}{\pi_i M_i'^*} \right)$$
$$\text{for } i = 1, 2, \dots, n. \qquad (24)$$

Notice that when both sides of (24) are divided by τ_i^{*o}, the trade policies enter this equation only in ratio form.[22]

---

[21] To establish this, use the properties of the price functions $\pi_i(\cdot)$ stated in n. 9.

[22] That is, X_i and M_i' are functions of $p_i = \tau_i \pi_i$, which is homogeneous of degree zero in τ_i and τ_i^*. Similarly, X_i^* and $M_i'^*$ are functions of $p_i^* = \tau_i^* \pi_i$, which is also homogeneous of degree zero in τ_i and τ_i^*. Finally, the term $\tau_i^* \pi_i$ appears directly in the denominator of both expressions in parentheses, once the equation has been divided through by τ_i^*. Thus they all can be expressed as functions of the ratio τ_i/τ_i^*.

Krasno, Jonathan S., and Green, Donald Philip (1988). Preempting quality challengers in House elections. *Journal of Politics* 50(4) (November): 920–936.

Long, Ngo Van, and Vousden, Neil (1991). Protectionist responses and declining industries. *Journal of International Economics* 30(1–2) (February): 87–103.

Magee, Stephen P., Brock, William A., and Young, Leslie (1989). *Black Hole Tariffs and Endogenous Policy Theory: Political Economy in General Equilibrium* (Cambridge: Cambridge University Press).

Magelby, David B., and Nelson, Candice J. (1990). *The Money Chase: Congressional Campaign Finance Reform* (Washington, D.C.: Brookings Institution).

Mayer, Wolfgang (1981). Theoretical considerations on negotiated tariff adjustments. *Oxford Economic Papers* 33(1) (March): 135–153.

Olson, Mancur (1965). *The Logic of Collective Action* (Cambridge, Mass.: Harvard University Press).

Rodrik, Dani (1986). Tariffs, subsidies, and welfare with endogenous policy. *Journal of International Economics* 21(3/4) (November): 285–296.

Stigler, George J. (1971). The theory of economic regulation. *Bell Journal of Economics* 2(1) (Spring): 359–365.

Wilson, John D. (1990). Are efficiency improvements in government transfer policies self-defeating in political equilibrium? *Economics and Politics* 2(3) (November): 241–258.

Five —————————————————————

Trade Wars and Trade Talks

1 Introduction

Recent events have highlighted the extent to which domestic politics condition international economic relations. Special-interest groups were visible and vocal in the weeks and years leading up to the Uruguay Round trade pact and the North American Free Trade Agreement. Similarly, industry representatives have been active participants in the ongoing trade conflict between the United States and Japan. There can

By Gene M. Grossman and Elhanan Helpman. Originally published in *Journal of Political Economy* 103 (August 1995): 675–708. Copyright © 1995 by the University of Chicago Press. Reprinted with permission. We thank the National Science Foundation and the U.S.-Israel Binational Science Foundation for financial support. Grossman also thanks the John S. Guggenheim Memorial Foundation, the Sumitomo Bank Fund, the Daiwa Bank Fund, and the Center of International Studies at Princeton University.

be little doubt that interest groups have influenced these and other policy outcomes.

In the political science literature, "statist" theories have dominated recent analysis of foreign economic policy (see Cowhey [1990]). Such theories cast an elite group of executive branch institutions and officials as relatively independent players in the international arena, setting policies to serve national objectives (such as balance-of-power diplomacy) while making only occasional and minimal concessions to domestic political groups. This approach has its counterpart in the economics literature on trade relations, which too has focused on the actions and interactions of autonomous governments. In his seminal paper on "Optimum Tariffs and Retaliation" (1954), Harry Johnson showed how policy interdependence between governments could be modeled as a noncooperative equilibrium of a two-country tariff game (see also Kuga [1973]; Riezman [1982]; Kennan and Riezman [1988]). Mayer (1981) and Riezman (1982) took a similar approach to negotiated trade agreements, viewing them as equilibrium outcomes to two-government bargaining games. While these authors surely are to be commended for emphasizing the international interactions that feature prominently in foreign policy determination, one cannot help but wonder whether their analyses capture the "true" objectives of real-world governments. In every case, the author has cast the government as a benevolent servant of the national interest.

It is now commonplace to view trade policy as an outgrowth of a political process that does not necessarily give rise to aggregate welfare maximization. A growing literature on endogenous policy formation treats interest groups (and sometimes voters) as participants in a competition for political favors, which are meted out by politicians serving their own selfish interests. However, this literature has focused exclusively on the case of a small or isolated country, one that sets trade policy without regard to the extant policies and possible reactions of its trade partners.

In this paper we develop a formal framework capable of capturing both strategic interaction between interest groups and politicians in the domestic arena and strategic interaction between governments in the international arena. In doing so, we follow the path suggested by Putnam (1988), who argued that international relations are best seen as just such a "two-level game." We study both noncooperative and cooperative tariff-setting games in a context in which domestic politics determine international objectives. Our goal is to understand how the political climate in one country conditions policy outcomes in another and how domestic political pressures on politicians condition their relations with foreign counterparts.[1]

In Section 2, we outline our model and discuss its relation to the existing literature. Section 3 spells out the formal assumptions of the model and the nature of a political equilibrium. In Sections 4 and 5, we study two-country policy games, assuming first that governments set their policies noncooperatively and then that they engage in international negotiations. Section 6 compares the predictions of our model with some of the findings in the empirical literature.

2 Model Outline and Relation to the Literature

In democracies, trade policies are set by elected representatives. Because the public typically is less than fully informed about trade issues and because most elections cover many issues, these representatives need not always select policies that maximize the welfare of the median voter. Other policies may better serve the politicians' goal of being reelected and any further objectives they may have. The literature on trade policy formation studies the choices made by elected representatives who may receive financial and other inducements from special-interest lobby groups.

One strand of literature began with Brock and Magee (1978) and is most fully articulated in Magee, Brock, and Young (1989). They consider an election between two parties representing protectionist and free-trade interests. Prior to the election, each party commits to a platform specifying the trade policy it would carry out if elected. Then, seeing these platforms, lobby groups representing capital (which would benefit from free trade) and labor (which would benefit from high tariffs) make campaign contributions to the respective parties championing their causes. The contributions finance campaign expenditures, which in turn affect the parties' probabilities of winning the election. Magee et al. study the Nash equilibrium platforms that emerge when the parties act as Stackelberg leaders vis-à-vis the lobbies.[2]

---

[1] Hillman and Moser (1995) also view trade policies as the outgrowth of interactions between politically motivated governments. Their analysis differs from ours inasmuch as they use reduced-form political support functions to describe the objectives of each government (see the discussion below). Our analysis goes further in explicitly modeling the behavior of special-interest groups that determines a specific relationship between policy choices and political support. Also, they study a single sector, whereas we consider the structure of protection in noncooperative and cooperative equilibria with many goods.

[2] Findlay and Wellisz (1982) developed a reduced form of the Brock and Magee approach. In their formulation, a *tariff formation function* summarizes the relationship between the contributions (or other spending) of the two lobbies and the policies that emerge from the political process. They study Nash equilibrium contributions by the lobbies, taking the policy function as given.

A second strand emanates from the writings of Stigler (1971) and Peltzman (1976) on domestic regulatory policy. Hillman (1982) applied these ideas to trade policy formation, with further elaboration by Long and Vousden (1991). Their approach sees an incumbent government that is in a position to choose trade policy but is constrained by the prospect of the next election. The government recognizes that favors granted to special-interest groups may elicit financial and other support but also may cause dissatisfaction among elements of the general electorate. While avoiding the details of motives and actions, the authors summarize the relevant trade-off in a *political support function*: the government's "support" depends directly on its policies (because they affect voter well-being) and indirectly on policy through its effect on the rents accruing to certain interests. The government selects a policy to maximize its political support.

Our own approach, first developed in Grossman and Helpman (1994), combines elements of these two. As in the political support approach, we focus on an incumbent government that is in a position to set its nation's trade policies. We go beyond that approach, however, by modeling the actions available to the organized special interests and the incentives they face in deciding their political involvement. In other words, rather than specify a support function exogenously, we derive one from the equilibrium actions of profit-maximizing lobby groups. The lobbies in our formulation, like those in the electoral competition models of Magee et al., decide what size campaign contributions to offer the political representatives. But whereas Magee et al. see lobbies as setting their contributions after policy positions have been taken and with the sole objective of influencing the election outcome, we see the lobbies as offering contributions with the aim of influencing the policy announcements themselves. In other words, our lobbies seek to curry favor with politicians who covet their financial support.[3]

Our model is outlined as follows. Lobby groups represent factor owners with stakes in certain industries. Each lobby confronts its national government with a campaign *contribution schedule*, that is, a schedule relating its promised gift to the action taken by the government.[4] These sched-

---

[3] In Grossman and Helpman (1994), we discuss the empirical evidence on campaign giving by political action committees in the United States. This evidence strongly suggests that "PAC money is interested money" with "more than electoral objective in mind" (Magelby and Nelson [1990], p. 55).

[4] An issue arises as to whether the industry lobbies can also offer contributions to politicians in the other country's government. Interest groups do sometimes try to influence a foreign government's policy choices. But politicians often view gifts from foreign sources as tainted money. We choose to focus in the text on the case in which lobbies contribute only to their own national governments, while treating the case with foreign contributions in a series of notes.

ules will not, of course, be formal contracts, nor will they often be explic-itly announced. Still, the government will know that an implicit rela-tionship exists between the way it treats each organized lobby and the contributions it can expect to receive from that group. We assume that the contribution schedules are set to maximize the aggregate welfare of the lobby group's members, taking as given the schedules offered by the other organized groups.

Faced with the contribution schedules of the various lobbies, the incumbents choose a vector of trade taxes and subsidies on the various import and export goods. Their objective in this is to maximize their own political welfare. We allow the politicians' utility to depend on the welfare of the average voter and the total amount of political contributions. Average welfare is included in the government's objective to reflect the likelihood that prospects for reelection depend on the well-being of the general electorate. Contributions enter the government's utility function because campaign funds can be used for political advertising and because the contributions sometimes augment the candidates' personal fortunes or provide them with other political benefits (see Grossman and Helpman [1994] for more on this point).

In our earlier paper, we followed the political economy literature in assuming that the government could take world prices as given. Accord-ingly, there was no scope for interaction between the governments and no possibility for the interest groups in one country to influence policy outcomes elsewhere. Here, in contrast, we focus on the interactions between countries. First we characterize the Nash equilibrium of a non-cooperative game between the two politically motivated governments. Then we consider a bargaining situation in which policies are set in an international negotiation.

3 The Formal Model

We consider the trade relations between two countries, "home" and "foreign." The countries have similar political and economic systems, although their tastes, endowments, and political conditions may differ. We describe in detail the political and economic structure of the home country.

Residents of the home country share identical additively separable preferences. Each individual maximizes a utility function of the form

$$u = c_Z + \sum_{i=1}^{n} u_i(c_{X_i}), \tag{1}$$

where c_Z is consumption of good Z and c_{X_i} is consumption of good X_i, $i = 1, 2, \ldots, n$. The functions $u_i(\cdot)$ are differentiable, increasing, and strictly concave. Good Z serves as a numeraire, with a world and domestic price equal to one. We denote by p_i the domestic price of good X_i in the home country, and π_i represents its offshore price.[5] With these preferences, each resident of the home country demands $d_i(p_i)$ units of good X_i, $i = 1, 2, \ldots, n$, where $d_i(\cdot)$ is the inverse of $u_i'(\cdot)$. The consumer devotes the remainder of his total spending of E to the numeraire good, thereby attaining the utility level

$$v(\mathbf{p}, E) = E + S(\mathbf{p}),\tag{2}$$

where $\mathbf{p} = (p_1, p_2, \ldots, p_n)$ is the vector of home prices of the non-numeraire goods and $S(\mathbf{p}) \equiv \sum_i u_i[d_i(p_i)] - \sum_i p_i d_i(p_i)$ is the consumer surplus enjoyed on these goods.

The numeraire good Z can be produced from labor alone, with constant returns to scale. We assume that the aggregate labor supply, l, is sufficiently large to ensure a positive output of this good. Then we can choose units so that the competitive wage rate equals one. Each of the other goods is manufactured from labor and a sector-specific input, also with constant returns to scale. The various specific inputs are available in inelastic supply. We denote by $\Pi_i(p_i)$ the aggregate rent accruing to the specific factor used in producing good X_i, and we note that the slope of this function gives the industry supply curve, that is,

$$X_i(p_i) = \Pi_i'(p_i).\tag{3}$$

The government has a limited set of policy instruments at its disposal. We allow it to tax or subsidize trade in any of the nonnumeraire goods and to collect revenues or distribute tax receipts using a (neutral) head tax or subsidy. In other words, the government must use trade policies to effect any income redistribution between groups in the economy. In reality, governments appear to have difficulty in using direct and transparent instruments to transfer income, so they resort to less direct means instead. Our model highlights the role of trade policy as a potential tool of income redistribution.

The ad valorem trade taxes or subsidies drive a wedge between domestic and offshore prices. We represent these policies by the parameters τ_i such that $p_i = \tau_i \pi_i$. Then $\tau_i > 1$ represents one plus the rate of tariff on an import good or one plus the rate of export subsidy on an export good. Similarly, $\tau_i < 1$ represents an import subsidy or an export tax. The vector of trade policies $\boldsymbol{\tau} = (\tau_1, \tau_2, \ldots, \tau_n)$ generates per capita government revenue of

$$r(\boldsymbol{\tau}, \boldsymbol{\pi}) = \sum_i (\tau_i - 1) \pi_i \left[d_i(\tau_i \pi_i) - \frac{1}{N} X_i(\tau_i \pi_i) \right],\tag{4}$$

where $\boldsymbol{\pi} = (\pi_1, \pi_2, \ldots, \pi_n)$ and N measures the total population, which we henceforth normalize to one. The government redistributes the tariff revenue evenly to the public.

Individuals collect income from several sources. Most earn wages as workers, and all receive the same transfer (possibly negative) from the government. In addition, some individuals own claims to one of the specific inputs. These assets are indivisible and nontradable (as, e.g., with claims to sector-specific human capital), so individuals cannot hold more than one type. Clearly, those who own some of the specific factor used in industry i will see their income tied to the domestic price of good X_i. These individuals have a direct stake in the trade policy τ_i, in addition to their general interest as consumers in all policies that affect domestic prices.

The owners of the specific input used in sector i, with their common desire for protection (or export subsidies) for their industry, may choose to join forces to express their policy wishes to the incumbent government. We assume that the various owners of some (or perhaps all) of the specific inputs form political action groups, but the owners of the remaining specific inputs (if any) fail to organize politically. The set of organized industries is taken as exogenous here. The organized groups enjoy a political advantage relative to individual factor owners inasmuch as the groups control substantially greater resources than most individuals. With these vast resources at their disposal, the lobbyists can gain access to politicians to communicate their political demands. We assume that the lobbies express their demands in the form of contribution schedules; that is, they offer to contribute to the campaign funds of the incumbent politicians an amount that depends on the particular policies implemented by the government, as well as perhaps the concessions that the politicians manage to extract from the foreign government in the course of any trade negotiation. While the unorganized individuals (including those individuals who own none of the specific inputs) might also wish to "bid" for trade policies in this way, we assume that the politicians will not take the time to hear their offers, which are likely to be small in view of the limited income of an individual factor owner and the limited stake that any one person has in the policy outcome. In short, we assume that politically unorganized individuals have no means to influence policy with their campaign contributions; they enter the political process only as voters.

The organized input owners coordinate their political activities so as to maximize their joint welfare. The lobby representing industry i submits the contribution schedule $C_i(\boldsymbol{\tau}, \cdot)$ that maximizes

$$v^i = \tilde{W}_i(\boldsymbol{\tau}, \boldsymbol{\pi}) - C_i(\boldsymbol{\tau}, \cdot), \tag{5}$$

where $$\tilde{W}_i(\boldsymbol{\tau}, \boldsymbol{\pi}) \equiv l_i + \Pi_i(\tau_i \pi_i) + \alpha_i[r(\boldsymbol{\tau}, \boldsymbol{\pi}) + S(\boldsymbol{\tau}\boldsymbol{\pi})], \tag{6}$$

α_i is the fraction of the population that owns the specific input used in sector i (also their measure, given that $N = 1$), and l_i is the joint labor endowment of these factor owners.[6] Equation (6) gives the total gross-of-contributions welfare of the α_i members of lobby group i, which they derive from wages, quasi rents, transfers from the government, and surplus from consuming the nonnumeraire goods (see eq. [2]). Notice that we have omitted all but one argument of the contribution schedule. This allows us to distinguish the case of a trade war, where the contribution schedule depends only on the actions of the home government, from that of trade talks, where the contributions may also depend on actions taken by the foreign government under any agreement.

Facing the contribution schedules offered by the various lobbies, the incumbents set trade policy—either unilaterally or through a process of international bargaining—so as to maximize their political welfare. We assume that the politicians care about the accumulation of campaign contributions and perhaps also about the welfare of the average voter. As we discussed in Section 2, the politicians may value contributions as a source of funding for campaign advertisements and possibly for other reasons. A concern for average welfare will arise if the prospects for reelection depend on the average voter's prosperity. We posit a linear form for the government's objective function, namely

$$G = \sum_{i \in L} C_i(\boldsymbol{\tau}, \cdot) + a\tilde{W}(\boldsymbol{\tau}, \boldsymbol{\pi}), \quad a \geq 0, \tag{7}$$

where L is the set of organized industries and

$$\tilde{W}(\boldsymbol{\tau}, \boldsymbol{\pi}) \equiv l + \sum_i \Pi_i(\tau_i \pi_i) + r(\boldsymbol{\tau}, \boldsymbol{\pi}) + S(\boldsymbol{\tau}\boldsymbol{\pi}) \tag{8}$$

measures average (gross) welfare. The parameter a in (7) represents the government's weighting of a dollar of social welfare compared to a dollar of campaign contributions, considering both the perceived political value of the funding and the indirect cost associated with the contributor's loss of welfare.

As we mentioned before, the foreign country has a similar political and economic structure, although the subutility functions $u_i^*(\cdot)$, the profit functions $\Pi_i^*(\cdot)$, the set of organized industries L^*, the number α_i^* of voters with claims to the specific input used in sector i, and the weight a^* that the government places on aggregate welfare relative to contributions may differ from those in the home country (the analogous functions and parameters have no asterisks). Equations analogous to (1)–(8) apply to the foreign country, where trade policies are $\boldsymbol{\tau}^* = (\tau_1^*, \tau_2^*, \ldots, \tau_n^*)$, internal prices are $\mathbf{p}^* = (p_1^*, p_2^*, \ldots, p_n^*)$, output in sector i is X_i^*, and so forth.

---

[6] In (6) we have used the notation $\boldsymbol{\tau}\boldsymbol{\pi}$ in the argument of $S(\cdot)$ to represent the vector $(\tau_1 \pi_1, \tau_2 \pi_2, \ldots, \tau_n \pi_n)$. Thus $\boldsymbol{\tau}\boldsymbol{\pi} = \mathbf{p}$ is the vector of home country prices.

Having specified the production and demand sides of each economy, we turn now to the international equilibrium. Net imports of good i in the home country are $M_i(p_i) = d_i(p_i) - X_i(p_i)$, and those in the foreign country equal $M_i^*(p_i^*) = d_i^*(p_i^*) - X_i^*(p_i^*)$. Recall that $p_i = \tau_i \pi_i$ and $p_i^* = \tau_i^* \pi_i$. Then world product markets clear when

$$M_i(\tau_i \pi_i) + M_i^*(\tau_i^* \pi_i) = 0, \quad i = 1, 2, \ldots, n. \tag{9}$$

This equation allows us to solve for the market-clearing price of good X_i as a function of the industry trade taxes or subsidies imposed by the two countries. We denote this functional relationship by $\pi_i(\tau_i, \tau_i^*)$. It follows from (9) that the functions $\pi_i(\cdot)$ are homogeneous of degree minus one; that is, if the home country were to increase its tariff on imports of some good and the foreign country increased its export subsidy by the same percentage amount, then the world price would fall so as to leave the domestic prices in each country unchanged.

Using (9), we can express the (gross-of-contributions) welfare levels of the organized interest groups and of the average voter in each country as functions of the trade policy vectors $\boldsymbol{\tau}$ and $\boldsymbol{\tau}^*$. For example, the expression in (6) for the gross welfare of owners of the specific factor used in home industry i becomes $W_i(\boldsymbol{\tau}, \boldsymbol{\tau}^*) \equiv \tilde{W}_i[\boldsymbol{\tau}, \boldsymbol{\pi}(\boldsymbol{\tau}, \boldsymbol{\tau}^*)]$, and the average welfare of home voters can be written as $W(\boldsymbol{\tau}, \boldsymbol{\tau}^*) \equiv \tilde{W}[\boldsymbol{\tau}, \boldsymbol{\pi}(\boldsymbol{\tau}, \boldsymbol{\tau}^*)]$. Inserting these functions into (5) and (7) and their foreign analogues gives the objectives of the lobbies and politicians as functions of the trade policy vectors in each country.

We describe finally the sequence of actions by the various agents in our two-country model. The lobbies in each country move first, setting contribution schedules that link their gifts to the various possible policy outcomes. The lobbies act simultaneously and noncooperatively, each taking as given the schedules of all other lobbies in the same and the other country. Then the governments set their national trade policies. In Section 4, where we study trade wars, these policies are set in a noncooperative, simultaneous-move game. In Section 5, which deals with international negotiations, the policies emerge from the specified bargaining process. In both cases, we assume that the implicit contracts between the politicians and interest groups in one country (i.e., the contribution schedules that have been communicated by the lobbyists to the government) are not observable to the government in the other. The importance of this assumption will become clear as we go along.

4 Trade Wars

We begin our analysis of the international economic relations between politically motivated governments with the case of a trade war. Here, the governments behave unilaterally, ignoring the impacts of their actions on political and economic agents in the opposite country. While purely non-cooperative outcomes are unlikely to emerge in a world with repeated interactions and many forums for trade discussions, the extreme case of noncooperation sheds light on the political forces that shape trade policies during the frequent departures from harmony and cooperation in the trading realm.

Let us define an *equilibrium response* by each country to an arbitrary policy choice of the other. We use the home country to illustrate, although a similar definition applies to the foreign country.

DEFINITION 1. Let $\boldsymbol{\tau}^*$ be an arbitrary trade policy vector of the foreign country. Then a set of feasible contribution functions $\{C_i^o\}_{i \in L}$ and a trade policy vector $\boldsymbol{\tau}^o$ are an equilibrium response to $\boldsymbol{\tau}^*$ if (a)

$$\boldsymbol{\tau}^o = \operatorname*{argmax}_{\boldsymbol{\tau}} \sum_{i \in L} C_i^o(\boldsymbol{\tau}; \boldsymbol{\tau}^*) + aW(\boldsymbol{\tau}, \boldsymbol{\tau}^*)$$

and (b) for every organized interest group $i \in L$ there does not exist a feasible contribution function $C_i(\boldsymbol{\tau}; \boldsymbol{\tau}^*)$ and a trade policy vector $\boldsymbol{\tau}^i$ such that (i)

$$\boldsymbol{\tau}^i = \operatorname*{argmax}_{\boldsymbol{\tau}} C_i(\boldsymbol{\tau}; \boldsymbol{\tau}^*) + \sum_{j \neq i, j \in L} C_j^o(\boldsymbol{\tau}; \boldsymbol{\tau}^*) + aW(\boldsymbol{\tau}, \boldsymbol{\tau}^*)$$

and (ii)

$$W_i(\boldsymbol{\tau}^i, \boldsymbol{\tau}^*) - C_i(\boldsymbol{\tau}^i, \boldsymbol{\tau}^*) > W_i(\boldsymbol{\tau}^o, \boldsymbol{\tau}^*) - C_i^o(\boldsymbol{\tau}^o, \boldsymbol{\tau}^*).$$

An equilibrium response comprises a set of feasible contribution schedules and a policy vector. Each contribution schedule prescribes a political donation for each trade policy vector $\boldsymbol{\tau}$ that the home government might select. Feasible schedules are those that promise only nonnegative offers that do not exceed the aggregate income of the group's members. Condition (a) of the definition stipulates that the politicians select the policy vector that best serves their own interest, given the policy of the foreign government and the contribution schedules offered by the domestic lobbies. Condition (b) states that, given the set of contributions offered by all lobbies other than itself, no individual lobby i can improve its lot by setting a contribution schedule $C_i(\cdot)$ different from $C_i^o(\cdot)$, thereby inducing the home government to choose the policy vector $\boldsymbol{\tau}^i$.

Several aspects of this definition bear further discussion. First, our definition supposes that the lobbies do not cooperate with one another. While it is occasionally the case that several lobbies in a country will coordinate their activities to pursue a common goal and even that lobbies in different countries will join forces, the norm is certainly for the various industry representatives to take independent political action. One explanation for this observation might be that pressure groups cannot write binding contracts specifying their contributions to politicians and other political activities. In the absence of such contracts, it would be difficult for the different lobby groups to enforce any cooperative agreement among themselves. Also, in our model, the scope for cooperation between lobbies in any one country is limited because the interests of different producers are mostly opposed to one another. Lobbies representing the same industry in different countries also have opposing views about desirable policy interventions, as we shall see.

Our definition also presumes that the lobbies condition their promised contributions on the expected policy choices of the other country's government. In other words, the lobbies take the other country's policy as given, even though these lobbies make their decisions before the governments make theirs. The lobbies certainly would wish to influence the choices of the other government if it were possible to do so. But here is where our assumption that a lobby's offers to its own government cannot be observed by the other government comes into play. If the home lobbies could make their promises observable to foreign politicians and if they could commit to their contribution schedules immutably, then the lobbies would set their schedules strategically in order to induce a favorable policy response by the foreign government. The situation would be similar to that analyzed by Fershtman and Judd (1987), who showed that the owners of a firm generally will want to set a compensation schedule that gives the firm's managers an incentive to act aggressively in oligopolistic competition against other firms. But, as Katz (1991) later argued, a strategic design of an agent's compensation schedule can bear fruit in a delegation game (i.e., a game in which agents play on behalf of principals) only if the contracts between principal and agent are observable to the opposing players. Otherwise, the opposing players will not be influenced by (unobserved) manipulation of the principal-agent contract, and so there can be no gain to the principals (in our case, the home lobbies) from such manipulation.

It is natural for us to assume that contribution schedules cannot be observed abroad, for at least two reasons. First, it might be problematic for special-interest groups to be open and explicit about their willingness to pay the government for favorable treatment. Second, even if the interest groups were to announce their intention to vary their support according to the positions taken by the politicians, these promises would not be legally binding and policy makers abroad would not know whether there were further details or subsequent agreements besides those that had been made public. In cases in which multiple agreements or renegotiation is possible, a lobby's announcement of its contribution schedule carries little commitment value (see Katz [1991]). Accordingly, we feel justified in studying an equilibrium in which the industry groups condition their lobbying strategies on what they expect will be the other government's policy choice, but do not see themselves as able to influence those policies by their own choice of contribution schedule.

To find the equilibrium responses for each country, we proceed as in Grossman and Helpman (1994). There we characterized equilibrium trade policies for a small country that takes external prices as given. We noted the applicability of the theory of common agency developed by Bernheim and Whinston (1986), wherein a single actor acts simultaneously as the agent for several different principals. In the present context, once we take the foreign policy vector as given, we have a situation in which the home government acts as an agent for the various special-interest groups in the home country. We have already derived the payoffs to the principals and the agent for every action open to the latter, so we can proceed to apply the Bernheim-Whinston results to characterize the equilibrium responses.

We know from lemma 2 in Bernheim and Whinston (1986) (or proposition 1 in Grossman and Helpman [1994]) that the equilibrium policy response to τ^* satisfies, in addition to condition (a) of definition 1, the following requirement that is implied by condition (b):[7]

$$\tau^o = \operatorname*{argmax}_{\tau} W_i(\tau, \tau^*) - C_i^o(\tau; \tau^*)$$

$$+ \sum_{j \in L} C_j^o(\tau; \tau^*) + aW(\tau, \tau^*) \quad \text{for every } i \in L. \qquad (10)$$

This condition has a simple interpretation: the equilibrium trade policy vector must maximize the joint welfare of each lobby i and the government, when the contribution schedules of all lobbies other than i are taken as given. If this were not the case, lobby i could reformulate its schedule to induce the government to choose the jointly optimal policy vector instead of the alternative, and it could do so in such a way as to share in the surplus from the switch in policy. In equilibrium there can exist no such possibilities for a lobby to improve its lot. Of course, the same holds true for the foreign lobbies, so that an equation analogous to (10) applies to τ^{*o}.

Let us assume now that the lobbies set contribution schedules that are *differentiable*, at least around the equilibrium point.[8] We have argued in

---

[7] This is a necessary condition for an equilibrium. All the necessary and sufficient conditions are given in proposition 1 of Grossman and Helpman (1994).

[8] Typically, the contribution schedules would not be differentiable where the constraint that payments must be nonnegative becomes binding, i.e., where $C_i(\cdot) = 0$. However, this is not a problem for our arguments since we shall assume differentiability only around equilibria in which $C_i^o(\tau^o; \tau^{*o}) > 0$ for all i.

Grossman and Helpman (1994) that there are compelling reasons for focusing on contribution schedules that have this property. For example, differentiable schedules may be robust to small calculation errors. With differentiability, a trade policy vector that satisfies (10) also satisfies the first-order condition

$$\nabla_\tau W_i(\tau^o, \tau^*) - \nabla_\tau C_i^o(\tau^o; \tau^*) + \sum_{j \in L} \nabla_\tau C_j^o(\tau^o; \tau^*) + a\nabla_\tau W(\tau^o, \tau^*) = 0$$

$$\text{for all } i \in L. \qquad (11)$$

The home politicians' utility maximization ensures, by part (a) of definition 1, that

$$\sum_{j \in L} \nabla_\tau C_j^o(\tau^o; \tau^*) + a\nabla_\tau W(\tau^o, \tau^*) = 0. \qquad (12)$$

Taken together, (11) and (12) imply

$$\nabla_\tau C_i^o(\tau^o; \tau^*) = \nabla_\tau W_i(\tau^o, \tau^*) \quad \text{for all } i \in L. \qquad (13)$$

That is, the contribution schedules are set so that the marginal change in the donation for a small change in home policy (with the foreign policy taken as given) matches the effect of the policy change on the lobby's gross welfare. In Grossman and Helpman (1994), we referred to this property of the equilibrium contribution schedules as *local truthfulness*.

We sum equation (13) over all i and substitute the result into (12) to derive

$$\sum_{j \in L} \nabla_\tau W_i(\tau^o, \tau^*) + a\nabla_\tau W(\tau^o, \tau^*) = 0. \qquad (14)$$

This equation allows us to compute the equilibrium home policy response to an arbitrary foreign policy vector τ^*. Similarly, we have

$$\sum_{i \in L^*} \nabla_{\tau^*} W_i^*(\tau^{*o}, \tau) + a^*\nabla_{\tau^*} W^*(\tau^{*o}, \tau) = 0, \qquad (14^*)$$

which gives the foreign equilibrium response to an arbitrary home policy vector.

At last we are ready to define a full equilibrium in the trade war. When the policies are set, each government makes an equilibrium response to what it expects the other's policy will be. We can invoke the concept of a Nash equilibrium as follows.

DEFINITION 2. A noncooperative trade policy equilibrium consists of sets of political contribution functions $\{C_i^o\}_{i \in L}$ and $\{C_i^{*o}\}_{i \in L^*}$ and a pair of trade policy vectors τ^o and τ^{*o} such that $[\{C_i^o\}_{i \in L}, \tau^o]$ is an equilibrium response to τ^{*o} and $[\{C_i^*\}_{i \in L^*}, \tau^{*o}]$ is an equilibrium response to τ^o.

We proceed now to characterize the equilibrium policy vectors by substituting τ^{*o} for τ^* in (14) and τ^o for τ in (14*) and then treating these equations as a system of simultaneous equations. We calculate the derivatives in (14) using (4), (6), (8), and the definitions of the import functions $M_i(\cdot)$ and the gross benefit functions $W_i(\cdot)$ and $W(\cdot)$. This gives

$$(I_{iL} - \alpha_L)(\pi_i + \tau_i^o \pi_{i1})X_i + (a + \alpha_L)$$
$$\times [(\tau_i - 1)\pi_i(\pi_i + \tau_i^o \pi_{i1})M_i' - \pi_{i1}M_i] = 0, \qquad (15)$$

where I_{iL} is an indicator variable that equals one if industry i is politically organized and zero otherwise, and $\alpha_L \equiv \sum_{j \in L} \alpha_j$ is the fraction of voters that are represented by a lobby. From (9) we find the partials of the world price functions, $\pi_j(\cdot)$.[9] Substituting them into (15) yields an expression for the home country's equilibrium policy, namely

$$\tau_i^o - 1 = -\frac{I_{iL} - \alpha_L}{a + \alpha_L} \frac{X_i}{\pi_i M_i'} + \frac{1}{e_i^*} \qquad \text{for } i = 1, 2, \ldots, n, \qquad (16)$$

where $e_i^* \equiv \tau_i^* \pi_i M_i^{*\prime}/M_i^*$ is the elasticity of foreign import demand or export supply (depending on whether M_i^* is positive or negative). An analogous equation describes the equilibrium foreign trade policy; that is,

$$\tau_i^{*o} - 1 = -\frac{I_{iL}^* - \alpha_L^*}{a^* + \alpha_L^*} \frac{X_i^*}{\pi_i M_i^{*\prime}} + \frac{1}{e_i} \qquad \text{for } i = 1, 2, \ldots, n, \qquad (16^*)$$

where $e_i \equiv \tau_i \pi_i M_i'/M_i$ is the home country's import demand or export supply elasticity.

Equations (16) and (16*) express the ad valorem trade tax and subsidy rates in each country as sums of two components. These components represent, respectively, the *political support* and *terms-of-trade* motives for trade intervention. The first component has exactly the same form as the expression in Grossman and Helpman (1994) for the equilibrium policy in a small country facing fixed world prices. It reflects a balancing of the deadweight loss associated with trade policies (given the terms of trade) and the income gains that special-interest groups can capture via such policies. The second component represents the familiar "optimum tariff" (or export tax) that applies in a large country with a benevolent dictator. Given the balancing of special and general interests implicit in the first term, this second term enters the political calculus as an added reason why noncooperating governments will wish to tax international trade.

It is apparent from (16) and (16*) that an organized import-competing industry emerges from a trade war with a protective tariff (since $e_i^* > 0$ when the foreign country exports good i), whereas an unorganized home export industry suffers an export tax (since $e_i^* < 0$ when the foreign country imports good i). In the former case, the terms-of-trade consid-

[9] We have $\pi_{i1}/\pi_i = -M_i'/(\tau_i M_i' + \tau_i^* M_i^{*\prime})$ and $\pi_{i2}/\pi_i = -M_i^{*\prime}/(\tau_i M_i' + \tau_i^* M_i^{*\prime})$.

erations reinforce the industry's lobbying efforts. In the latter case, the government's desire to drive up the world price with an export tax finds support from all organized groups, whose members are consumers of the exportable good. Only in cases of organized export sectors and unorganized import sectors do the special and general interests come into conflict—at least as far as the sign, as opposed to the size, of the desired trade policy is concerned.

Consider, for example, an organized export industry (so that $e_i^* < 0$ and $I_{iL} = 1$). The industry's prospects for securing an export subsidy are better the greater is industry output, the smaller are the price sensitivities of domestic supply and demand, and the smaller is the weight a that home politicians place on average welfare. A large domestic output raises the stakes for owners of the specific input and makes them willing to bid more for support. Such bids have a greater influence on the politicians when they are less concerned with the public interest and when the deadweight loss associated with a given departure from free trade is small (i.e., $|M_i'|$ is small). On the other hand, for a given value of a and given conditions in the domestic market, the more inelastic the foreign import demand curve, the more inclined the home government will be to choose an export tax as its equilibrium policy. This accords with intuition since the home country's market power in trade varies with the inverse of the foreign elasticity, so the potential social gains from trade taxes become larger as $|e_i^*|$ declines. We note that the second term can outweigh the first even if the government pays no attention whatsoever to national welfare (i.e., $a = 0$). The reason is that the members of the various interest groups themselves share in the terms-of-trade gains from trade taxes, and they may collectively bid for an export tax for industry i even though the lobby that represents the industry presses for a subsidy.[10]

---

[10] In the case in which lobbies can contribute to foreign politicians as well as to their own national government, the lobbies still find it optimal to be locally truthful in their contribution offers *to each government*. The implication is that the left-hand side of (15) has some additional terms representing the effect of a marginal change in the home tariff on the aggregate welfare of foreign interest group members. To calculate the domestic tariff response functions, we would need to add to the left-hand side of (15) the following expression:

$$(I_{iL}^* - \alpha_L^*)\tau_i^*\pi_{i1}X_i^* + \alpha_L^*[(\tau_i^* - 1)\pi_i\tau_i^*M_i^{*\prime} - M_i^*]\pi_{i1}.$$

The resulting analogue to the tariff formula (16) is somewhat complicated but is easily interpreted for the case in which the lobby groups are a negligible fraction of the voting population in each country; i.e., $\alpha_L = \alpha_L^* = 0$. In this special case, the home country's equilibrium tariff is given by

$$\tau_i^o - 1 = -\frac{I_{iL}}{a}\frac{X_i}{\pi_i M_i'} + \frac{I_{iL}^*}{a}\frac{X_i^*}{\pi_i M_i^{*\prime}} + \frac{1}{e^*} \qquad (16')$$

(continued next page)

It is interesting to compare the policy outcomes in our model with those derived by Johnson (1954) under the assumption that governments maximize social welfare. This comparison allows us to isolate the role that domestic politics play in determining the outcome of a trade war. We note that our model reproduces the Johnson equilibrium as a limiting case when the governments care overwhelmingly about voters' welfare (so that a and a^* approach infinity).[11] Then the governments apply the familiar inverse elasticity rules in setting trade taxes.

In making the comparison, we focus on a special case in which both countries have constant trade elasticities. We may limit our attention to the outcome in a single industry because the equilibrium policy responses depend only on the characteristics of industry i and aggregate variables (see [16] and [16*]). For concreteness, we make the home country the importer of good X_i. Then its import demand curve is given by $M = m(\tau\pi)^{-\varepsilon}$, with $m > 0$ and $\varepsilon = -e_i > 1$.[12] The foreign country's export supply function has the form $-M^* = m^*(\tau^*\pi)^{\varepsilon^*}$, with $m^* > 0$ and $\varepsilon^* = e_i^* > 0$.

Figure 1 shows the Johnson equilibrium at point J. This point lies at the intersection of two best-response functions, BB for the home country and B^*B^* for the foreign country, where B refers to the benevolent dictators that rule each country. The curves are vertical and horizontal, respectively, in the constant elasticity case. The inverse elasticity rule gives the equilibrium policies in the Johnson equilibrium, $\tau_J = 1 + (1/\varepsilon^*)$ and $\tau_J^* = 1 - (1/\varepsilon)$. These are, of course, a tariff at home ($\tau_J > 1$) and an export tax abroad ($\tau_J^* < 1$).

In the trade war between politically motivated governments, the market-clearing world price for good i can be found using (9) and the

---

when there are contributions by both national *and foreign* lobbies. Comparing (16) and (16'), we see that influence-seeking by foreign lobbies serves to reduce the size of the home tariff response to any given foreign tariff, the more so the greater the foreign industry's output and the less price responsive the foreign country's export supply. The foreign output X_i^* measures the size and hence political clout of the foreign industry, and the slope of the foreign export supply measures the home government's willingness to accede to its wishes for a smaller tariff, in view of the induced effect on the international price.

[11] The Johnson equilibrium also obtains when all voters belong to a lobby group and all industries are politically organized. In this case, all individuals are able to express their political demands to the politicians, and so all are equally represented in the political process. The opposing interest groups neutralize one another in their attempts to transfer income to themselves, and what remains is only the terms-of-trade motive for trade policy that potentially benefits them all. Becker (1983) derives a similar neutrality result in a somewhat different model of the political process.

[12] We omit the industry subscript for the time being since all parameters and variables refer to industry i.

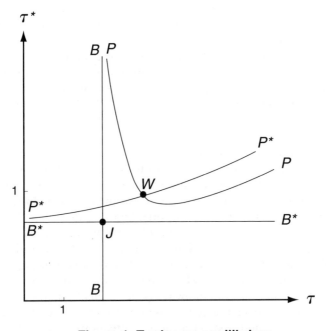

Figure 1. Trade war equilibrium

expressions that define the constant elasticity import demand and export
supply functions. We find

$$\pi(\tau, \tau^*) = \left(\frac{m}{m^*}\right)^{1/(\varepsilon + \varepsilon^*)} \left(\frac{1}{\tau}\right)^{\varepsilon/(\varepsilon + \varepsilon^*)} \left(\frac{1}{\tau^*}\right)^{\varepsilon^*/(\varepsilon + \varepsilon^*)} \tag{17}$$

Also, (16) and (16*) give the equilibrium policy responses, which in the
constant elasticity case can be written as

$$\tau = \left(1 + \frac{1}{\varepsilon^*}\right)\left[1 - \frac{I_L - \alpha_L}{a + \alpha_L} \frac{X(\tau\pi)}{\varepsilon m(\tau\pi)^{-\varepsilon}}\right]^{-1} \tag{18}$$

and

$$\tau^* = \left(1 - \frac{1}{\varepsilon}\right)\left[1 - \frac{I_L^* - \alpha_L^*}{a^* + \alpha_L^*} \frac{X^*(\tau^*\pi)}{\varepsilon^* m^*(\tau^*\pi)^{\varepsilon^*}}\right]^{-1}, \tag{18*}$$

where the π in (18) and (18*) represents the equilibrium $\pi(\tau, \tau^*)$ given
in (17).

Figure 1 shows the equilibrium responses for an industry with active
lobby groups in both countries (i.e., $I_L = I_L^* = 1$). The home country's
equilibrium response function (18) is represented by PP (P for political)
and the foreign country's (18*) by P^*P^*. The PP curve lies everywhere

to the right of BB and has a U-shape: it asymptotes to BB at $\tau = 1 + (1/\varepsilon^*)$ and to a ray from the origin as τ grows large.[13] The P^*P^* curve lies everywhere above B^*B^* and always slopes upward.[14]

Point W depicts the political equilibrium in the trade war.[15] This point lies to the northeast of the Johnson equilibrium at point J. Evidently, the politically motivated governments tilt trade policies in favor of their organized special interests; the home tariff is higher in the political equilibrium than in the Johnson equilibrium, whereas the foreign export tax is lower or possibly even a subsidy.[16]

Next we examine how the policy outcome changes when the political climate does. Suppose that the home politicians were to become less sensitive to the public interest and more concerned with their campaign finances; that is, consider a decrease in a. For the case of a home import good with active lobbies in each country, Figure 1 describes the initial equilibrium. A decline in a causes the PP curve to shift up, moving the equilibrium up and to the right along the fixed P^*P^* schedule.[17] The new equilibrium entails a higher home tariff and a lower foreign export tax (or higher export subsidy). The increase in the tariff comes about in the first instance because the lobby perceives a smaller marginal cost of "buying" protection from the government. Since the foreign lobbies and the foreign government expect a more protectionist stance from the home government, the political calculus changes there as well. In par-

---

[13] From (18) we see that $\tau \to \infty$ if and only if the term in brackets on the right-hand side approaches zero. Since $X(\tau\pi)/(\tau\pi)^{-\varepsilon}$ is an increasing function of $\tau\pi$, this gives a unique value for $\tau\pi$ and therefore τ/τ^* (see [17]) as τ grows large.

[14] The right-hand side of (18*) declines in the foreign price $p^* = \tau^*\pi$ because foreign exports ($m^*p^{*\varepsilon'}$), which are the difference between foreign output and demand, are more sensitive to p^* than foreign supply (X^*). But, from (17), we see that the foreign price $\tau^*\pi$ increases in τ^*/τ. It follows that P^*P^* must slope upward. We note that the slope would be ambiguous if the sector's input owners were unorganized (i.e., if $I_L^* = 0$).

[15] The diagram shows a unique equilibrium, which exists when the P^*P^* curve is steeper than the PP curve for τ and τ^* large. If the PP curve becomes steeper as τ and τ^* grow large, then the curves have either zero or two intersections. In the event that there are two, our remarks apply only to the equilibrium associated with the first crossing.

[16] The trade war generates both higher import tariffs and higher export taxes than the Johnson equilibrium for industries in which the import-competing interests are organized but the export interests are not. Where the export interests are organized and the import-competing interests are not, the trade taxes are lower in both countries than at J and may even turn to subsidies in one or both countries. Finally, import tariffs are lower and export taxes higher than at J in industries that have organized lobbies in neither country; then the organized groups representing other industries bid unopposed for lower consumer prices, at the expense of the unrepresented specific factor owners.

[17] Given τ, eq. (18) requires an increase in τ^* in response to a decline in a, so that π rises and X/M falls.

ticular, a higher domestic tariff means, ceteris paribus, a lower world price for the good. This decreases both the private benefit and social cost of an export subsidy, but the latter falls by proportionately more. Thus the industry's willingness to pay for a subsidy (or to resist a tax) declines by less than the cost to the government of providing the favor. The new foreign policy is more favorable to the foreign industry.

We note that the rise in the import tariff and the fall in the export tax have offsetting implications for internal prices in each country. The increase in the home tariff raises the home price despite the resultant improvement in the terms of trade, but the fall in the foreign export tax pushes the home price down via its effect on π. Similarly, the increase in τ^* puts upward pressure on p^*, but the terms-of-trade movement associated with the rise in τ works in the opposite direction. The figure shows, however, that τ/τ^* must rise.[18] Since $\tau\pi$ is an increasing function of τ/τ^* and $\tau^*\pi$ is a decreasing function of this same ratio, the decline in a causes the internal price of a home import good to rise at home and to fall abroad.

The change in the political environment affects organized export industries in much the same way. Figure 2 shows the policy outcome for such a sector. Since our labeling convention makes the foreign country the exporter of the good in question, we represent a reduction in the government's concern about aggregate welfare by a cut in a^*. This shifts the P^*P^* curve to the left. The export tax (or subsidy) may rise or fall, whereas the import tariff always falls. But no matter which way the exporting country's policy changes, τ/τ^* must fall, so again the internal price rises in the country that experiences the change in its political environment and falls in the other. In both the export and import cases, an increased government sensitivity to the concerns of special interests in one country raises the profits of the organized factor owners in that country at the expense of their counterparts abroad.

The analysis shows how the domestic political environments color the strategic interactions between countries. We have seen that a decline in the home parameter a induces a change in the foreign country's policy that improves the home country's terms of trade. This raises the potential for a political paradox: *a government that is unresponsive to the public interest might actually serve the general voter well, because the self-interested government can credibly commit to a policy of aggressive support for the domestic industry.*

5 Trade Talks

We have portrayed the interactions between government officials in different countries who pursue their selfish interests while setting their

---

[18] At each point along P^*P^*, the curve is flatter than a ray to that point from the origin. This implies that τ^*/τ falls as we move out and to the right along the curve.

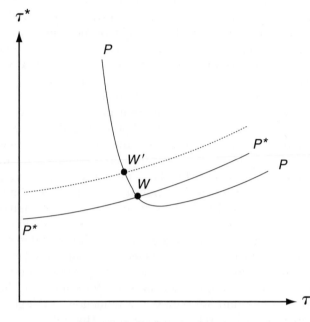

Figure 2. Decrease in *a**

nations' trade policies. These officials are willing to impose deadweight losses on their constituencies as a means of amassing campaign contributions. Thus the economic inefficiency of the political equilibrium will not be a matter of overriding concern to them. However, there is another sort of inefficiency inherent in the equilibrium of Section 4 that may be of greater concern. By choosing their national policies noncooperatively, the incumbent politicians impose avoidable political costs on one another. If the politicians recognize this, they may be willing and indeed anxious to enter into a multilateral trade negotiation. In this section we study equilibria that emerge from trade talks between politically motivated governments.

We allow the two governments to bargain over the trade policy schedules τ and τ^*. For the moment, we also allow them to negotiate a transfer payment R (positive or negative) that the foreign country pays to the home country as part of the negotiated agreement.[19] Some trade pacts such as the European Community's common agricultural policy actually call for such intercountry transfers. However, as we shall see below, the

---

[19] While we allow official, government-to-government transfers, we do not allow side payments (i.e., kickbacks) from one set of politicians to the other.

bargaining game has essentially the same equilibrium when R is constrained to zero. Thus our results apply also when transfers are infeasible.

It proves convenient for the exposition to begin with a case in which organized owners of specific factors constitute a negligible fraction of the voters in each country. With $\alpha_L = \alpha_L^* = 0$, the members of lobby groups enjoy a negligible share of the surplus from consuming non-numeraire goods, and they pay a negligible fraction of the head taxes levied by the governments. Thus the interest groups worry only about their factor incomes and the amounts of their political contributions. In the negotiation game, the organized lobbies tie their contributions to the policies that emerge from the international talks; that is, contributions are functions of τ and τ^*. In general, the lobbies might also condition their contributions on the size of the international transfer. But they need not do so here because their members are so few in number that they receive or contribute only a negligible fraction of any payment that is made.

Confronted with the set of contribution schedules $\{C_i(\tau, \tau^*)\}$, the home government comes to the bargaining table with the goal of maximizing

$$G = \sum_{i \in L} C_i(\tau, \tau^*) + a[W(\tau, \tau^*) + R]. \tag{19}$$

The first term in (19) is the total amount of campaign contributions. The second term represents per capita welfare weighted by the parameter a reflecting the government's concern for the public interest. Notice that the transfer R has been added to the previously defined measure of average gross welfare. This reflects our assumption that transfer payments are combined with any net revenue from trade taxes and subsidies and that the government redistributes the surplus (or collects the shortfall) on an equal per capita basis. The same is true of the foreign government, so its objective becomes

$$G^* = \sum_{i \in L^*} C_i^*(\tau^*, \tau) + a^*[W^*(\tau^*, \tau) - R]. \tag{19*}$$

For now, we do not commit ourselves to any particular bargaining procedure. Rather we assume only that the politicians settle on an outcome that is efficient from their own selfish perspectives. In other words, we assume that the trade policies that emerge from the negotiation are such that G could not be raised without lowering G^*. The Nash bargaining solution and Rubinstein's (1982) noncooperative bargaining equilibrium, among others, have this efficiency property. Efficiency requires the governments to choose the trade policy vectors to maximize the weighted sum

$$a^*G + aG^* = a^* \sum_{i \in L} C_i(\tau, \tau^*) + a \sum_{i \in L^*} C_i^*(\tau^*, \tau)$$
$$+ a^*a[W(\tau, \tau^*) + W^*(\tau^*, \tau)]. \tag{20}$$

Once this sum has been maximized, the governments can use the international transfer to select (almost) any utility pair (G, G^*) on the straight line defined by (20).[20]

We are now in a position to define an equilibrium in the two-stage game in which lobbies set contribution schedules noncooperatively in the first stage and the governments bargain over trade policies in the second.

DEFINITION 3. An equilibrium trade agreement consists of sets of political contribution functions $\{C_i^o\}_{i \in L}$ and $\{C_i^{*o}\}_{i \in L^*}$ and a pair of trade policy vectors $\boldsymbol{\tau}^o$ and $\boldsymbol{\tau}^{*o}$ such that

(i) $(\boldsymbol{\tau}^o, \boldsymbol{\tau}^{*o}) = \underset{(\boldsymbol{\tau}, \boldsymbol{\tau}^*)}{\text{argmax}}\ a^* \sum_{i \in L} C_i^o(\boldsymbol{\tau}, \boldsymbol{\tau}^*)$

$$+ a \sum_{i \in L^*} C_i^{*o}(\boldsymbol{\tau}^*, \boldsymbol{\tau}) + a^* a[W(\boldsymbol{\tau}, \boldsymbol{\tau}^*) + W^*(\boldsymbol{\tau}^*, \boldsymbol{\tau})];$$

(ii) for every organized lobby $i \in L$, there does not exist a feasible contribution function $C_i(\boldsymbol{\tau}, \boldsymbol{\tau}^*)$ and a pair of trade policy vectors $(\boldsymbol{\tau}^i, \boldsymbol{\tau}^{*i})$ such that (a)

$$(\boldsymbol{\tau}^i, \boldsymbol{\tau}^{*i}) = \underset{(\boldsymbol{\tau}, \boldsymbol{\tau}^*)}{\text{argmax}}\ a^*[C_i(\boldsymbol{\tau}, \boldsymbol{\tau}^*) + \sum_{j \neq i, j \in L} C_j^o(\boldsymbol{\tau}, \boldsymbol{\tau}^*)]$$

$$+ a \sum_{j \in L^*} C_j^{*o}(\boldsymbol{\tau}^*, \boldsymbol{\tau}) + a^* a[W(\boldsymbol{\tau}, \boldsymbol{\tau}^*) + W^*(\boldsymbol{\tau}^*, \boldsymbol{\tau})]$$

and (b)

$$W_i(\boldsymbol{\tau}^i, \boldsymbol{\tau}^{*i}) - C_i(\boldsymbol{\tau}^i, \boldsymbol{\tau}^{*i}) > W_i(\boldsymbol{\tau}^o, \boldsymbol{\tau}^{*o}) - C_i^o(\boldsymbol{\tau}^o, \boldsymbol{\tau}^{*o});$$

(iii) for every organized lobby $i \in L^*$, there does not exist a feasible contribution function $C_i^*(\boldsymbol{\tau}^*, \boldsymbol{\tau})$ and a pair of trade policy vectors $(\boldsymbol{\tau}^i, \boldsymbol{\tau}^{*i})$ such that (a)

$$(\boldsymbol{\tau}^i, \boldsymbol{\tau}^{*i}) = \underset{(\boldsymbol{\tau}, \boldsymbol{\tau}^*)}{\text{argmax}}\ a^* \sum_{j \in L} C_j^o(\boldsymbol{\tau}, \boldsymbol{\tau}^*)$$

$$+ a[C_i^*(\boldsymbol{\tau}^*, \boldsymbol{\tau}) + \sum_{j \neq i, j \in L^*} C_j^{*o}(\boldsymbol{\tau}^*, \boldsymbol{\tau})]$$

$$+ a^* a[W(\boldsymbol{\tau}, \boldsymbol{\tau}^*) + W^*(\boldsymbol{\tau}^*, \boldsymbol{\tau})]$$

and (ii)

$$W_i^*(\boldsymbol{\tau}^{*i}, \boldsymbol{\tau}^i) - C_i^*(\boldsymbol{\tau}^{*i}, \boldsymbol{\tau}^i) > W_i^*(\boldsymbol{\tau}^{*o}, \boldsymbol{\tau}^o) - C_i^{*o}(\boldsymbol{\tau}^{*o}, \boldsymbol{\tau}^o).$$

Condition (i) of the definition stipulates that the settlement is efficient from the point of view of the two negotiating governments. Note that efficiency here means maximization of the joint welfare of the two sets of politicians, not Pareto efficiency for voters. Condition (ii), analogous to the similarly labeled condition of definition 1, requires that it be impos-

---

[20] Equation (20) is derived as a weighted sum of (19) and (19*), after R is canceled. The only restriction on feasible (G, G^*) is that neither government can promise to transfer to the other country more than the entirety of the national product.

sible for any organized lobby group in the home country to gain by restructuring its contribution schedule, considering that the two governments will settle on a different agreement when one of them faces an altered set of political incentives. The same must be true for organized interest groups in the foreign country, which is the meaning of condition (iii). The equilibrium trade agreement also entails a certain transfer, R^o, the size of which will depend on the details of the bargaining process.

This two-country game has a structure almost identical to the one that characterizes policy setting in a small country (see Grossman and Helpman [1994]). In the case of a small country, the organized lobbies set contribution schedules that induce their common agent (the government) to take a policy action in light of the perceived costs to the agent. The various schedules are set simultaneously, and each constitutes a best response to the others. Here there are two sets of organized lobbies, but still they set their schedules simultaneously and noncooperatively. While there is no identifiable common agent, the objective function in (20) can be interpreted as being that of an "as if" mediator or a surrogate world government. In other words, the equilibrium trade agreement is the same one that would arise if a single decision maker had the preferences given on the right-hand side of (20) and a large set of interest groups constituting the organized lobbies of both countries bid to influence this agent's decisions. Once again, the equilibrium policies can be found by application of lemma 2 in Bernheim and Whinston (1986). That is, we replace conditions (ii) and (iii) of definition 3 by the requirement—analogous to (10)—that the negotiated policy outcome must maximize the joint welfare of each organized lobby and the hypothetical mediator, when the contribution schedules of all other lobbies are taken as given. This requirement can be written as

$$(\boldsymbol{\tau}^o, \boldsymbol{\tau}^{*o}) = \operatorname*{argmax}_{(\boldsymbol{\tau}, \boldsymbol{\tau}^*)} a^*[W_j(\boldsymbol{\tau}, \boldsymbol{\tau}^*) - C_j^o(\boldsymbol{\tau}, \boldsymbol{\tau}^*)]$$
$$+ a^* \sum_{i \in L} C_i^o(\boldsymbol{\tau}, \boldsymbol{\tau}^*) + a \sum_{i \in L^*} C_i^{*o}(\boldsymbol{\tau}^*, \boldsymbol{\tau})$$
$$+ a^* a[W(\boldsymbol{\tau}, \boldsymbol{\tau}^*) + W^*(\boldsymbol{\tau}^*, \boldsymbol{\tau})] \quad \text{for all } j \in L \qquad (21)$$

and

$$(\boldsymbol{\tau}^o, \boldsymbol{\tau}^{*o}) = \operatorname*{argmax}_{(\boldsymbol{\tau}, \boldsymbol{\tau}^*)} a[W_j^*(\boldsymbol{\tau}^*, \boldsymbol{\tau}) - C_j^{*o}(\boldsymbol{\tau}^*, \boldsymbol{\tau})]$$
$$+ a \sum_{i \in L} C_i^o(\boldsymbol{\tau}, \boldsymbol{\tau}^*) + a \sum_{i \in L^*} C_i^{*o}(\boldsymbol{\tau}^*, \boldsymbol{\tau})]$$
$$+ a^* a[W(\boldsymbol{\tau}, \boldsymbol{\tau}^*) + W^*(\boldsymbol{\tau}^*, \boldsymbol{\tau})] \quad \text{for all } j \in L^*. \qquad (21^*)$$

Now we introduce the assumption, as we did before, that all contribution schedules are differentiable around the equilibrium point. Then we can make use of the first-order conditions that characterize the solutions to the maximization in condition (a) of definition 3 and the maximizations in (21) and (21*). Combining these, we find that the equilibrium contribution schedules again are locally truthful and that the agreed-on policies must satisfy

$$
a^* \sum_{i \in L} \nabla_\tau W_i(\tau^o, \tau^{*o}) + a \sum_{i \in L^*} \nabla_\tau W_i^*(\tau^{*o}, \tau^o)
$$
$$
+ a^* a [\nabla_\tau W(\tau^o, \tau^{*o}) + \nabla_\tau W^*(\tau^{*o}, \tau^o)] = 0 \qquad (22)
$$

and

$$
a^* \sum_{i \in L} \nabla_{\tau^*} W_i(\tau^o, \tau^{*o}) + a \sum_{i \in L^*} \nabla_{\tau^*} W_i^*(\tau^{*o}, \tau^o)
$$
$$
+ a^* a [\nabla_{\tau^*} W(\tau^o, \tau^{*o}) + \nabla_{\tau^*} W^*(\tau^{*o}, \tau^o)] = 0. \qquad (22^*)
$$

It is straightforward to calculate the partial derivatives in (22) and (22*). Substituting these expressions, we obtain

$$
a^* [I_{jL} X_j + a(\tau_j^o - 1) \pi_j M_j'] (\pi_j + \tau_j^o \pi_{j1})
$$
$$
+ a [I_{jL}^* X_j^* + a^* (\tau_j^{*o} - 1) \pi_j M_j^{*'}] \tau_j^{*o} \pi_{j1} = 0 \quad \text{for } j \in L \qquad (23)
$$

and

$$
a [I_{jL}^* X_j^* + a^* (\tau_j^{*o} - 1) \pi_j M_j^{*'}] (\pi_j + \tau_j^{*o} \pi_{j2})
$$
$$
+ a^* [I_{jL} X_j + a(\tau_j^o - 1) \pi_j M_j'] \tau_j^o \pi_{j2} = 0 \quad \text{for } j \in L^*. \qquad (23^*)
$$

Equations (23) and (23*) are two sets of equations that, if independent, might be used to solve for τ^o and τ^{*o}. However, these equations are linearly dependent.[21] In other words, the equilibrium requirements that we have stated so far determine only the ratios $\tau_1^o/\tau_1^{*o}, \tau_2^o/\tau_2^{*o}, \ldots,$ τ_n^o/τ_n^{*o}, but not τ^o and τ^{*o} separately. We shall explain the meaning of this finding presently, but first we derive from (23) and (23*) the following equation that implicitly gives the equilibrium policy ratio in industry i:

$$
\tau_i^o - \tau_i^{*o} = \left(-\frac{I_{iL}}{a} \frac{X_i}{\pi_i M_i'} \right) - \left(-\frac{I_{iL}^*}{a^*} \frac{X_i^*}{\pi_i M_i'^*} \right)
$$
$$
\text{for } i = 1, 2, \ldots, n. \qquad (24)
$$

Notice that when both sides of (24) are divided by τ_i^{*o}, the trade policies enter this equation only in ratio form.[22]

---

[21] To establish this, use the properties of the price functions $\pi_i(\cdot)$ stated in n. 9.

[22] That is, X_i and M_i' are functions of $p_i = \tau_i \pi_i$, which is homogeneous of degree zero in τ_i and τ_i^*. Similarly, X_i^* and $M_i'^*$ are functions of $p_i^* = \tau_i^* \pi_i$, which is also homogeneous of degree zero in τ_i and τ_i^*. Finally, the term $\tau_i^* \pi_i$ appears directly in the denominator of both expressions in parentheses, once the equation has been divided through by τ_i^*. Thus they all can be expressed as functions of the ratio τ_i/τ_i^*.

On reflection, it is clear why definition 3—which we have used to characterize an equilibrium trade pact—pins down only the ratio of the two countries' trade policies and not the levels of those policies. The definition stipulates that the equilibrium must be efficient for the two governments without specifying how the surplus will be divided between them. But the ratio τ_i/τ_i^* determines the internal prices p_i and p_i^*, which in turn determine industry outputs, demands, trade flows, and factor prices in each country. In short, the allocation of resources does not depend separately on τ_i and τ_i^*, and neither does the joint welfare available to the two sets of politicians.[23]

This brings us to an important point: *Equation (24) must characterize the equilibrium trade agreement even if intercountry transfer payments are constrained to be zero.* Since allocations do not depend separately on the sizes of the policy wedges in the two countries, the governments can mimic any international transfer payment by increasing (or decreasing) some τ_i and τ_i^* while holding their ratio constant. Consider what this would do to trade tax revenue in each country. The revenues that the home country derives from the tax or subsidy in industry i total $r_i = (\tau_i - 1)\pi_i M_i$, and those that the foreign country collects amount to $r_i^* = (\tau_i^* - 1)\pi_i M_i^*$. An equiproportionate increase in τ_i and τ_i^* leaves $\tau_i\pi_i$, $\tau_i^*\pi_i$, M_i, and M_i^* unchanged. Therefore, tax receipts must rise in the country that imports good X_i and fall in the country that exports this good. Moreover, the offsetting changes in government revenue have exactly the same size. Thus an equiproportionate increase in τ_i and τ_i^* is in every way equivalent to a direct transfer from the exporting country to the importing country. It follows that a bargain that is efficient when transfers are feasible remains so when they are not.[24]

Recall that we have so far restricted attention to the case in which lobby group members constitute a negligible fraction of the total voting

---

[23] Mayer (1981) noted this point in his discussion of efficient bargaining between two aggregate-welfare-maximizing governments.

[24] In the event that lobbies can offer contributions to politicians in either country, all campaign giving will be concentrated on the single government that is more easily swayed by such gifts. That is, each industry, no matter where it is located, will offer nothing to the government that places the greater weight on its average voter's welfare and will devote all its efforts to influencing the negotiating position of the government that more readily trades off voter well-being for campaign funds. The upshot is that, instead of (24), the negotiated tariff schedule will satisfy

$$\tau_i^o - \tau_i^{*o} = \left(-\frac{I_{iL}}{\tilde{a}}\frac{X_i}{\pi_i M_i'}\right) - \left(-\frac{I_{iL}^*}{\tilde{a}}\frac{X_i^*}{\pi_i M_i^{*\prime}}\right) \quad \text{for } i = 1, 2, \ldots, n, \qquad (24')$$

where $\tilde{a} = \min(a, a^*)$.

population. We can now extend the analysis to the more general case. When $\alpha_L \geq 0$ and $\alpha_L^* \geq 0$, the following formula applies in place of (24):

$$\tau_i^o - \tau_i^{*o} = \left(-\frac{I_{iL} - \alpha_L}{a + \alpha_L} \frac{X_i}{\pi_i M_i'} \right) - \left(-\frac{I_{iL}^* - \alpha_L^*}{a^* + \alpha_L^*} \frac{X_i^*}{\pi_i M_i^{*'}} \right)$$

$$\text{for } i = 1, 2, \ldots, n. \qquad (25)$$

This can be derived in one of two ways. First, we can impose $R = 0$ and solve the common agency problem involving lobbies with objectives $v^i = W_i(\boldsymbol{\tau}, \boldsymbol{\tau}^*) - C_i(\boldsymbol{\tau}, \boldsymbol{\tau}^*)$ and $v^{*i} = W_i^*(\boldsymbol{\tau}^*, \boldsymbol{\tau}) - C_i(\boldsymbol{\tau}^*, \boldsymbol{\tau})$, and a hypothetical mediator who maximizes the right-hand side of (20). The derivation proceeds as before. Alternatively, we can allow $R \neq 0$, but then we must permit the lobbies to condition their contributions on the sizes of the transfers obtained by their governments as part of the trade agreement. If we allow for this dependence and write $C_i(\cdot) = \tilde{C}_i(\boldsymbol{\tau}, \boldsymbol{\tau}^*) + \lambda_i R$, and similarly for the foreign lobbies, then we can once again derive (25) as the outcome of the common agency problem.[25]

Equation (25) reveals that, relative to free trade, the negotiated trade agreement favors the industry group that has greater political clout. We have $\tau_i/\tau_i^* > 1$ when the first term in parentheses on the right-hand side exceeds the second and $\tau_i/\tau_i^* < 1$ when the second exceeds the first. Since $\tau_i/\tau_i^* = 1$ in free trade and the home (foreign) domestic price is an increasing (decreasing) function of τ_i/τ_i^*, it is the politically stronger industry that winds up with greater profits under the agreement as compared to free trade.

Several components enter into the measurement of political power. First and foremost, political power derives from representation in the political process. If the specific factor owners in industry i are organized in one country and not in the other, then the organized group always secures from the trade agreement a gain relative to free trade. When both countries' specific factor owners are organized in some industry, then the more powerful group is the one with the greater stake in the negotiation (i.e., X_i vs. X_i^*), the one with the government that places less weight on average welfare (i.e., a vs. a^*), and the one in the country in which a smaller fraction of the voting population bids for policies (i.e., α_L vs. α_L^*). Also, an industry interest group at home gains a political advantage relative to its foreign counterpart if the home import demand or export supply is less price sensitive than that abroad. A high price sensitivity raises the cost to a government of distorting prices and thus makes the government less open to the industry's bids for protection.

---

[25] We can also show that no lobby can improve its lot by deviating to an arbitrary contribution function $C_i(\boldsymbol{\tau}, \boldsymbol{\tau}^*, R)$ in place of the one with the form $\tilde{C}_i(\boldsymbol{\tau}, \boldsymbol{\tau}^*) + \lambda_i R$.

When the interest groups in industry i enjoy equal political power in the two countries, a negotiated agreement gives rise to equal rates of import tax and export subsidy. In the event, internal prices, world prices, and industry outputs and profit levels will be the same as in free trade. This finding points to the conclusion that whatever aggregate efficiency losses result from the negotiated trade agreement, they stem not from the mere existence of special-interest politics in the two countries, but from differences in the extent of the political pressures that the interest groups can bring to bear. A trade negotiation pits the powerful lobbies in one country against those in another and thereby neutralizes (to some extent) the power of each one.

Notably absent from the formula in (25) is any measure of the relative market power of the two countries. That is, the foreign trade elasticities—which fully determine the Johnson equilibrium and appear as components of the trade war equilibrium discussed in Section 4—are neglected by the hypothetical mediator of the trade agreement. As is well known, policy-induced terms-of-trade movements benefit one country at the expense of the other and impose a deadweight loss on the world economy. An efficient negotiation will eliminate this source of deadweight loss while perhaps compensating the party that otherwise would have captured the benefits.

It is time now to introduce a specific bargaining procedure in order to show how this determines the division of surplus between the two negotiating parties. For illustrative purposes, we adopt the Rubinstein (1982) bargaining model, as extended by Binmore, Rubinstein, and Wolinsky (1986) and Sutton (1986), to incorporate the risk that negotiations might break down at any moment when an agreement has not yet been reached.

Suppose that the two governments meet at the bargaining table with the trade war equilibrium of Section 4 as the status quo ante. The governments take turns proposing vectors of trade policies τ and τ^* to replace those in the noncooperative equilibrium. When one government makes an offer, the other can accept or reject. If it accepts, the agreement goes into effect immediately. If it rejects, then a period of time passes during which the policies given in (16) and (16*) remain in force. At the end of this period the talks may terminate exogenously or else the second government will get an opportunity to make a counterproposal. Termination happens with probability $1 - e^{-\beta\Delta}$, where Δ represents the length of a bargaining period and β is a parameter measuring the likelihood of a breakdown per unit of time. The process of alternating proposals continues until either an agreement is reached or a breakdown occurs. In the event of the latter, the noncooperative equilibrium continues indefinitely.

In this setting, there are two costs of failing to reach an immediate agreement. First, the noncooperative equilibrium applies during the bargaining period. Second, the parties face the risk that the talks will come to an end. To capture the cost of delay, we introduce discount rates ρ and ρ^* for the two governments. They could arise, for example, if politicians and factor owners have the same discount rates and if the politicians did not collect their promised gifts until after the talks were completed.[26] The discount rates imply that the home government perceives the value of an agreement reached after k rounds of bargaining to be $e^{-\rho\Delta(k-1)}$ times as great as the value of an agreement with identical provisions that is signed immediately

In this bargaining game, neither government has an incentive to offer a set of policies when another set would provide strictly greater welfare to both governments. In other words, the offers must maximize the right-hand side of (20). Let the maximal value for this expression be $\overline{G}$. Then we can think of the governments as bargaining directly over the instantaneous welfare levels G and G^* subject to the constraint that $a^*G + aG^* = \overline{G}$. Once a distribution of welfare has been agreed on, the governments can implement the agreement by choosing policies that satisfy (25) and that divide the trade tax revenues as required by the agreement.

We can solve the bargaining game in the manner suggested by Sutton (1986). Let the home country make the first offer, and denote its proposed division of the surplus by (G_H, G_H^*). Of course the proposal must satisfy

$$a^*G_H + aG_H^* = \overline{G}. \tag{26}$$

Moreover, the offer will be such as to induce immediate acceptance while leaving the foreign government with no extra surplus relative to what it could achieve by refusing the offer. If the foreign government accepts, it receives G_H^* forever. If it rejects, the noncooperative equilibrium continues on for a period of at least Δ. Then, with probability $1 - e^{-\beta\Delta}$, the negotiations end and the noncooperative equilibrium persists forever; with probability $e^{-\beta\Delta}$, the foreign government gets the opportunity to make a counteroffer, which we denote by (G_F, G_F^*). The foreign government would always choose an offer that would (just) be accepted, so it can count on a flow of utility G_F^* after the delay of Δ, if the talks do not break down. The home offer that makes the foreign government just indifferent between accepting and rejecting satisfies

---

[26] The governments' discount factors also reflect the fact that the incumbent politicians may not remain in power forever. We view the discount factors as a simple way to capture whatever costs the governments perceive to be associated with delay in reaching an agreement.

$$\frac{G_H^*}{\rho^*} = \frac{1 - e^{-\rho^*\Delta}}{\rho^*} \; G_N^* + \left[\frac{(1 - e^{-\beta\Delta})e^{-\rho^*\Delta}}{\rho^*} \; G_N^* + \frac{e^{-\beta\Delta}e^{-\rho^*\Delta}}{\rho^*} \; G_F^*\right],$$

where G_N^* is the flow of utility to the foreign government in the noncooperative equilibrium of Section 4. The two terms on the right-hand side represent, respectively, the present value of the utility flow during the period before the first possible counteroffer (from time 0 to time Δ) and the expected value of the flow from that time onward. Rearranging this equation gives

$$G_H^* = [1 - e^{-(\beta + \rho^*)\Delta}]G_N^* + [e^{-(\beta + \rho^*)\Delta}]G_F^*. \tag{27}$$

We now derive the offer that the foreign government would make were it to reach the stage of counterproposing. The counteroffer (G_F, G_F^*) satisfies

$$a^*G_F + aG_F^* = \overline{G}, \tag{26*}$$

and it provides the home politicians with just enough utility to make them indifferent between accepting the offer and waiting for the chance of still another bargaining round. This indifference condition implies

$$G_F = [1 - e^{-(\beta + \rho)\Delta}]G_N + [e^{-(\beta + \rho)\Delta}]G_H, \tag{28}$$

where G_N is the flow of utility to the home government in a trade war.

We solve the four equations (26), (26*), (27), and (28) for the offer (G_H, G_H^*) and the counteroffer (G_F, G_F^*). Since the initial offer is always accepted, we can readily calculate the division of surplus in the modified Rubinstein game. As is usual in such games, the outcome of the bargaining depends on which government can make the initial offer. However, the advantage from going first disappears as the time between offers shrinks to zero. With continuous bargaining (i.e., $\Delta \to 0$), the equilibrium trade pact yields the following flows of utility to the two governments:

$$G = \frac{1}{2 + \gamma + \gamma^*}\left[\frac{1 + \gamma^*}{a^*} \; \overline{G} + (1 + \gamma)G_N - \frac{a}{a^*}(1 + \gamma^*)G_N^*\right] \tag{29}$$

and

$$G^* = \frac{1}{2 + \gamma + \gamma^*}\left[\frac{1 + \gamma}{a} \; \overline{G} + (1 + \gamma^*)G_N^* - \frac{a^*}{a}(1 + \gamma)G_N\right], \tag{29*}$$

where $\gamma = \rho/\beta$ and $\gamma^* = \rho^*/\beta$. Here, the division of surplus depends on the fallback positions. That is, each government captures more of the gains from cooperation the greater its measure of political welfare in the trade war equilibrium. As usual, higher welfare in the status quo ante gives a negotiator a stronger position at the bargaining table. Each government also gains more from the trade agreement the more patient it can be while bargaining. Patience gives a negotiator a credible threat to decline a low offer, and thus her rival must offer more to ensure an agreement without delay.

6 Conclusions

In this paper we have introduced special-interest politics into the analysis of international trade relations. Our model features campaign contributions by industry lobbies that induce policy preferences in self-interested politicians. We have used the model to study policy formation in cooperative and noncooperative international settings.

Our approach rests on the key assumption that interest groups contribute to politicians with the intention of influencing their policy choices. This assumption finds support in the evidence presented by Magelby and Nelson (1990) and Snyder (1990). Moreover, econometric studies of congressional voting behavior suggest that such investments bear fruit. For example, Baldwin (1985) found that a congressperson was more likely to vote against the Trade Act of 1974 the greater the contributions he or she received from major labor unions opposed to the bill; Tosini and Tower (1987) found a positive association between a vote in favor of the protectionist Textile Bill of 1985 and the size of donations received from companies and unions in the textiles and apparel industries.

When governments set their trade policies noncooperatively, each party neglects the impact of its policies on factor owners and politicians abroad. Our model predicts that in such circumstances higher tariff rates will emerge in industries that are politically organized, all else equal. Rates of protection should vary positively with the stake of the specific factor in trade policy relative to that of the average voter (i.e., with the ratio of output to imports) and inversely with the sizes of the elasticities of foreign export supply and home import demand.

It is difficult to evaluate how well these predictions are borne out by the empirical evidence. While there have been many econometric studies of the determinants of protection across industries, most suffer from a number of serious shortcomings. First, it has been common practice to include a long list of regressors when "explaining" the level of protection in an industry. Often each regressor bears only a loose relationship to some theoretical concept, and different interpretations can be ascribed to the same right-hand-side variable. Second, many of the (collinear) regressors are intended to proxy the same thing, so it is difficult to give meaning to the coefficient on one of them when others are implicitly being held constant. Third, almost all the regressions have been estimated by ordinary least squares, despite the fact that levels of protection

clearly influence many of the supposedly exogenous right-hand-side variables.[27] Finally, none of the studies includes any regressors relating to
foreign political and economic conditions, and thus they implicitly
assume that international interdependence is unimportant or that
foreign industry conditions are uncorrelated with those at home.

   With these caveats in mind, the evidence does suggest a positive association between levels of protection and the extent to which an industry
is politically organized. Lavergne (1983), Baldwin (1985), and Trefler
(1993) have proxied political activism by the economic and geographic
concentration of firms, since they presumably affect the ease of organ-
izing politically. These authors find one or both of these variables to be a
positive and significant influence on the levels of tariffs or nontariff barriers. As for our prediction that tariffs will be higher in industries with
more to gain from protection, the evidence here is ambiguous. Riedel
(1977), Baldwin (1985), and others find that protection is higher in
industries with greater levels of employment. While consistent with our
prediction (more employment means a larger stake, all else equal), this
result is difficult to interpret because these same authors include the
share of labor in value added and the import-penetration ratio as separate explanatory variables. Several studies find that import-penetration
ratios are positively related to the level of protection. Our model predicts
that the opposite should be true, but again it is difficult to know what
the empirical results mean, both because import penetration should
really be treated as endogenous and because the regressions hold constant several variables related to the size of the domestic industry. Finally,
as for the effects of the elasticities of import demand and export supply,
they have not been examined in any of the existing empirical work.

   Our model also yields predictions about the outcome of trade negotiations. For example, when governments bargain efficiently, the resulting
trade policies for a given industry should not reflect the countries' market
power in trade. In other words, the foreign export supply elasticities that
should enter into each country's tariff rates in a noncooperative equilibrium should have no bearing on these rates in a cooperative settlement. With international bargaining, rates of protection should reflect
not only the political strength of the special interest group at home—as
indicated by the extent of its political activism, by the ratio of domestic
output to net trade, and by the size of the home import demand or
export supply—but also the political strength of the interest group in the
same industry abroad. Protection should be especially high where the

---

[27] An exception to this rule is the paper by Trefler (1993), who estimates an equation
   explaining the level of nontariff barriers jointly with one explaining the pattern of trade.
   He finds substantial evidence of simultaneity in these two equations.

home interest group is strong and the foreign group in the same industry is weak. When both are equally strong, their political influences will cancel, and international prices under a trade agreement should be equal to those that would prevail under totally free trade.

There is some scant evidence that such international bargaining considerations do affect U.S. trade policies. For example, Lavergne (1983) finds that U.S. tariff cuts have been largest in industries in which Canadian producers enjoy the biggest U.S. market share. He interprets this as reflecting the outgrowth of pressures brought by the Canadian government on behalf of its industry interests and the willingness of the U.S. government to concede in the light of corresponding concessions offered U.S. exporters. Still, much remains to be done in testing whether and how the policies prescribed by trade treaties reflect the political pressures that the governments faced when they negotiated the pacts.

References

Baldwin, Robert E. (1985). *The Political Economy of U.S. Import Policy* (Cambridge, Mass.: MIT Press).

Becker, Gary S. (1983). A theory of competition among pressure groups for political influence. *Quarterly Journal of Economics* 98 (August): 371–400.

Bernheim, B. Douglas, and Whinston, Michael D. (1986). Menu auctions, resource allocation, and economic influence. *Quarterly Journal of Economics* 101 (February): 1–31.

Binmore, Ken, Rubinstein, Ariel, and Wolinsky, Asher (1986). The Nash bargaining solution in economic modelling. *RAND Journal of Economics* 17 (Summer): 176–188.

Brock, William A., and Magee, Stephen P. (1978). The economics of special interest politics: The case of the tariff. *American Economic Review Papers and Proceedings* 68 (May): 246–250.

Cowhey, Peter F. (1990) "States" and "politics" in American foreign economic policy. In John S. Odell and Thomas D. Willett (eds.). *International Trade Policies: Gains from Exchange between Economics and Political Science* (Ann Arbor: University of Michigan Press).

Fershtman, Chaim, and Judd, Kenneth L. (1987). Equilibrium incentives in oligopoly. *American Economic Review* 77 (December): 927–940.

Findlay, Ronald, and Wellisz, Stanislaw (1982). Endogenous tariffs, the political economy of trade restrictions, and welfare. In Jagdish N. Bhagwati (ed.). *Import Competition and Response* (Chicago: University of Chicago Press, for NBER).

Grossman, Gene M., and Helpman, Elhanan (1994). Protection for sale. *American Economic Review* 84 (September): 833–850.

Hillman, Arye L. (1982). Declining industries and political-support protectionist motives. *American Economic Review* 72 (December): 1180–1187.

Hillman, Arye L., and Moser, Peter (1995). Trade liberalization as politically optimal exchange of market access. In Matthew Canzoneri et al. (eds.). *The New Transatlantic Economy* (Cambridge: Cambridge University Press).

Johnson, Harry G. (1954). Optimum tariffs and retaliation. *Review of Economic Studies* 21 (2): 142–153.

Katz, Michael L. (1991). Game-playing agents: Unobservable contracts as precommitments. *RAND Journal of Economics* 22 (Autumn): 307–328.

Kennan, John, and Riezman, Raymond (1988). Do big countries win tariff wars? *International Economic Review* 29 (February): 81–85.

Kuga, Kiyoshi (1973). Tariff retaliation and policy equilibrium. *Journal of International Economics* 3 (November): 351–366.

Lavergne, Réal P. (1983). *The Political Economy of U.S. Tariffs: An Empirical Analysis* (Toronto: Academic Press).

Long, Ngo Van, and Vousden, Neil (1991). Protectionist responses and declining industries. *Journal of International Economics* 30 (February): 87–103.

Magee, Stephen P.; Brock, William A.; and Young, Leslie (1989). *Black Hole Tariffs and Endogenous Policy Theory: Political Economy in General Equilibrium* (Cambridge, Mass.: MIT Press).

Magelby, David B., and Nelson, Candice J. (1990). *The Money Chase: Congressional Campaign Finance Reform* (Washington, D.C.: Brookings Institution).

Mayer, Wolfgang (1981). Theoretical considerations on negotiated tariff adjustments. *Oxford Economic Papers* 33 (March): 135–153.

Peltzman, Sam (1976). Toward a more general theory of regulation. *Journal of Law and Economics* 19 (August): 211–240.

Putnam, Robert D. (1988). Diplomacy and domestic politics: The logic of two-level games. *International Organization* 42 (Summer): 427–460.

Riedel, James C. (1977). Tariff concessions in the Kennedy Round and the structure of protection in West Germany: An econometric assessment. *Journal of International Economics* 7 (May): 133–143.

Riezman, Raymond (1982). Tariff retaliation from a strategic viewpoint. *Southern Economic Journal* 48 (January): 583–593.

Rubinstein, Ariel (1982). Perfect equilibrium in a bargaining model. *Econometrica* 50 (January): 97–109.

Snyder, James M., Jr. (1990). Campaign contributions as investments: The U.S. House of Representatives, 1980–1986. *Journal of Political Economy* 98 (December): 1195–1227.

Stigler, George J. (1971). The theory of economic regulation. *Bell Journal of Economics and Management Science* 1 (Spring): 1–21.

Sutton, John (1986). Non-cooperative bargaining theory: An introduction. *Review of Economic Studies* 53 (October): 709–724.

Tosini, Suzanne C., and Tower, Edward (1987). The textile bill of 1985: The determinants of congressional voting patterns. *Public Choice* 54, no. 1: 19–25.

Trefler, Daniel (1993). Trade liberalization and the theory of endogenous protection: An econometric study of U.S. import policy. *Journal of Political Economy* 101 (February): 138–160.

Six

Politics and Trade Policy

1 Introduction

Economists have devoted much effort to the study of *efficiency* properties of trade policies. These efforts have produced a coherent body of literature that describes how trade policy instruments—such as tariffs, export subsidies, quotas, or voluntary export restraints—affect economies that trade with each other. And they produced empirical models that have been extensively used to evaluate the efficiency losses from trade policies, on the one hand, and prospective gains from trade reforms, on the other.

By Elhanan Helpman. Originally published in *Advances in Economics and Econometrics: Theory and Applications*, Vol. 1, D. M. Kreps and K. F. Wallis, eds. 19–45. Copyright © 1997 by Cambridge University Press. Reprinted with permission. I am grateful to the National Science Foundation for financial support and to Gene Grossman and Alan Winters for comments.

Examples include quantitative studies of the single-market program in Europe (e.g., Flam [1992]) and of NAFTA (e.g., Garber [1993]).

At the same time another strand of the literature has examined possible explanations for prevailing trade policies. Here efficiency considerations have not played center stage. Many policies—such as quotas and voluntary export restraints—impose large burdens on society. Therefore research looked for objectives of the policy makers other than overall efficiency in order to explain them. This literature emphasizes distributional considerations. It views trade policy as a device for income transfers to preferred groups in society. And it explains the desire of a policy maker to engage in this sort of costly transfer by means of political arguments in her objective function (see Hillman [1989] for a review).

Political economy explanations of trade policies are important, because they help to understand the structure of protection as well as major public policy debates. It would be impossible, in fact, to understand such debates without paying close attention to political considerations. Examples include the debate about NAFTA in the U.S., in which special interests—such as the sugar industry—were able to effectively voice their concerns in Congress. Or the debate about the Uruguay Round in France, that brought farmers out into the streets. Quite often countries design their trade policies in a way that yields to pressure from special-interest groups, and trade negotiations at the international arena respond similarly.

As important as the political economy of trade policy seems to be, however, there exists no coherent theory to explain it. Models that underline some features of the policy formation process have been designed by economists and political scientists. But they do not add up as yet to a coherent theory. One reason for this state of affairs is that there exists no agreed-upon theory of domestic politics. This reflects partly the fact that there are many channels through which residents convey their desires to policy makers, and these ways differ across issues and across concerned groups in society. Moreover, political institutions vary across countries and they affect the ways in which influence works through the system. As a result, there are potentially many modes of interaction that require close scrutiny. Special-interest politics are prevalent, however, and economists need to understand these processes in order to better predict policy outcomes and to better design feasible policy options.

My purpose is to describe in this chapter a number of political economy approaches that have been developed to explain trade policies. I present these approaches in Section 2, using a unified framework that helps to identify the key differences among them. These comparisons revolve around tariff formulas that are predicted by the political equilibria. A typical formula explains cross-sectoral variations in rates of protection as well as differences in average rates of protection across countries. Section 3 then reviews a set of results that emerge from a new approach to the interaction of international economic relations with domestic politics. Importantly, there are two-way interactions in such systems, as pointed out by Putnam (1988). They link the formation of trade policies in the international arena with the activities of domestic special-interest groups. The use of a framework of this sort is essential for a proper analysis of a host of important problems, such as negotiations about tariff levels or the formation of free trade areas. Recent studies have developed suitable tools for this purpose, as I will argue in Section 3.

2 Political Economy Approaches

I briefly describe in this section some of the leading political economy approaches to the formation of trade policies.

2.1 Direct Democracy

Wolfgang Mayer (1984) proposed to view trade policy as the outcome of majority voting over tariff levels. There are, of course, very few countries in which direct democracy is applied to a broad range of issues, Switzerland being the prime example. Nevertheless, there exists a view that in representative democracies policy outcomes are reasonably close to what is supported by a majority of the voters. In such cases the simple analysis of majority voting serves as a good approximation. There remain, of course, the difficulties involved in voting over multi-dimensional issues, that have not yet been resolved (see Shepsle [1990]). And these difficulties apply to trade policies, which are often multi-dimensional in character. Witness, for example, the various rounds of trade liberalization under the auspices of the GATT (the Uruguay round being the last one), in which the removal of many tariffs and other trade barriers were negotiated simultaneously. Nevertheless, we may be able to learn something useful from the direct democracy approach.

The essence of Mayer's approach is quite simple. Suppose that a country has to decide the level of a particular tariff rate. We shall denote by τ_i one plus the tariff rate on product i.[1] Then we can derive a reduced-form indirect utility function for each voter j, $\hat{v}_i(\tau_i, \gamma^j)$, where γ^j is a vector of the voter's characteristics. These characteristics may include his

---

[1] When τ_i is larger than one and the good is imported, we have a proper tariff. Alternatively, when τ_i is smaller than one and the good is imported, we have a subsidy to imports. If the good is exported and τ_i is larger than one we have an export subsidy and if τ_i is smaller than one and the good is exported we have an export tax.

endowment(such as his skills, his ownership of shares in companies) or
parameters describing his preference for consumption. Naturally, the
shape of $\hat{v}_i(\cdot)$ depends on various details of the economy's structure. If
individual j was asked to choose the tariff level that he prefers most, he
would choose τ_i that maximizes $\hat{v}_i(\tau_i, \gamma^j)$.[2] Let $\hat{\tau}_i(\gamma^j)$ describe the solution
to this problem as a function of the individual's characteristics. The
assumption that $\hat{\tau}_i(\cdot)$ is a function means that individual preferences over
tariff rates are single peaked. Under these circumstances voting over
pairs of alternative tariff rates leads to the adoption of τ_i^m, which is most
preferred by the median voter. Namely, it is the tariff rate that has the
property that the number of voters who prefer a higher rate equals the
number of voters who prefer a lower rate. As a result no other tariff
obtains more votes in a competition with τ_i^m.

Mayer studied properties of the equilibrium rate of protection τ_i^m in a
Heckscher–Ohlin type two-sector two-factor economy, in which all individuals have the same homothetic preferences, every sector produces a
homogeneous product under constant returns to scale, and people differ
in their relative endowment of the two factors. Taking labor and capital
to be the two factors, γ^j represents the capital–labor ratio owned by individual j. Then, assuming that tariff revenue is redistributed to the public
in proportion to income, he was able to derive the most preferred tariff
rate of the median voter and to study its characteristics.

As an example of tariffs determined by direct voting, I now develop a
model that will also be used for future purposes. Consider an economy
with a continuum of individuals. Each individual has the utility function

$$u(c) = c_0 + \sum_{i=1}^{n} u_i(c_i), \tag{1}$$

where c_i is consumption of product i and $u_i(\cdot)$ is an increasing concave
function. Population size equals one.

Let there be labor and a sector-specific input in each sector i. Aggregate labor supply is normalized to equal one. Individual j owns the fraction γ_L^j of labor.[3] The numeraire good, indexed 0, is produced only with
labor, using one unit of labor per unit output. Each one of the remaining goods is produced with labor and the sector-specific input. We shall
measure all prices in terms of the numeraire. Then the wage rate equals

one and the reward to the sector-specific input in sector i, $\Pi_i(p_i)$, is an increasing function of the producer price of product i, p_i. Now normalize all foreign prices to equal one. Then $p_i = \tau_i$. Next let γ_i^j represent the fraction of the sector-i specific input owned by individual j.[4] Finally, suppose that the government redistributes tariff revenue in a lump-sum fashion and equally to every individual. It then follows that the reduced-form indirect utility function is given by

$$\hat{v}(\tau, \gamma^j) = \gamma_L^j + \sum_{i=1}^{n} (\tau_i - 1) M_i(\tau_i) + \sum_{i=1}^{n} \gamma_i^j \Pi_i(\tau_i) + \sum_{i=1}^{n} S_i(\tau_i), \quad (2)$$

where $M_i(\tau_i)$ represents aggregate imports of product i.[5] The first term on the right-hand side represents labor income. The second term represents income from the government's transfer, and the third term represents income from the ownership of sector-specific inputs. The last term represents consumer surplus.

It is evident from (2) that individual j's preference for the tariff rate in sector i depends only on his fraction of ownership of the sector-specific input in that sector. This preference function can be represented by $\hat{v}_i(\tau_i, \gamma_i^j) = (\tau_i - 1) M_i(\tau_i) + \gamma_i^j \Pi_i(\tau_i) + S_i(\tau_i)$.[6] As a result we have $\partial \hat{v}_i(\tau_i, \gamma_i^j) \partial \tau_i = (\tau_i - 1) M_i'(\tau_i) + (\gamma_i^j - 1) X_i(\tau_i)$, where $X_i = \Pi_i'$ represents the output level in sector i. Since imports decline with the tariff, it follows that individuals with above-average ownership of the sector-specific input vote for a tariff while individuals with below-average ownership vote for an import subsidy.[7] And an individual's most preferred tariff is higher the larger his ownership share of the sector-specific input. It follows that voting on the tariff level in sector i leads to a tariff rate that is most preferred by the individual with the median value of γ_i^j. The larger this median value γ_i^m, the higher the resulting tariff rate. When the median voter's most-preferred tariff rate is not on the boundary of the feasible set, it can be calculated from the condition $\partial \hat{v}_i(\tau_i, \gamma_i^m)/\partial \tau_i = 0$, which yields the following formula for the equilibrium tariff:[8]

---

[4] I.e., $\int_j \gamma_i^j dj = 1$ for every $i = 1, 2, \ldots, n$.

[5] When there are trade taxes only, the consumer price equals the producer price. As is well known, the utility function (1) has an associated standard indirect utility function $v(p, E) = E + \sum_{i=1}^{n} S_i(p_i)$, where E represents total spending and $S_i(p_i) = u_i[d_i(p_i)] - p_i d_i(p_i)$ is the consumer surplus from product i, where $d_i(p_i)$ is the demand function for product i. Imports of product i are given by $M_i(\tau_i) = -[S_i'(\tau_i) + \Pi_i'(\tau_i)]$.

[6] Namely, the reduced form indirect utility function (2) is given by $\hat{v}(\tau, \gamma^j) = \gamma_L^j + \sum_{i=1}^{n} \hat{v}_i(\tau_i, \gamma_i^j)$.

[7] I use the term "tariff" to mean $\tau_i > 1$ independently of whether the good is imported or exported. Also observe that under our normalization of the population size—i.e., that the population equals one—the average ownership share of a sector-specific input equals one.

[8] Output and the slope of the import demand function depend on the tariff rate, but these arguments have been suppressed in the following formula for convenience.

$$\tau_i - 1 = (\gamma_i^m - 1) \frac{X_i}{(-M_i')}.$$ (3)

The tariff rate is higher when the median voter's share of ownership of the sector-specific input is higher, and it also is higher the larger the sector in terms of output and the smaller the slope of the import demand function. Larger output levels imply higher stakes for the industry, which makes it more profitable to have a high tariff (as long as γ_i^m is above average), while the less elastic the import demand function, the lower the excess burden of a tariff. Part of this excess burden is born by the median voter. Therefore he prefers a higher tariff rate the lower this marginal cost. This is, of course, a standard consideration in Ramsey pricing.

One last point should be noted concerning equilibrium tariff rates in a direct democracy. My discussion assumed that the ownership of the sector-specific inputs is thinly dispersed in the population. Occasionally (or perhaps even often) this is not the case. So consider the other extreme case, in which, say, the ownership of the sector-specific input in sector k is highly concentrated, up to the point that it is owned by a negligible fraction of the population. Under these circumstances a member of this minority group, who owns a finite amount of the sector-specific input, wants the tariff rate to be as high as possible. On the other hand, an individual who has no ownership of this input whatsoever wants an import subsidy. Since the latter type of people represent almost 100 percent of the voters, the median voter most prefers to subsidize imports. More generally, it is clear from this example that under majority voting we should not observe tariffs but rather import subsidies in sectors with a highly concentrated ownership. If anything, the opposite seems to be true. As argued by Olson (1965), however, in sectors with a highly concentrated ownership it is relatively easy to overcome the free-rider problem and to form pressure groups whose purpose it is to protect sector-specific incomes. Therefore we need to consider the role of such organizations in the shaping of trade policies, to which we will turn at a later stage.

2.2 Political Support Function

An alternative approach was proposed by Hillman (1982). Borrowing from the theory of economic regulation, as developed by Stigler (1971) and Peltzman (1976), he suggested that we could view the choice of a tariff rate as the solution to an optimizing problem in which the government trades off political support from industry interests against the dissatisfaction of consumers. Industry interests provide more support the higher the industry's profits, while the government gains more support from consumers the lower the consumer price. In the event, by raising domestic prices higher tariffs bring about more support from industry interests—whose profits rise—and less support from consumers—whose real income declines. And the government chooses a tariff level that maximizes aggregate support.

Hillman postulated a reduced-form aggregate support function for a tariff in sector i, $P_i[\Pi_i(p_i) - \Pi_i(p_i^*), p_i - p_i^*]$, in which the first argument represents the gain in profits from a trade policy that raises the domestic price from the free-trade price p_i^* to p_i, while the second term represents the loss in consumer welfare that results from the same price increase. Political support rises in the first argument, and it declines in the second argument for $p_i^* < p_i$. Hillman used this approach to study the trade policy response to a declining foreign price. In particular, he showed that under mild assumptions a decline in the foreign price leads to higher domestic protection, but the resulting tariff increase does not fully compensate for the fall in the foreign price. As a result, the decline in the foreign price leads to a decline in the domestic price as well, but to a lesser degree.

I will now reformulate the political-support function approach in order to derive a formula for equilibrium tariff rates that is comparable with (3). For this purpose suppose that the economic structure is the same as in Section 2.1. In this event we can use (2) to calculate aggregate welfare, by integrating the individual welfare functions over the entire population. The result is

$$W(\tau) = 1 + \sum_{i=1}^{n} (\tau_i - 1)M_i(\tau_i) + \sum_{i=1}^{n} \Pi_i(\tau_i) + \sum_{i=1}^{n} S_i(\tau_i). \qquad (4)$$

Next, suppose that the government's political support for a policy is an increasing function of the income gains of sector-specific inputs and of the aggregate welfare gain. For simplicity assume that this function is linear;[9] i.e.,

$$\hat{P}(\tau) = \sum_{i=1}^{n} \frac{1}{a_{pi}} [\Pi_i(\tau_i) - \Pi_i(1)] + [W(\tau) - W(1, 1, \ldots, 1)]. \qquad (5)$$

The parameter a_{pi} represents the marginal rate of substitution in the government's political support function between aggregate welfare and profits of special interests in sector i. These parameters are allowed to vary across sectors. The larger a_{pi}, the more willing is the government to

[9] The assumption of linearity is inconsequential for our purpose. With a nonlinear political support function, the formula of the tariff rate has a marginal rate of substitution a_{pi} that depends on the levels of income of sector-specific inputs and on aggregate welfare.

give up profits of sector-i interests in exchange for aggregate welfare. The government chooses rates of protection to maximize its political support, as measured by $\hat{P}(\tau)$. Using (4) and (5), an interior solution to this maximization problem implies the following tariff rates:[10]

$$\tau_i - 1 = \frac{1}{a_{pi}} \frac{X_i}{(-M_i')}. \qquad (6)$$

Comparing this formula with (3), we see that they are the same, except for the fact that the parameter $1/a_{pi}$ replaces $(\gamma_i^m - 1)$. Namely, in both cases the tariff is higher the larger the sector's output level and the flatter the import demand function. Importantly, however, while the political-support function approach implies that each sector in which special interests count (i.e., in which a_{pi} is finite) will be protected and no sector will be afforded negative protection, direct voting over tariff rates brings about positive protection in sectors with median ownership of sector-specific inputs larger than the average, but negative protection in sectors in which median ownership of sector-specific inputs falls short of the average. It follows that in a direct democracy the distribution of ownership has an important effect on the structure of protection, while in a representative democracy—in which the government evaluates a political-support function in its design of trade policy—the political-support function's marginal rates of substitution between the well-being of consumers and sectoral interests importantly affect the structure of protection. Evidently, building on the political-support function's approach, a better understanding of the forces that shape the structure of protection requires some insights on what determines the marginal rates of substitution between aggregate welfare and special interest profits. Unfortunately, the theory is not particularly helpful on this critical point.

2.3 Tariff-Formation Function

The political-support function summarizes a trade-off between the support that a government obtains from special interests, on the one hand, and the support of consumers, on the other. Under this approach, a government designs its trade policy so as to balance the conflict between these opposing groups in a way that serves it best. Considerations of this sort are, of course, quite common in representative democracies, and

---

[10] Observe that by substituting (4) into (5) we obtain an objective function in which every dollar of real income obtains a weight of 1, except for income from a sector-specific input that obtains a weight of $1 + 1/a_{pi}$. These differential weights on different sources of real income drive the results. Long and Vousden (1991) have proposed a somewhat different approach to the formulation of political support functions, in which the weights vary across individuals rather than across sources of income.

even in totalitarian regimes rulers tend to listen to the concerns of the general public. But competition for preferential treatment very often takes on an active form, rather than the passive form envisioned in the political-support function approach. Lobbying for the protection of real incomes is prevalent, and many interest groups participate in this process.

To deal with the active seeking of protection of real incomes, Findlay and Wellisz (1982) proposed the use of tariff-formation functions. A function of this sort describes the level of protection afforded to an industry as depending on the amount of resources devoted to lobbying by a group of supporters of protection, on the one hand, and by the lobbying efforts of opposers, on the other. According to this view, the level of protection reflects the outcome of a contest between interest groups on the opposing sides of the issue.[11] More precisely, let $T_i(C_i^S, C_i^O)$ describe the tariff formation function in sector i, where C_i^S represents the lobbying expenditure of the proprotectionist interest group and C_i^O represents the lobbying expenditure of the antiprotectionist interest group. The resulting rate of protection is higher the larger the expenditure of the former group and the lower the expenditure of the latter. In the political equilibrium, $\tau_i = T_i(C_i^S, C_i^O)$.

In order to derive the equilibrium level of protection, we need to describe the incentives of the various interest groups. So suppose that the benefits of the proprotectionist lobby are given by the increasing function $W_i^S(\tau_i)$ while the benefits of the opposition are given by the declining function $W_i^O(\tau_i)$, both measured in terms of numeraire income. Then the lobbying expenditure levels are determined as the Nash equilibrium of a noncooperative game in which each interest group chooses its lobbying expenditure so as to maximize net benefits, which are $W_i^S[T_i(C_i^S, C_i^O)] - C_i^S$ for the proprotectionist lobby and $W_i^O[T_i(C_i^S, C_i^O)] - C_i^O$ for its rival. Findlay and Wellisz developed a two-sector specific-factor model, in which the owners of the specific factor in the import-competing industry lobby for import protection while the owners of the specific factor in the exporting industry oppose protection. As is well known, in an economy of this type the former group gains from protection while the latter group loses (see Jones [1971]); therefore they naturally take the opposite sides of the protection issue. In this framework Findlay and Wellisz have investigated the determinants of the equilibrium rate of protection. Given that the results depend on the shape of the tariff formation function, however, and the fact that their theory has little to say about this shape, they were unable to derive sharp predictions.

[11] Feenstra and Bhagwati (1982) take a similar approach, except that they view the government as the defender of the public interest. As a result, the lobbying costs of the proprotectionist coalition rise with the price distortion. We will come back to this point at a later stage.

In order to relate this approach to my previous discussion, let us consider a somewhat different variant of the tariff formation model. Suppose that the economy is the same as in Section 2.1. Also suppose that the owners of the sector-i specific factor form an interest group that lobbies for protection. The purpose of the lobby is to maximize the individuals' joint welfare. Joint welfare maximization is suitable whenever the interest group can resolve its internal conflicts, such as ensuring the participation of all factor owners and the distribution of the burden of the lobbying expenses among them. If these owners constitute a fraction α_i of the population, then the joint welfare that they derive from sector i can be represented by [see (2)]:[12]

$$W_i^S(\tau_i) = \Pi_i(\tau_i) + \alpha_i[(\tau_i - 1)M_i(\tau_i) + S_i(\tau_i)].$$

The first term on the right-hand side represents income of the sector-specific input while the second term describes the share of the lobby in the tariff rebate and in consumer surplus. So this describes the benefit function of the protectionist lobby. Marginal benefits of protection equal $W_i^{S\prime} = (1 - \alpha_i)X_i + \alpha_i(\tau_i - 1)M_i'$, which are positive for values of τ_i that are not too large.

Next suppose that there exists a lobby that opposes protection, which consists of all the other individuals in the economy.[13] The joint welfare that this group derives from a given tariff level equals

$$W_i^O(\tau_i) = (1 - \alpha_i)[(\tau_i - 1)M_i(\tau_i) + S_i(\tau_i)].$$

Namely, they obtain a fraction $1 - \alpha_i$ of the tariff rebate and the same fraction of consumer surplus. To this group the marginal benefit of protection equals $W_i^{O\prime} = (1 - \alpha_i)[-X_i + (\tau_i - 1)M_i']$, which is negative for positive rates of protection (i.e., for $\tau_i > 1$).

Finally, consider an interior equilibrium to the noncooperative game between the interest groups. The first-order conditions for the choice of lobbying expenditures that maximize net benefits are given by $[(1 - \alpha_i)X_i + \alpha_i(\tau_i - 1)M_i']T_{iS} = 1$ for the protectionist lobby and by $(1 - \alpha_i)[-X_i + (\tau_i - 1)M_i']T_{iO} = 1$ for its rival. T_{iS} and T_{iO} represent partial derivatives of the tariff formation function with respect to the spending levels of the proprotectionist lobby and the antiprotectionist lobby, respectively. In the first condition, the left-hand side represents the marginal benefit of an additional dollar spent to promote protection, which consists of the product of the marginal benefit of protection and the marginal gain in protection from a dollar of spending. The right-

[12] I exclude the constant term for labor income from this formula.
[13] It is, of course, not realistic to assume that the antiprotectionist lobby consists of all other individuals in the economy. But it simplifies the exposition.

hand side represents the marginal cost. A proprotectionist lobby chooses
its spending level so as to balance costs and benefits at the margin. A
similar interpretation can be given to the second condition, which applies
to the interest group that opposes protection. Together these conditions
yield

$$\tau_i - 1 = \frac{(1 - \alpha_i)(b_i - 1)}{\alpha_i b_i + (1 - \alpha_i)} \frac{X_i}{(-M_i')} , \tag{7}$$

where $b_i = -T_{iS}/T_{i0} > 0$ represents the marginal rate of substitution
between the spending levels on lobbying in the tariff-formation function.[14] When $b_i > 1$, a marginal dollar of spending on lobbying by the
proprotectionist interest group raises the tariff by more than it declines
as a result of an extra dollar of spending on lobbying by the antiprotectionist interest group. We see from this equation that the sector is protected if and only if $b_i > 1$. And if a marginal lobbying dollar of one
interest group is as effective as a marginal lobbying dollar of the other
interest group, then there is free trade. Importantly, whenever the sector
is protected, the rate of protection is higher the more effective a lobbying dollar of the proprotectionist interest group is relative to a lobbying
dollar of the antiprotectionist interest group, and the smaller the fraction of people that belong to the former group. The last result implies
that the more highly concentrated the ownership of a sector-specific
factor is, the higher the rate of protection afforded to this sector will be.
This result—which is just the opposite from the prediction of the direct
voting model—stems from the fact that the fewer the owners of the sector-
specific input, the less account does the lobby take of the excess burden
produced by protection. In the extreme case, when the entire population has a stake in the sector, free trade prevails, because the lobby inter-
nalizes all welfare considerations. Finally, as in the previously discussed
cases, the rate of protection is higher the larger the output level and the
flatter the import demand function.

Formula (7) results partly from the assumption that the opposition
to the proprotectionist lobby consists of all the other individuals in
the economy. This is obviously not the typical case. The important
point is, however, that the welfare of at least some fraction of the
general public counts in the design of a trade policy. Those members
of society may be represented by an organized group or by the government itself. In the latter case the government's motivation may be
the desire to do good or just cool political calculus. Indeed, Feenstra

---

[14] If only a fraction $\alpha_i^o < 1 - \alpha_i$ of individuals belong to the antiprotectionist lobby, then
the first term on the right-hand side of (7) should be replaced with $[(1 - \alpha_i)(b_i - 1) + 1 - \alpha_i - \alpha_i^o]/(\alpha_i b_i + \alpha_i^o)$.

and Bhagwati (1982) have used a tariff-formation function with a government that cares about welfare of the general public. Under these circumstances the desire to minimize excess burden plays an important role.

2.4 Electoral Competition

Unlike most other approaches to the politics of trade policy, Magee, Brock, and Young (MBY) (1989) advocate an emphasis on electoral competition.[15] According to this view interest groups give contributions to political parties and candidates in order to improve their chances of being elected. This contrasts with the tariff-formation function approach in which contributions influence policy choices. For this reason MBY construct a model in which two parties compete in an election. Each one commits to a policy *before* the choice of contributions by special interests. As a result, the choice of contributions does not affect policy choices and their only role is to improve the likelihood of one or the other party being elected. Anticipating the electoral motive in campaign giving, however, the parties—which are interested in maximizing their electoral prospects at the polls—choose policies that correctly anticipate future campaign contributions.

Somewhat more formally, suppose that there are two political parties and two lobbies. Each lobby is aligned with one party. In MBY there is a procapital party with which the lobby of capital owners is aligned and a prolabor party with which labor is aligned. Other alignments are of course possible, depending on context. For present purposes let us be agnostic about the precise interpretation of these allegiances, and let us have party A and party B, and lobby 1 and lobby 2. Lobby 1 is aligned with party A while lobby 2 is aligned with party B. Party A gets elected with probability $q\left(\sum_{i=1}^{2} C_i^A, \sum_{i=1}^{2} C_i^B, \tau^A, \tau^B \right)$, where C_i^K stands for the contribution of lobby i to the political campaign of party K and τ^K is the trade policy of party K. This probability is higher the more contributions party A amasses, the less contributions party B amasses, the less distortive the trade policy of party A is, and the more distortive the trade policy of party B is.

In the second stage of the game, after the parties have committed to their trade policies, the lobbies decide on campaign contributions. Let $W_i(\tau)$ be the benefit function of lobby i when the trade policy is τ. Then

---

[15] Electoral competition is implicit in both the political-support function and the tariff-formation function approaches, while in the Magee, Brock, and Young (1989) approach it plays center stage.

this lobby expects the benefit level $W_i(\tau^A)$ with probability $q(\cdot)$ and the benefit $W_i(\tau^B)$ with probability $1 - q(\cdot)$. Lobbies choose their contributions noncooperatively. Therefore, contributions are a Nash equilibrium of the game in which each lobby maximizes its expected net benefit. Namely, the best response of lobby i to the contribution levels of the other lobby is given by the solution to the following problem:

$$\max_{C_i^A \geq 0, C_i^B \geq 0} \quad q\left(\sum_{i=1}^{2} C_i^A, \sum_{i=1}^{2} C_i^B, \tau^A, \tau^B\right) W_i(\tau^A)$$

$$+\left[1 - q\left(\sum_{i=1}^{2} C_i^A \sum_{i=1}^{2} C_i^B, \tau^A, \tau^B\right)\right] W_i(\tau^B) - \sum_{K=A,B} C_i^K.$$

In the resulting Nash equilibrium the contribution levels are functions of the tax policies. Substituting these functions into $q(\cdot)$ yields a reduced-form probability function that depends only on the trade policies, $\tilde{q}(\tau^A, \tau^B)$. The function $\tilde{q}(\cdot)$ anticipates the contribution game that will be played by the lobbies for each policy choice by the parties. In the first stage the parties play a noncooperative game. Each one chooses its policy so as to maximize its probability of winning the election. Therefore party A chooses τ^A so as to maximize $\tilde{q}(\tau^A, \tau^B)$ while party B chooses τ^B so as to maximize $1 - \tilde{q}(\tau^A, \tau^B)$. The Nash equilibrium of this game identifies the equilibrium levels of the rates of protection.

Mayer and Li (1994) have reexamined the MBY analysis, using probabilistic voting theory as the microfoundations. Probabilistic voting allows for preferences of voters that depend on economic policies as well as on other attributes of political parties, such as their positions on social issues or political ideology. Preferences over noneconomic issues are diverse and parties know only their distribution in the voting population (see Coughlin [1992]). Mayer and Li also assume that voters are not sure about the economic policy stance of the parties, and that each party can use campaign contributions in order to clarify its position. Each party chooses its policy so as to maximize the probability of being elected.

Their analysis supports some of MBY's conclusions, but not all. For example it supports the result that a lobby will contribute to at most one political party; i.e., lobbies specialize in campaign giving. Unfortunately, this result does not fare well on empirical grounds; it is quite common in parliamentary systems for lobbies to contribute to the two major political parties (e.g., Israel). On the other hand, Mayer and Li find that both lobbies may end up contributing to the same political party, while MBY *assume* that each lobby is aligned with one party only. My conclusion from the Mayer–Li analysis is that it is indeed important to develop more detailed models in order to deal satisfactorily with the role of the electoral motive for campaign contributions in the political economy of trade policies. More about this in the next section.

2.5 Influence-Driven Contributions

Political contributions that influence election outcomes are a desirable feature of trade policy models. They seem to emphasize, however, a motive for contributions that is at most secondary. To be sure, from the point of view of politicians and their political parties the total amount of contributions serve an important role in enhancing their chances of being elected or reelected. But this does not mean that the individual contributors view the improved chance of a candidate as a major consideration in their giving. For one thing, there typically exist many contributors with the contribution of each one being small relative to the total. This is particularly true in countries with legal limits on contributions, but not only in countries of this type. As a result, each contribution has a marginal effect on the election outcome. Under these circumstances it is more likely that contributions are designed to influence the choice of policy than to influence election outcomes. Namely, having a choice between an emphasis on the electoral motive for contributions (as in MBY) and an influence motive, the latter seems to be more attractive on theoretical grounds. This point is made explicit in the detailed model of electoral competition and special interest politics by Grossman and Helpman (1996), in which they show that with a large number of organized interest groups the electoral motive for campaign contributions is negligible.[16]

At the same time the empirical literature also supports the view that the influence motive is more prominent. For example, Magelby and Nelson (1990) report that: (a) political action committees (PACs) in the U.S. gave more than three quarters of their total contributions in the 1988 congressional campaign to incumbent candidates; (b) not counting elections for open seats, incumbents receive over six times as much as challengers; (c) over 60 percent of the campaign contributions by PACs occurred in the early part of the election cycle, often before a challenger had even been identified; (d) PACs switch their contributions to the winner even if they supported the loser to begin with. In addition, in parliamentary democracies, interest groups often contribute simultaneously to more than one major political party.

Relying on these considerations, Grossman and Helpman (1994) have developed a theory that puts the influence motive at the heart of cam-

---

[16] The influence motive generates benefits to the lobbies that are of the same order of magnitude as their contributions. This feature makes it desirable to exploit this motive for contributions even when there exists a large number of interest groups.

paign contributions. According to this approach, interest groups move first, offering politicians campaign contributions that depend on their policy stance. Special interests seek to maximize the well-being of their members. Then the politicians choose policy stances, knowing how their contributions depend on the selected polices. Politicians seek to maximize a political objective function that depends on contributions and on the well-being of the general public.[17]

A political objective function that depends on contributions and the well-being of voters is consistent with electoral competition. Grossman and Helpman (1996) have shown that it emerges in a political system in which special interests design contributions in the above described way, and two parties compete for seats in parliament.[18]

So suppose again that the economy is the same as in Section 2.1, but that the policy maker's objective function is $C + aW$, where C stands for campaign contributions that he amasses, W represents aggregate welfare (or per capita welfare), and a is a parameter that represents the marginal rate of substitution between welfare and contributions. The larger a, the more weight is placed on the well-being of voters relative to contributions.[19] Contributions depend on the policy choice and so does welfare, and the policy maker maximizes this political objective function.

---

[17] The political-support function approach can be interpreted as a reduced form of the influence-driven contributions approach. For some purposes the details of the influence-driven contributions approach are not needed. For other purposes, however, they are essential.

[18] Each party seeks to maximize its expected number of seats. The probability of successfully promoting a policy depends on the number of seats in command. A party uses contributions from special interests to influence the voting pattern of uninformed or "impressionable" voters. On the other hand, each informed voter casts her ballot on the basis of whichever party commits to a policy that she most prefers. Each voter may however have preferences between the parties that are based on other considerations as well, such as their positions on noneconomic issues. This leads to probabilistic voting. In this framework a party can choose a policy that is desirable to the general public and thereby secure the support of informed voters. Instead it can tilt its policy position in favor of special interests in order to gain campaign contributions. In this event it loses the support of some of the informed voters, but it can use the contributions to gain support from the impressionable voters. This trade-off between the support of the two groups of voters and a party's objective to attain as many seats as possible in parliament translates into a desire to maximize an objective function that is increasing in contributions and in the well-being of the general public. This function is linear in income when the distribution of preferences over noneconomic issues is uniform. The parameters of the political objective function depend on the degree of dispersion of these preferences, on the noneconomic bias in the preferences of voters, the number of informed relative to uninformed voters in the population, and the effectiveness of campaign spending in attracting impressionable voters.

[19] As explained in the previous footnote, in the Grossman and Helpman (1996) model of electoral competition with special interests a depends on a variety of the underlying parameters.

Now consider the special interest groups. Suppose that in some subset of sectors, denoted by $\mathcal{L} \subset \{1, 2, \ldots, n\}$, the owners of the sector-specific inputs form lobby groups. Let α_i represent (as before) the fraction of people who own the input in sector i. Also assume that each person owns at most one type of sector-specific input. Then the aggregate well-being of the individuals that belong to lobby i is given by

$$W_i(\boldsymbol{\tau}) = l_i + \Pi_i(\tau_i) + \alpha_i \sum_{j=1}^{n} [(\tau_j - 1) M_j(\tau_j) + S_j(\tau_j)]. \tag{8}$$

The first term on the right-hand side represents their share in labor supply, the second term represents their income from the sector-specific factor, and the last term represents their share in tariff rebates and in consumer surplus.[20] The lobby's purpose is to maximize $W_i(\boldsymbol{\tau}) - C_i$, where $C_i \geq 0$ is the contribution of lobby i. How should the lobby design its contributions?

Interest group i takes the contribution functions $C_j(\boldsymbol{\tau})$ of all the other interest groups $j \neq i$ as given. Therefore it knows that if it does not lobby, the policy maker will attain the political welfare $G_{-i} = \max_{\boldsymbol{\tau}}[\sum_{j \neq i} C_j(\boldsymbol{\tau}) + aW(\boldsymbol{\tau})]$; i.e., the policy maker will choose a policy vector $\boldsymbol{\tau}$ that maximizes its objective function, disregarding lobby i's preferences.[21] It follows that if lobby i wishes to affect the policy outcome, it needs to offer a contribution function that induces a policy change and provides the policy-maker with at least G_{-i}. Namely, its contribution function has to satisfy

$$C_i(\boldsymbol{\tau}) \geq G_{-i} - \left[\sum_{j \neq i} C_j(\boldsymbol{\tau}) + aW(\boldsymbol{\tau}) \right] \tag{9}$$

in order to implement $\boldsymbol{\tau}$. This is the standard participation constraint in principal-agent problems. Naturally, the interest group has no desire to give the policy maker more than necessary in order to induce a policy change. Therefore it choose a contribution function that satisfies (9) with equality at the equilibrium point. The policy vector that maximizes the lobby's objective function $W_i(\boldsymbol{\tau}) - C_i$ is then

$$\boldsymbol{\tau}^i \in \operatorname*{argmax}_{\boldsymbol{\tau}} W_i(\boldsymbol{\tau}) + \left[\sum_{j \neq i} C_j(\boldsymbol{\tau}) + aW(\boldsymbol{\tau}) \right].$$

The contribution function is designed to *implement* this policy vector, and there typically exist many contribution functions that do it. Although

[20] Observe that unlike the example of the tariff formation function here we include contributions to welfare by all goods, not only the product of sector i. The reason is that we shall allow each interest group to lobby for trade taxes in all sectors (i.e., not only the sector in which they have a stake in the sector-specific factor). More on this point later.

[21] In order to simplify notation, I use $\sum_{j \neq i} C_j(\boldsymbol{\tau})$ as shorthand for the sum of contributions of all organized interest groups other than i.

POLITICS AND TRADE POLICY

lobby i is indifferent as to which contribution function it uses to implement this policy vector, its choice may affect the decision problems of
other lobbies. Therefore there often exist many contribution functions
that implement the equilibrium policy vector as well as equilibria with
different policy vectors (see Bernheim and Whinston [1986]). An equi-
librium consists of feasible contribution functions $\{C_j^o(\cdot)\}_{j \in \mathcal{L}}$ and a policy
vector $\boldsymbol{\tau}^o$ such that: (a) $\boldsymbol{\tau}^o \in \mathrm{argmax}_\tau\ W_i(\boldsymbol{\tau}) + [\sum_{j \neq i} C_j^o(\boldsymbol{\tau}) + aW(\boldsymbol{\tau})]$ for
all $i \in \mathcal{L}$; (b) $C_j^o(\cdot)$ implements $\boldsymbol{\tau}^o$ for all $j \in \mathcal{L}$; and (c) $\sum_{j \in \mathcal{L}} C_j^o(\boldsymbol{\tau}^o) + aW(\boldsymbol{\tau}^o)$
$= G_{-i}$ for all $i \in \mathcal{L}$.

To illustrate some of the relevant considerations, first suppose that
there is only one organized interest group, say in sector i. Then the equi-
librium policy vector maximizes $W_i(\boldsymbol{\tau}) + aW(\boldsymbol{\tau})$. Using (4) and (8) this
implies

$$\tau_j - 1 = \frac{I_j - \alpha_i}{a + \alpha_i} \frac{X_j}{(-M_j')},$$

where I_j equals one for $j = i$ and zero otherwise. First note that only
sector i, which is represented by an organized interest group, is protected. All other sectors are afforded negative protection. The reason is
that the special interest group lobbies the policy maker for high prices
in sector i, in which it is a net seller, and for low prices in all other sectors,
in which it is a net buyer. The rate of protection in sector i is higher the
more concentrated the ownership of the sector-specific factor in that
sector is (because the less the lobby cares then about excess burden), the
less weight the policy maker places on welfare relative to contributions
(because the cheaper it is then to influence the policy maker with contributions), the larger the output level of the sector (because it raises the
benefit of the influence motive), and the flatter the import demand function (because the lower is then the excess burden imposed on society,
about which the policy maker cares). Observe that the effects of output
and the slope of the import demand function are the same as in the formulas that we derived from the direct democracy approach, the politi-
cal- support function approach, and the tariff-formation function
approach. In addition, the effect of the degree of concentration of ownership is similar to the tariff-formation function approach, while the role
of the marginal rate of substitution between welfare and contributions
plays a similar role to the marginal rate of substitution between welfare
and profits in the political-support function approach. These analogies
are not accidental. I have purposely constructed variants of the other
approaches that enable us to draw these analogies with the influence–motive
approach.

What happens when there is more than one organized interest group?
Grossman and Helpman (1994) have shown that if we restrict the

contribution functions to be differentiable around the equilibrium vector
$\tau°$, then they have to be locally truthful; i.e., the gradient of $C_j^o(\cdot)$ has to
equal the gradient of $W_i(\cdot)$ at $\tau°$. This leads to the tariff formula

$$\tau_j - 1 = \frac{I_j - \alpha_{\mathscr{L}}}{a + \alpha_{\mathscr{L}}} \frac{X_j}{(-M_j')}, \tag{10}$$

where $\alpha_{\mathscr{L}} = \Sigma_{j\in\mathscr{L}}\alpha_j$ stands for the fraction of people that own sector-
specific inputs. The difference between this formula and the previous
one, which was derived for the case in which only one sector had an
organized lobby, is the replacement of α_i with $\alpha_{\mathscr{L}}$. Therefore the interpretation remains very much the same. Importantly, now all sectors with
organized pressure groups enjoy protection while sectors without lobbies
are afforded negative protection. In the extreme case, when all sectors
have organized pressure groups and every individual has a stake in some
sector, there is free trade. Under these circumstances the lobbies battle
for protection of their own interests and neutralize each other in the
process. Despite the fact that none of them succeeds in securing higher
prices for their clients, they typically spend resources in the process (as
can be confirmed from the participation constraint). The role of the
contributions in this case is to avoid being harmed by the other lobbies.

Formula (10) describes the resulting rates of protection when each
lobby conditions its contributions on the entire tariff vector. In practice
this may not be the case. A lobby of the textile industry is obviously very
much concerned with the protection of textiles, but its interest in subsi-
dizing imports of tea is much smaller. In the event, it may choose to
neglect the conditioning of its contributions on the policy toward tea,
especially if it is costly to spread the lobbying effort across a large number
of policy instruments. A complete model of the political process should
include a specification of the lobbying technology, which will then determine relative costs of lobbying. We would then expect pressure groups
to focus on their core activity and get involved in the design of other policies only when the direct or indirect benefits from doing so would be
large or when the marginal cost of doing so would be small. To see what
difference a focused lobbying effort can make, suppose that the lobby of
sector i conditions its contributions only on τ_i, for $i \in \mathscr{L}$. In this event
there will be free trade in each sector that does not have an organized
interest group while in the sectors with pressure groups the rates of protection will be

$$\tau_j - 1 = \frac{1 - \alpha_j}{a + \alpha_j} \frac{X_j}{(-M_j')} \text{ for } j \in \mathscr{L}.$$

We see that the effects of the sector's size and the slope of its import
demand function are the same as in the other formulas. Compared with

the case in which pressure groups lobby for all policies, however, there are two major differences. First, now unorganized sectors are not protected while in (10) they are afforded negative protection. Second, now the rate of protection of an organized sector depends on the fraction of voters who have a stake in the industry (i.e., α_i) while in (10) it depends on the fraction of voters who belong to any lobby, not necessarily the lobby of the industry under consideration (i.e., $\alpha_{\mathcal{L}}$). The implication is that now the degree of concentration of ownership in a sector has a direct effect on its rate of protection; sectors with higher concentration of ownership attain higher protection. This is a desirable feature, as it finds support in reality.

My discussion has focused on trade taxes. It should be clear, however, that the same tools of analysis can be applied to other policy instruments as well.[22] There is a major question, however, concerning the choice of instruments of protection. Why use tariffs rather than output subsidies, for example, when the latter instrument is more desirable on efficiency grounds? Partial answers, based on political economy considerations, are provided by Rodrik (1986) and Grossman and Helpman (1994). But as Rodrik (1995) argues forcefully, the choice of instrument is a central question that has received only limited attention. Since good answers to this question are not yet available, I shall proceed to the next topic.

3 Double-Edged Diplomacy

We have so far examined situations in which trade policies are pursued by a single country facing constant world prices. This simplification helped us to focus on the internal politics; i.e., the interaction between lobbies and policy makers. Much of trade policy is affected, however, by international constraints. As a result, even when a country sets its own trade policy agenda it has to consider the international repercussions. This is particularly so for large countries. But countries also negotiate trade rules, tariff reductions, voluntary export restraints, free trade areas, and other items. Therefore an analysis of the formation of trade policies is incomplete without paying attention to international interactions.

In view of these remarks it is only appropriate to consider the formation of trade policies in a framework that emphasizes two levels of strategic interaction. On the one hand, governments set trade policies facing each other in the international arena. On the other hand, each government has to deal with its internal political system. This type of two-level interaction produces a simultaneous dependence between the internal

---

[22] See, for example, Dixit (1995) for an application to commodity taxation. Similar methods can be used to deal with quotas and other forms of quantitative restrictions.

and the external politics. A government that, say, negotiates a free trade agreement, is aware in its dealings with the foreign government of the domestic consequences of such an agreement. At the same time, domestic pressure groups that wish to influence the policy outcome are aware of the negotiation process, and of the pros and cons of alternative results. These dependencies are the source of the title of this section, which is taken from the title of a book by Evans, Jacobson, and Putnam (1993). Their book describes a series of case studies, building on the conceptual framework that was developed by Putnam (1988), in order to study situations of this sort. The rest of this section describes three examples that build on two-level interactions: noncooperative tariff setting, negotiated tariffs, and negotiated free trade agreements.

3.1 Trade Wars

Grossman and Helpman (1995a) have extended the influence-driven contributions approach to a setting with two countries that set trade policies noncooperatively. In each country the economy is structured as in Section 2.1, pressure groups lobby the domestic policy maker in the manner described in Section 2.5, and the policy maker maximizes a political objective function that is linear in contributions and aggregate welfare.[23] Both the lobbies and the policy maker take as given the policy vector of the other country. But they do take into account the fact that domestic policies affect the terms of trade. In particular, denoting the countries by A and B and the international price by π_i, the world market-clearing condition for product i, $\sum_{K = A,B} M_i^K(\tau_i^K \pi_i) = 0$, defines implicitly the international price as a function of the trade policies in the two countries. Using this relationship, it is possible to derive a set of contribution schedules and a domestic policy vector that are the political response to the trade policy of the other country. A similar political response can be defined for the other country. An equilibrium consists of contribution schedules and a policy vector for each country, such that the contribution schedules and the policy vector of each country represent a political response to the trade policy of the other country. These equilibrium trade policies satisfy

$$\tau_j^K - 1 = \frac{I_j^K - \alpha_{\mathscr{L}}^K}{a^K + \alpha_{\mathscr{L}}^K} \frac{X_j^K}{(-\pi_j M_j^{K\prime})} + \frac{1}{e_j^L} \quad \text{for } K, L = A, B \text{ and } L \neq K, \quad (11)$$

where e_j^L is the export supply elasticity of country L in sector j (this elasticity is negative if the country imports the product). This formula has

---

[23] It is also possible to allow pressure groups to lobby foreign governments, as shown in Grossman and Helpman (1995a).

two parts: a political power index that is identical to (10) and a second part that captures terms-of-trade considerations. The latter, which is well known from Johnson (1953–1954) and the now-standard optimal-tariff formula, states that a tariff should be higher the less elastic is the foreign export supply function.

The tax rate of country K in sector i, as given by (11), depends on the trade policy in the other country (i.e., it depends on it through the international price π_j). This interdependence has some interesting implications. In particular, for constant elasticity import demand and output supply functions, it implies that a lower weight on welfare relative to contributions in the political objective function of the importing country leads it to take a more aggressive policy stance. As a result its terms of trade improve, its tariff is higher—and sufficiently so as to secure a higher domestic price for the protected industry—and the domestic price in the exporting country is lower. It follows that the same industry in the exporting country receives less protection, or that it is afforded more negative protection. This example demonstrates how a change in the political environment in one country affects the resulting degree of protection in each one of them. Evidently, this type of analysis helps to see how trade policies of one country depend on the political environment in the other.

3.2 Trade Talks

In Section 3.1 trade taxes were set noncooperatively. As a result, policymakers inflicted deadweight loss not only on the residents of the two countries, but also on each other. To avoid some of this political damage they can set trade policies cooperatively, as governments often do.

When governments negotiate trade policies they are aware of the political repercussions at home, including those that are related to special-interest groups. These repercussions affect their strategy. At the same time, campaign contributions of special-interest groups are designed differently when they expect the policy makers to negotiate than when they expect them to set policies noncooperatively. In anticipation of negotiation a lobby designs its contribution schedule so as to tilt the agreement in its favor. The best schedule depends on the institutional framework in which the negotiations take place. As shown in Grossman and Helpman (1995a), however, as long as the negotiating procedure allows policymakers to choose from the outcomes that are efficient from their own perspective, the resulting equilibrium policy vectors satisfy

$$\tau_j^A - \tau_j^B = \frac{I_j^A - \alpha_{\mathscr{L}}^A}{a^A + \alpha_{\mathscr{L}}^A} \frac{X_j^A}{(-\pi_j M_j^{A\prime})} - \frac{I_j^B - \alpha_{\mathscr{L}}^B}{a^B + \alpha_{\mathscr{L}}^B} \frac{X_j^B}{(-\pi_j M_j^{B\prime})}. \tag{12}$$

This formula determines only the relative values τ_j^A/τ_j^B, which are independent of the negotiation procedure. They ensure that the outcome is on the efficiency frontier of the governments. It is then possible to use the levels of these policy variables, or direct transfers between the governments (as in the Common Agricultural Policy in Europe) to select a particular distribution of gains on the efficient frontier.[24] Which particular distribution the governments choose depends on the negotiation procedure, as well as on a variety of economic and political variables.[25]

Importantly, an industry is protected in country A but not in B if and only if the political power index of this industry is larger in A. Negotiations over trade taxes bring special interests of an industry from the two countries to take opposing sides of the issue; each one of them wants to be protected at the expense of the other. As a result they exert opposing pressures on the negotiating parties and the winner is the lobby with the larger political clout. Thus, for example, if the textile industry is organized in country A but not in B, textiles will obtain positive protection in A and negative protection in B, relative to free trade. Formula (12) also shows that the governments will agree on free trade in textiles (or the same internal price in both countries) if and only if the political power indexes of the textile lobbies are the same in both countries.

Finally, observe that contrary to (11), no export supply elasticities appear in (12). This stems from the fact that in a trade war each government is using trade taxes to better its nation's terms of trade. When the governments negotiate, however, the use of terms of trade as a means of income transfer is politically inefficient. Therefore they do not use them in the cooperative design of trade taxes.

3.3 Free Trade Agreements

Another important example of negotiated trade policies is provided by free trade agreements (FTAs). Unlike negotiated trade taxes, however, FTAs involve discrete choices (although some continuity is available via the specified terms). The GATT article of agreement XXIV allows countries to form a free trade area in exception to the "most favored nation" clause if the agreement eliminates duties and restrictions on "substantially all trade" among the contracting parties. Grossman and Helpman (1995b) have studied the political economy of such agreements when interest groups that represent various industries express their concerns by means of campaign contributions. Each interest group can voice its

---

[24] See also Mayer (1981) on this issue.

[25] See Grossman and Helpman (1995a) for an example.

support or opposition to an agreement by contributing money in case an FTA forms or in case the FTA is rejected.

First, suppose that a country contemplates joining a free trade area with well-specified terms that it cannot affect. Each sector is represented in the debate over the agreement, and the representatives of an industry seek to maximize the return to the sector-specific input. The government seeks to maximize $C + aW$, as in Section 2.5. The economic model is the same as in Section 2.1. In these circumstances the policy maker has to choose one of two regimes: regime F (i.e., joining the free trade area), or regime N (i.e., not joining). Sector-specific income in regime $R = F, N$ equals Π_{iR} in sector i, and welfare is given by W_R. Lobby i offers a pair of contributions (C_{iF}, C_{iN}), the first one representing an offer in case regime F is adopted and the second one representing an offer in case regime N is adopted. One of the offers equals zero.

The first question to ask is: What types of political equilibria arise in these circumstances? Grossman and Helpman show that two types may arise. If the regime that provides the higher aggregate welfare level generates a large enough welfare gain relative to the alternative, then there exists a political equilibrium in which the welfare superior regime is chosen by the government and all lobbies contribute zero. The welfare gain is large enough for this purpose if the product of a with the welfare gain exceeds the largest loss that a single sector experiences when the welfare superior regime is selected.[26] Clearly, with no contributions the government selects the welfare-superior regime. The point is, however, that under the specified circumstances no lobby stands to gain enough from inducing the government to choose the welfare-inferior regime in order to make it worthwhile for the lobby to contribute the required minimum that induces the policy maker to switch regimes. Evidently, this equilibrium builds on a lack of coordination among the lobbying groups, and each one separately does not have a big enough stake to induce a switch of regimes on its own.

Minimal coordination by pressure groups, in the form of nonbinding prior communication about preferable outcomes, leads to an equilibrium that is *coalition-proof*. In such equilibria the policy maker chooses the regime that provides the highest joint welfare to the organized interest groups and the government.[27] Moreover, every equilibrium in which contributions by at least one lobby support the selected regime

---

[26] Let R be the welfare-superior regime; i.e., $W_R > W_K$, $R \neq K$. Then there exists an equilibrium in which contributions are zero and the government chooses R whenever $a(W_R - W_K) \geq \max[0, \max_i(\Pi_{iK} - \Pi_{iR})]$.

[27] Regime R is selected in this case if $\sum_{j \in \mathscr{L}} \Pi_{jR} + aW_R \geq \sum_{j \in \mathscr{L}} \Pi_{jK} + aW_K$.

is of this nature. In these equilibria contributions by opposing interest groups make the government just indifferent between the alternative regimes. The implication is that a delicate balance prevails in these equilibria, in the sense that about equal political strength supports each side of the issue.[28]

These results can be used to examine what pairs of countries are likely candidates for free trade agreements. An agreement requires both countries to select regime F in the political equilibrium. For this purpose enough support in favor of the agreement has to be amassed in each country.

Now, support for an agreement can come from one of two sources. Either F provides higher welfare, in which case the government will be happy to sign an agreement in order to please its voters. Or potential exporters to the free trade area, who expect to sell at higher prices in the partner country, are willing to contribute enough money in order to open those markets. Sectors that expect to face fiercer import competition in the free trade area oppose the agreement.

If the initial rates of protection reflect a political balance of power of the type described in Section 2.5, then each country needs enough potential exporters that support the FTA in order to overcome the opposing political pressures. This means that the imbalance of trade between the countries has to be small enough, because one country's exports into the free trade area are the other's imports. Unfortunately, potential exporters that support the agreement do so because they expect to be able to charge higher prices, and higher prices are bad for welfare. As a result, free trade agreements are most viable in situations in which the two countries are most likely to suffer joint welfare losses.[29]

Both countries are more likely to endorse an FTA if some politically sensitive sectors can be excluded from the agreement and allowed to maintain the original rates of protection. Given a choice, each country prefers to exclude sectors for which the free trade area produces the largest loss of welfare plus lobby income per unit of the overall constraining factor, where the constraining factor represents the interpretation of the term "substantially all trade" in article XXIV. Examples of the constraining factor include the fraction of industries that can be excluded from the agreement or the fraction of trade that takes place in exempted products. All sectors can be ranked accord-

---

[28] The fact that NAFTA barely passed during the vote in U.S. Congress can be interpreted as a reflection of this sort of equilibrium.

[29] In this statement welfare is measured by W, and it does not include the well-being of the government.

ing to this criterion and the cutoff point then determined by the overall constraint.[30]

It is quite unlikely, however, that both countries will have the same ranking of sectors according to this criterion. Under these circumstances a conflict arises over the set of exemptions and the countries need to reach a compromise in order to enact an FTA. Grossman and Helpman show that if the two governments engage in Nash bargaining over the exemptions, then they agree to exclude a set of sectors that is ranked according to a weighted average of the criterion that each country would like to use on its own.[31] The weights reflect the relative bargaining powers of the two governments. And a cutoff point is determined by the overall constraint imposed by the term "substantially all trade."

These examples show the power of an approach that emphasizes two-way interactions between internal politics and international economic relations. They also show that—complications generated by such interactions notwithstanding—this approach yields interesting insights about important policy issues. Further enrichment of this framework is needed, however, in order to address problems of institutional design that are at the heart of the current debate about rules concerning trade, direct foreign investment, and intellectual property rights.

[30] Suppose there exists a continuum of sectors and that the overall constraint is given by $\int_{i\in E} T_i di \leq T$, where E represents the set of exempt sectors, T_i represents the contribution of sector i to the overall constraint, and T represents the overall constraint. If, for example, the overall constraint is on the number of sectors that can be granted an exemption, then $T_i = 1$ for every sector and T stands for the largest measure of sectors that are allowed to be excluded from the FTA under article XXIV. On the other hand, if the constraint is on the trade volume, then T_i stands for the trade volume in sector i and T represents the maximum trade volume that can be excluded from the agreement. The ranking of industries builds on the index $g_i = (a\Delta W_i + \Delta\Pi_i)/T_i$, where ΔW_i represents the welfare gain in sector i from the FTA and $\Delta\Pi_i$ represents lobby i's income gain from the FTA. Indexing the sectors in an increasing order of g_i, the government wants to exclude the sectors for which g_i is negative, up to the constraint permitted by $\int_{i\in E} T_i di \leq T$.

[31] Namely, sectors are ranked according to $\omega^A g_i^A + \omega^B g_i^B$, where ω^K is the weight of country K. The overall constraint remains the same as in the previous footnote.

References

Bernheim, Douglas B., and Whinston, Michael D. (1986). Menu auctions, resource allocation, and economic influence. *Quarterly Journal of Economics* 101: 1–31.

Coughlin, Peter J. (1992). *Probabilistic Voting Theory* (Cambridge: Cambridge University Press).

Dixit, Avinash (1995). Special-interest lobbying and endogenous commodity taxation. Mimeo, Princeton University.

Evans, Peter, Jacobson, Harold, and Putnam, Robert (eds.). (1993) *Double-Edge Diplomacy* (Berkeley: University of California Press).

Feenstra, Robert C., and Bhagwati, Jagdish N. (1982). Tariff seeking and the efficient tariff. In Bhagwati, Jagdish N. (ed.). *Import Competition and Response* (Chicago: University of Chicago Press).

Findlay, Ronald, and Wellisz, Stanislaw (1982). Endogenous tariffs, the political economy of trade restrictions, and welfare. In Bhagwati, Jagdish N. (ed.). *Import Competition and Response* (Chicago: University of Chicago Press).

Flam, Harry (1992). Product markets and 1992: Full integration, large gains? *Journal of Economic Perspectives* 6: 7–30.

Garber, Peter M. (ed.). (1993). *The Mexico-US Free Trade Agreement* (Cambridge, Mass.: MIT Press).

Grossman, Gene M., and Helpman, Elhanan (1994). Protection for sale. *American Economic Review* 84: 833–850.

———. (1995a). Trade wars and trade talks. *Journal of Political Economy* 103: 675–708.

———. (1995b). The politics of free trade agreements. *American Economic Review* 85: 667–690.

———. (1996). Electoral competition and special interest politics. *Review of Economic Studies* 63: 269–286.

Hillman, Arye L. (1982). Declining industries and political-support protectionist motives. *American Economic Review* 72: 1180–1187.

———. (1989). *The Political Economy of Protection* (Chur: Harwood).

Hillman, Arye L., and Ursprung, Heinrich (1988). Domestic politics, foreign interests, and international trade policy. *American Economic Review* 78: 729–745.

Johnson, Harry G. (1953–1954). Optimal tariffs and retaliation. *Review of Economic Studies* 21: 142–153.

Jones, Ronald W. (1971). A three factor model in theory, trade and history. In Bhagwati, Jagdish N., *et al.* (eds.). *Trade, Growth and the Balance of Payments: Essays in Honor of C. B. Kindleberger* (Amsterdam: North-Holland).

Long, Ngo Van, and Vousden, Neil (1991). Protectionist responses and declining industries. *Journal of International Economics* 30: 87–103.

Magee, Stephen P., Brock, William A., and Young, Leslie (1989). *Black Hole Tariffs and Endogenous Policy Formation* (Cambridge: Cambridge University Press).

Magelby, David B., and Nelson, Candice J. (1990). *The Money Chase: Congressional Campaign Finance Reform* (Washington, D.C.: The Brookings Institution).

Mayer, Wolfgang (1981). Theoretical considerations on negotiated tariff adjustments. *Oxford Economic Papers* 33: 135–153.

———. (1984). Endogenous tariff formation. *American Economic Review* 74: 970–985.

Mayer, Wolfgang, and Li, Jun (1994). Interest groups, electoral competition, and probabilistic voting for trade policies. *Economics and Politics* 6: 59–77.

Olson, Mancur (1965). *The Logic of Collective Action* (Cambridge, Mass.: Harvard University Press).

Peltzman, Sam (1976). Toward a more general theory of regulation. *Journal of Law and Economics* 19: 211–240.

Putnam, Robert (1988). Diplomacy and domestic politics: The logic of two-level games. *International Organization* 42: 427–460.

Rodrik, Dani (1986). Tariffs, subsidies, and welfare with endogenous policy. *Journal of International Economics* 21: 285–296.

———. (1995). Political economy of trade policy. In Grossman, Gene M., and Rogoff, Kenneth (eds.). *Handbook of International Economics,* vol. III (Amsterdam: North-Holland.)

Shepsle, Kenneth A. (1990). *Models of Multiparty Electoral Competition* (Chur: Harwood).

Stigler, George (1971). The theory of economic regulation. *Bell Journal of Economics* 2: 3–21.

Seven

The Politics of Free Trade Agreements

Governments have been meeting frequently of late to discuss the possibility of their forming bilateral or regional trading arrangements. The United States has concluded bilateral agreements with Israel, Canada, and Mexico and will pursue talks with Chile and perhaps other Latin American nations. The European Union expanded its membership to include Greece, Portugal, and Spain and has discussed preferential arrangements with many Central and Eastern European countries. Some

By Gene Grossman and Elhanan Helpman. Originally published in *American Economic Review* 105 (September 1995): 667–690. Copyright © 1995 by the American Economic Association. Reprinted with permission. Financial support was provided by the National Science Foundation, the U.S.-Israel Binational Science Foundation, and the CEPR. Grossman also gratefully acknowledges the John S. Guggenheim Memorial Foundation, the Sumitomo Bank Fund, the Daiwa Bank Fund, and the Center of International Studies at Princeton University. We thank Raquel Fernandez, Paul Krugman, Torsten Persson, Dani Rodrik, and two anonymous referees for helpful comments.

members of the Association for South East Asian Nations (ASEAN) have
been calling for the formation of a Pacific free trade area. And Argentina,
Brazil, Paraguay, and Uruguay have banded together to form the Southern Common Market (MERCOSUR).

These trade negotiations have never been easy, nor have they always
been successful. One need only reflect on the recent debates in the
United States concerning NAFTA or those in Europe over accession to
the EU to recognize the political hackles raised by prospective trade
agreements. In this paper we attempt to analyze some of the political pressures that are brought to bear on a government as it contemplates
whether to enter into a new trading arrangement. In particular, we
address the following problem. Suppose that an opportunity arises for
two countries to negotiate a free trade agreement (FTA) between themselves. Will an FTA between these countries be politically viable? If so,
what form will the agreement take?

These questions take us into the realm of international relations. Tra-
ditionally, studies of international relations in both political science and
economics have adopted a "statist" mode of analysis (see the discussion
of this point in Peter F. Cowhey [1990]). In this approach, states are seen
as unified rational actors pursuing some well-defined objective. In economic analysis, for example, it is common to assume that the state seeks
to maximize aggregate national welfare. Then the analysis focuses on the
nature of the game between governments. We, like Robert Putnam
(1988), would rather regard international relations as involving two distinct stages of strategic interaction. First, there is an initial stage during
which political competition between the different interests in each
country determines the government's policy preferences. Then there is
a subsequent stage of give-and-take that determines international equilibrium. We would argue, moreover, that neither stage can be meaning-
fully analyzed without reference to the other. Inevitably, international
interdependence sets the parameters for the domestic political contest,
while the domestic political environment constrains the actions that governments can take internationally. Here and in a paper that examines
multilateral negotiations over levels of nondiscriminatory tariffs (Grossman and Helpman [1995]), we implement this perspective, by incor-
porating the two stages of strategic interaction into a single, sequential
game.

In treating the rivalry between competing interests in a single country
we use the analytical framework that we developed in Grossman and
Helpman (1994a). This framework emphasizes the interaction between
lobby groups representing industry special interests and an incumbent
government. In our model, lobby groups offer policy-contingent campaign contributions to politicians, who make decisions that serve their

own political objectives. In this setting, a country's policy stance reflects the relative political power of its organized special interests and also the extent of the government's concern for the plight of the average voter.

The paper is organized as follows. Section 1 develops the analytical framework, describing both the economic and political interactions and the effects of an FTA on the welfare of the various agents. In Section 2 we focus on "the initial stage," asking when the government of one country might be willing to endorse an agreement calling for complete and immediate liberalization of all bilateral trade with some partner. This forms the basis for our discussion in Section 3 of the outcome of a bilateral negotiation between two countries. In Section 4 we allow for the possibility that an FTA may exclude a few especially sensitive sectors, or that it may allow for some extended periods of adjustment. We show how a more liberal interpretation of GATT rules about the types of permissible FTAs may enhance political viability and examine the politics that determine which industries gain exemptions under the agreement. The concluding section summarizes our findings.

1 Analytical Framework

We examine the trade policy of two small countries that interact with one another and the rest of the world. The countries produce and trade many goods, all of whose international prices are normalized to 1. Initially, each country imposes the same tariff on all imports of a good regardless of source, in keeping with the "most favored nation" (MFN) clause of the GATT articles of agreement. The two countries now have the opportunity to discuss an FTA. Our aim is to identify the political and economic conditions in the two countries that would make it possible for their politically minded governments to conclude such an agreement.

We suppose that there is a numeraire good 0 that is untaxed in each country and n other goods. Some of these goods are imported by one or both of the small countries in the initial equilibrium, while others may be exported. In recognition of GATT rules, we exclude the possibility that the countries subsidize their exports. We also ignore export taxes, which are unconstitutional in the United States and rarely used elsewhere. Thus, we assume that the initial domestic price in either country of any good that is exported by that country is 1. As for import goods, these may be subject to arbitrary import tariffs. We let τ_i^j represent 1 plus the initial tariff rate on good i in country j, for $j = $ A, B. With our normalization of international prices, these are also the domestic prices in country j for the import goods.[1]

---

[1] We adopt the convention that $\tau_i^j = 1$ for the numeraire good 0 and for any goods that are exported by country j in the initial equilibrium.

Article XXIV of the GATT articles of agreement permits certain exceptions to the principle of MFN. Countries may enter bilateral or regional agreements if they eliminate "duties and other regulations of commerce" on "substantially all trade" among themselves. The GATT rules allow for both *customs unions,* in which member countries impose a common external tariff on trade with the rest of the world, and *free trade areas,* in which the countries maintain separate external tariffs and enforce them with rules of origin. In this paper we study only the latter type of agreement. GATT rules further stipulate that the external tariffs imposed must be no higher than those that were in force beforehand. While the practical meaning of this requirement remains in doubt (see John McMillan [1993]), we appeal to it as loose justification for supposing that the initial tariffs τ_i^j continue to apply to imports from the rest of the world under any FTA that might be formed.[2]

The phrase "substantially all trade" in GATT article XXIV has been interpreted to allow some latitude in the structuring of trade agreements. Regional and bilateral trade agreements typically exclude a few politically sensitive sectors and specify prolonged phase-in periods for some others. At first, we shall ignore this limited degree of flexibility and interpret the GATT rules as requiring that all goods be freely traded between the parties to any agreement. But later we will relax this assumption and suppose that the countries can exclude some sectors from the agreement. Then we will have the initial MFN tariffs remain in force on trade between A and B in the excluded goods.

1.1 Objectives of Economic and Political Agents

The qualitative features of the two small economies are similar. We describe the structure of one of these countries but omit, for the time being, the country superscripts that implicitly are attached to every function and variable.

The country has a voting population of size 1. Individuals within the country have identical preferences $u(\mathbf{c}) = c_0 + \sum_{i=1}^{n} u_i(c_i)$, where c_i denotes consumption of good i and $u_i(\cdot)$ is an increasing and concave function. These preferences give rise to the per capita demands $D_i(q_i)$ for goods $i = 1, \ldots, n$ and the demand $y - \sum_{i=1}^{n} q_i D_i(q_i)$ for good 0, where q_i is the domestic consumer price of good i and y is the individual's spend-

---

[2] We recognize that this assumption is not without fault. Martin Richardson (1993) has shown, for example, that countries may have reason to *lower* their external tariffs after completing a trade agreement. A more complete analysis—which would allow for an additional stage of tariff-setting after the FTA issues were resolved—would certainly be desirable but is beyond the scope of the present paper.

ing. The same demands apply in the aggregate, except that individual spending is replaced by aggregate spending in the demand for good 0.

The production of good 0 uses only labor, with one unit of labor required per unit of output. Each other good is manufactured with constant returns to scale by labor and a sector-specific factor. Since the domestic price of good 0 has been normalized to 1, the competitive wage must equal 1 in any equilibrium in which this good is produced. Then the specific factor used in industry i earns the reward $\Pi_i(p_i)$, where p_i is the domestic producer price. Aggregate supply of good i is $X_i(p_i) = \Pi_i'(p_i) > 0$ for $i = 1, \ldots, n$.

We assume that the ownership of the specific factors is highly concentrated in the population. In fact, we take an extreme case where these factor owners comprise a negligible fraction of the total number of voters. The owners of a particular factor have a common interest in seeing a high domestic price for the good they produce and so favor protection from foreign competition. We assume, perhaps because they are few in number, that they can overcome the "collective-action problem" described by Mancur Olson (1965) and that they work together for their common political goals. The owners of the factor used in sector i form a special-interest group that takes political action to maximize joint welfare.[3]

As in Grossman and Helpman (1994a, 1995), we suppose that the incumbent government is in a position to set trade policy, which means here that it can either work toward a free trade agreement or terminate the discussions. The politicians may receive contributions from the various interest groups, hoping to influence their decision. The politicians value these contributions—because they can help them to get reelected or for other reasons—but they may also care about the well-being of the average voter. Per capita welfare will enter the incumbent government's objective function if, for example, some voters are well informed about the effects of trade policy and base their votes partly on their standard of living. We assume that the government's objective has a simple linear form, $G \equiv \sum_i C_i + aW$, where C_i is the campaign contribution of the lobby representing industry i, W is aggregate (and per capita) welfare, and a is a parameter (possibly zero) reflecting the government's sensitivity to the average voter's well-being relative to its taste for campaign contributions.[4]

---

[3] In Grossman and Helpman (1994a, 1995) we allow for the possibility that some sectors may fail to organize for political action, although we take the set of organized lobbies as exogenous in our analysis. Here, for simplicity, we assume that all sectors are organized.

[4] Alternatively, we could use the welfare of the median voter, rather than that of the mean voter, as an argument in the government's objective function. The difference is that the median individual owns none of any industry-specific factor. The analysis would proceed similarly, except that W would be defined in (1) to exclude aggregate profits. See Grossman and Helpman (1994a) for further discussion of the government's objective function.

Each individual enjoys surplus of $S_i(q_i) \equiv u_i[D_i(q_i)] - q_i D_i(q_i)$ from consuming good i, $i = 1, \ldots, n$. He or she also receives a lump-sum transfer from the government, representing a share of the total tariff revenue, which is rebated to the public on an equal, per capita basis. Aggregate welfare of voters is given by

$$W = L + \sum_{i=1}^{n} \Pi_i(p_i) + \sum_{i=1}^{n} (\tau_i - 1) M_i + \sum_{i=1}^{n} S_i(q_i), \qquad (1)$$

where L is aggregate labor supply and the right-hand side of (1) therefore represents the sum of labor income, profits, tariff revenues, and total consumer surplus. In the initial situation with MFN tariffs, $p_i = q_i = \tau_i$ and $M_i = D_i - X_i$, so W is maximized when $\tau_i = 1$ for all i. As usual, the small country suffers an aggregate welfare loss whenever its politics generate a deviation from free trade.

The small number of owners of the input used in industry i capture a negligible fraction of the consumer surplus in the economy and receive only a negligible fraction of the rebated tariff revenue. Thus, the objective of these factor owners can be closely approximated by $\Pi_i(p_i) - C_i$, their profits net of political contributions. We will use Π_{iN} to represent gross industry profits in the event that no agreement is reached, in which case output continues to sell for $p_i = \tau_i$. Similarly, we let Π_{iF} denote industry profits under an FTA, which depend of course on the producer prices that would prevail in the event of an agreement. In a moment, we will consider what these prices must be. But first we describe the nature of the political game.

1.2 The Political Game

Interest groups move first in the political game. They offer financial support to incumbent politicians in their home country but link their contributions to the actions taken by the government with respect to the trade agreement.[5] This follows Grossman and Helpman (1994a), where we applied B. Douglas Bernheim and Michael D. Whinston's (1986) notion of a menu auction to the problem of tariff formation. In our earlier paper, we allowed interest groups to design *contribution schedules* that made each campaign gift a function of the trade tax vector chosen by the government. Here the government has only two options: to pursue

[5] We choose to ignore in the main text the possibility that interest groups may offer contributions to a foreign government. Although such contributions do sometimes occur, the scope for interest groups to influence a foreign government's decisions generally is quite limited. This may be because politicians regard foreign gifts as tainted money and so place a lower value on them in their political objective function. In any event, we discuss the differences that arise when interest groups can give to either government in the appendix.

an agreement or not. It follows that a policy-contingent contribution schedule need only comprise two numbers, C_{iF} and C_{iN}, which are the gifts associated with the realization of an FTA and with a continuation of the status quo, respectively.

In fact, it is never optimal for a lobby to promise positive gifts for both policy outcomes, because then it could cut back equally on both of its offers without affecting the government's decision. And a lobby surely does not wish to give the government added incentive to choose the outcome that is contrary to its interests. Thus, each lobby need only quote a single number, representing its donation in the event that its preferred outcome is chosen. We limit each lobby to offer no more than what it stands to gain in profits if the government were to follow its bidding.[6]

The lobbies set their contributions noncooperatively (although we will at times allow them to communicate first). Then, faced with the set of offers, the government takes a position on the trade accord. The government endorses the FTA if and only if $\sum_i C_{iF} + aW_F \geq \sum_i C_{iN} + aW_N$ (where W_R is aggregate welfare under regime R, R = F,N). Otherwise, it rejects the agreement.

1.3 Economic Equilibrium Under an FTA

Before we proceed to characterize the outcome of this political game, we discuss what effects the FTA would have on the voters and special-interest groups in each country. Our economic analysis builds on Martin Richardson (1992).

We focus on one particular product i. If both countries happen to export this good in the initial equilibrium, then each has a domestic price equal to 1, and the FTA will have no effect on outputs, profits, or consumption levels. The more interesting cases arise when at least one of the countries initially imports the good subject to a positive MFN tariff. Without loss of generality we consider an industry in which $\tau_i^A > \tau_i^B \geq 1$.

Figure 1 depicts the demand for imports by country A and three possible locations of the *total* supply curve for country B. Suppose that B's endowment of the specific factor is relatively small, as with $X_i^B[1]$, so that the total amount of that country's supply at price τ_i^A does not suffice to satisfy A's import demand at that price. Then A must continue to import from the rest of the world under an FTA, and its domestic price must remain at τ_i^A. The producers in B prefer to sell in A's market at the high price τ_i^A rather than to sell at the lower price τ_i^B (which may equal 1, if

[6] For each lobby, the strategy of bidding zero for all outcomes weakly dominates any strategy with a bid in excess of what the lobby stands to gain under its preferred regime. Our assumption serves to rule out weakly dominated strategies.

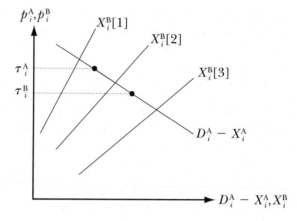

Figure 1. Industry effects of an FTA

this is initially an export good) prevailing at home. These producers divert all of their output to country A after the conclusion of the FTA, and consumers in B satisfy all of their demands by importing from the rest of the world. The FTA has no effect on producer or consumer prices in country A, or on consumer prices in country B. It serves only to raise the prices paid to producers in the low-tariff country, who in effect would capture the protection of the high-tariff country (see Anne O. Krueger [1993] on a related point). We will refer to this as the case of *enhanced protection*.

At the opposite extreme, the endowment of the specific factor in B may be so large that this country's output would satisfy A's import demand at the lower price τ_i^B. In this case, represented by $X_i^B[3]$ in the figure, the domestic price in country A falls to τ_i^B. Now B is the source for all of A's imports, and producers in country B also sell in their home market. Consumers in B pay τ_i^B for the good just as they did before the agreement, and producers there continue to receive this sum. But producers in A receive less than before. This is a case of *reduced protection*.

Finally, the curve $X_i^B[2]$ represents an intermediate case in which B's supply curve intersects A's import demand at a price between τ_i^A and τ_i^B. In this case, when producers in B divert their output to the higher-priced market, this output is just sufficient to meet import demand at a price where there is no residual demand for imports from the rest of the world. Producers in B receive the equilibrium price in A's market, which is higher than τ_i^B but lower than τ_i^A. Consumers in B import from the rest of the world, paying the same price τ_i^B as they did before the agreement.

TABLE 1.   OUTCOMES UNDER AN FTA $(\tau_i^A > \tau_i^B)$

Outcome	Enhanced protection	Intermediate case	Reduced protection
A imports from rest of world?	yes	no	no
B consumes own output?	no	no	yes
Producer price in A ⎤ Consumer price in A ⎬ Producer price in B ⎦	τ_i^A	$>\tau_i^B$ $<\tau_i^A$	τ_i^B
Consumer price in B	τ_i^B	τ_i^B	τ_i^B

The main point here is that, depending on the size of B's potential output, the marginal good produced there may be sold in A's protected market, in B's less protected market, or possibly even on the world market. The price that B's producers receive and that all agents face in country A varies accordingly. Table 1 summarizes these findings.

1.4 Effects of an FTA on Economic Interests

We are now ready to describe how an FTA affects the profits of specific factor owners and the welfare of the average voter in each country. We continue to focus on a single industry in which $\tau_i^A > \tau_i^B \geq 1$. Of course the effect of an agreement on aggregate welfare reflects the sum of its effects in the various industries, including those in which $\tau_i^B > \tau_i^A \geq 1$.

Consider first an industry that experiences *enhanced protection*. Producers in country B benefit from their preferential access to A's highly protected market. Their gain amounts to $\Delta\Pi_i^B = \Pi_i^B(\tau_i^A) - \Pi_i^B(\tau_i^B)$. Producers in A are unaffected, since the domestic price there does not change. As for welfare, the only effect in A is the loss of tariff revenue. This country, which collects duties on all of its imports in this industry under the MFN tariff, does not collect any on its imports of $X_i^B(\tau_i^A)$ from its partner under the FTA. The welfare change in A amounts to

$$\Delta W_i^A = -(\tau_i^A - 1)X_i^B(\tau_i^A).$$

This welfare loss corresponds, of course, to the adverse effects of *trade diversion*, which are familiar from the literature on customs unions.

In country B the contribution of the industry under consideration to aggregate welfare rises. There are two components of this gain. First, as we have noted, profits in the industry increase. Second, the country imports from the rest of the world to replace sales formerly made by domestic producers. Assuming that $\tau_i^B > 1$, the country collects added tariff revenue on these new imports. The change in welfare equals $\Delta W_i^B = \Delta\Pi_i^B + (\tau_i^B - 1)X_i^B(\tau_i^B)$. We note that A's welfare loss exceeds B's welfare gain, reflecting the global efficiency cost associated with trade diversion.

For an industry that experiences *reduced protection*, the price obtained by producers in the low-tariff country does not change. These exporters gain nothing from the agreement, while the producers in country A suffer from the increased import competition. The expression for the profit change is $\Delta\Pi_i^A = \Pi_i^A(\tau_i^B) - \Pi_i^A(\tau_i^A) < 0$. Tariff proceeds in the industry fall to zero in country A, as all imports now originate in the partner country. But voters gain qua consumers from the fall in the domestic price of the good. The contribution of the industry to the change in aggregate welfare is $\Delta\Pi_i^A = \Delta\Pi_i^A - (\tau_i^A - 1)M_i^A(\tau_i^A) + S_i^A(\tau_i^B) - S_i^A(\tau_i^A)$, which may be positive or negative, depending on the relative sizes of the gains from trade creation and the losses from trade diversion. Country B captures only the extra tariff revenue in this case $[\Delta W_i^B = (\tau_i^B - 1)M_i^A(\tau_i^B)]$, but joint welfare gains for the two countries are assured.

The intermediate case combines elements of the other two. Producers gain in country B and lose in country A. Aggregate welfare rises in B and may rise or fall in A. The effect on joint welfare of the two countries is ambiguous. As there is nothing new in this case, we will not consider it any further.

To summarize, an FTA can have any of several combinations of impacts on the economic actors with interests in a particular industry. Producers in the country that exports to its partner under an FTA sometimes gain and never lose. These producers are one potential source of political support for an agreement. On the other hand, the producers in the country that imports from its partner under the agreement never gain and sometimes lose. Here we find potential resistance. The stake of the general public in an FTA is less clear-cut. If most goods will be exported to the partner country, then aggregate welfare must rise, as consumer surplus never falls in the exporting country, and tariff revenues generally increase. If most goods will be imported, the aggregate welfare effect depends on the relative strength of the forces of trade creation and trade diversion, as is well known from the theory of discriminatory tariffs.

2 Unilateral Stances

We are ready to begin our search for equilibrium outcomes. We focus first on the political interactions in a single country. These determine the nation's *unilateral stance*, that is, the position that the government would adopt if it believed its decision would determine the fate of the agreement. We aim to describe the policy positions that can be supported as optimal government responses to equilibrium behavior by the country's interest groups. To this end, we propose the following definition.

DEFINITION 1. A choice of regime $R \in \{N, F\}$ is a *unilateral stance* if there exists a set of political contributions $\{C_{iN}, C_{iF}\}$, one for each lobby i, such that:

(a) $C_{iK} \geq 0$ for $K = N,F$ and for all i;
(b) $C_{iK} \leq \max(0, \Pi_{iK} - \Pi_{ij})$ for $J = N,F$; $K = N,F$; $J \neq K$;
(c) $\sum_i C_{iR} + aW_R \geq \sum_i C_{iK} + aW_K$ for $K = N,F$;
(d) for every lobby i there exist no contributions $\hat{C}_{iN} \geq 0$ and $\hat{C}_{iF} \geq 0$ and no regime $\hat{R}_i \in \{N,F\}$ such that:

(i) $\hat{C}_{i\hat{R}_i} + \sum_{j \neq i} C_{j\hat{R}_i} + aW_{\hat{R}_i} \geq \hat{C}_{iK} + \sum_{j \neq i} C_{jK} + aW_K$ for $K = N,F$

and

(ii) $\Pi_{i\hat{R}_i} - \hat{C}_{i\hat{R}_i} > \Pi_{iR} - C_{iR}$.

The definition stipulates that the political contributions supporting a unilateral stance must be nonnegative and no greater than what a lobby stands to gain under its preferred regime. The contributions induce the government to take the position R rather than the alternative, in the light of its own political objectives. And there are no alternative offers available to any lobby that, given the contribution schedules of the other lobbies and the anticipated optimization by the politicians, would leave the lobby with greater net welfare.

We will find that there are two generic types of unilateral stances that may exist for a given set of parameter values. We refer to a stance as *unpressured* if the government takes the chosen position despite there being no offers of contributions that encourage it to do so. By contrast, a *pressured* stance is one that the government takes partly in response to offers of interest-group support. We now derive the following result.

RESULT 1. There exists an unpressured stance in support of regime R if and only if

$$a(W_R - W_{\tilde{R}}) \geq \max\left[0, \max_i (\Pi_{i\tilde{R}} - \Pi_{iR})\right], \tag{2}$$

where $\tilde{R}$ is the alternative to regime R.

The result says that, in an unpressured stance, the government prefers the regime R to the alternative on grounds of public welfare. Moreover, there is no single lobby favoring the alternative policy that stands to lose so much under R that it would unilaterally sway the government from its concern for the plight of the average voter.

The proof is straightforward. First, suppose that all contribution offers are zero (i.e., $C_{iR} = C_{i\tilde{R}} = 0$ for all i). Then the government chooses the socially preferred position and, if (2) is satisfied, no single lobby finds it profitable given the zero offers of the others to induce the government to change its stance. This establishes that (2) is sufficient for an unpressured stance in favor of R. As for necessity, it is obvious that we must have $W_R - W_{\tilde{R}} \geq 0$ if the government is to choose R in the absence of any contributions in support of that position. And if $a(W_R - W_{\tilde{R}}) < \Pi_{i\tilde{R}} - \Pi_{iR}$ for any i, then lobby i could profitably deviate by bidding something more than $a(W_R - W_{\tilde{R}})$ but less than $\Pi_{i\tilde{R}} - \Pi_{iR}$, thereby inducing the government to choose $\tilde{R}$.

Next we examine stances that feature campaign giving by the prospective beneficiaries of the chosen regime. When $C_{iR} > 0$ for at least one lobby i, the government must be left indifferent between the two policy choices (i.e., $\sum_i C_{iR} + aW_R = \sum_i C_{i\tilde{R}} + aW_{\tilde{R}}$). Otherwise, one of the lobbies offering a positive contribution in support of R could reduce its offer without affecting the final outcome, thereby increasing its net income. Once we know that the government is left indifferent, we also know that every lobby on the losing side (i.e., those preferring $\tilde{R}$ to R) bids for $\tilde{R}$ the full amount of what it stands to lose under R; otherwise one such lobby would find it profitable to raise its offer for $\tilde{R}$ slightly, thereby tipping the balance to that policy. Of course, no lobby on the winning side offers more than the extra profits it earns under R, and each lobby contributes nothing if the government's choice is counter to its interests. Together, these considerations establish our second result.

RESULT 2. If there exists a pressured stance in support of regime R, then

$$\sum_i \Pi_{iR} + aW_R \geq \sum_i \Pi_{i\tilde{R}} + aW_{\tilde{R}}. \tag{3}$$

Condition (3) states that the regime supported in a pressured stance maximizes the sum of aggregate profits and a times average welfare. It follows that, if such a stance exists, the policy outcome it selects is (generically) unique. Existence requires

$$aW_R < aW_{\tilde{R}} + \sum_{i \in S_{\tilde{R}}} (\Pi_{i\tilde{R}} - \Pi_{iR}),$$

where $S_{\tilde{R}}$ is the set of lobbies that prefer regime $\tilde{R}$, and R is the regime that satisfies (3). In other words, a pressured stance exists whenever positive contributions by the supporters of regime R are needed to induce the government to choose this stance when each opponent of R bids its maximum willingness to pay for the alternative. When this inequality fails, the proponents of R can refrain from offering any contributions with the assurance that the government will nonetheless choose their preferred stance.

It is possible that both a pressured and an unpressured stance will exist for some parameter values. In that event, the two stances may select the same policy outcome. But this need not be the case. Whereas the unpressured stance always endorses the socially preferred regime, the pressured stance may select the regime that harms the average voter. This happens any time the aggregate profit gain from R relative to $\tilde{R}$ exceeds a times the social welfare loss.

In cases where pressured and unpressured stances both exist and support different policy positions, there may be compelling reasons to focus primarily on the pressured stance. In these circumstances, the unpressured stance does not survive as an equilibrium when we allow a limited degree of coordination among the lobbies. In particular, consider the notion of a *coalition-proof equilibrium*, as discussed by Bernheim et al. (1987). This refinement of Nash equilibrium rejects any outcome for which there exists a set of actions by some coalition of players such that (i) each member of the coalition attains a payoff as high or higher than in the Nash equilibrium, given the actions of nonmembers of the coalition; and (ii) the proposed action of each coalition member is a best response to the proposed or given actions of the others. The refinement applies best to situations where players can communicate but cannot make binding agreements. The communication could be used to spell out the entire list of proposed plays by coalition members, so that each would realize that it could gain by following the proposal and that it and the others have no incentive to cheat, assuming that all members do as proposed.

The unpressured stance will fail to be coalition-proof whenever it selects a regime different from the pressured stance. To see why, suppose that (2) is satisfied for R and (3) is satisfied for $\tilde{R}$. In the unpressured stance, all supporters of R contribute nothing. An industry that is harmed by R could propose a coalition comprising all such industries. It could propose that the members jointly contribute enough so that the total contributions just overcome the government's sensitivity to voter opposition, with no member being asked to contribute more than what it has to gain. Then, given the zero contributions of the nonmembers of this coalition, the government would be induced to choose $\tilde{R}$. Each member of the coalition would benefit from this deviation, and each would see itself as pivotal and so would have no incentive to cheat. Since we have assumed that (3) is satisfied for $\tilde{R}$, the collective gains of the coalition members are large enough to allow such a proposal to be designed. Evidently, the unpressured stance rests in these circumstances on the inability of opponents of the chosen regime to coordinate their political activity.

Bernheim and Whinston (1986) have shown that all coalition-proof equilibria in menu auctions select an action from among the set of actions that maximizes the joint welfare of the principals and the agent, and also that any element in this set can be supported as a coalition-proof equilibrium. Here, the government acts as agent for the many interest groups, and condition (3) expresses the requirement for joint welfare maximization. Since the regime that maximizes joint welfare always exists, we have proved the following.

RESULT 3.   A coalition-proof stance always exists. This stance supports regime R if and only if condition (3) is satisfied.

Results 2 and 3 imply immediately that *all pressured stances are coalition-proof.*

This completes our discussion of the equilibrium interactions in a single polity. To summarize, there always exists at least one unilateral stance. This stance may be pressured or unpressured. When a pressured stance exists, it always supports the (generically) unique regime that maximizes the joint welfare of lobbies and politicians. When an unpressured stance exists, it supports the regime that benefits the average voter. When both exist, they may or may not endorse the same outcome. If they do not, then only the pressured stance will be coalition-proof. In these situations, it will be possible for a coalition of lobbies to upset the unpressured stance by minimal coordination of their political activities.

3 Equilibrium Agreements

We turn now to the international negotiation. Our prohibition on exclusions leaves the two governments with little to negotiate about. In principle, they could discuss compensation payments that would be made from one treasury to the other under the terms of a potential agreement. Such compensation schemes do play a part in some regional trade agreements, such as the European Common Market. But transfers still seem the exception rather than the rule (for example, they are not included in the terms of NAFTA), and even where they are used, they often are limited in scope. While we could include (limited or full) opportunities for compensation in our analysis of FTAs, we choose to focus on the case where such opportunities are unavailable to avoid a cumbersome taxonomy.

In the absence of transfers, an FTA requires the unilateral support of both governments. If the lobbies in each country anticipate that the other government will pursue the agreement, they will expect that their own country's political deliberations will determine its fate. Then they will act exactly as described in our analysis of unilateral stances in Section 2.[7] In a subgame-perfect Nash equilibrium, all expectations about the

---

[7] If the Nash equilibrium entails a continuation of the status quo, then lobbies in at least one country must expect that the other government will oppose the FTA at the international talks. These lobbies will contribute nothing to block the agreement, because they will believe it to be doomed in any case. This means that a pressured stance against an FTA will be observed in an international equilibrium in at most one country.

behavior of the other government are fulfilled. This justifies the following definition.

DEFINITION 2. An FTA is an *equilibrium agreement* if and only if $R = F$ is a unilateral stance in both countries.

Our objective in this section is to characterize the economic and political conditions in the two countries under which an FTA can arise as an equilibrium outcome.

A central theme will emerge from our analysis. We will argue that the political viability of an FTA requires sufficient "balance" in the potential trade between the parties to the agreement. To motivate this idea, it helps to begin with an extreme case. Suppose that all goods exported by country A in the status quo ante are also exports of country B and that country A has the higher MFN tariff in all of its import-competing sectors. Then country A would not export to country B at all in the event of an agreement. This means that none of the lobbies in A would support the agreement. If most industries would experience enhanced protection, then welfare in A would be likely to fall, in which case there could be no unilateral stance in A in support of the FTA. On the other hand, if most industries would experience reduced protection, then the potential opposition to the agreement from the special interests would be great. The only chance for an FTA in this case of extreme imbalance in potential trade would be if the agreement happened to be welfare-improving and the opposing interests failed to coordinate their lobbying activities or if they were unable to muster enough opposition to block the accord. And even this last scenario would be unlikely, if the initial MFN tariffs also were the outgrowth of a political process.[8]

In order to be more precise about what we mean by balance and also to see how industry conditions influence the political outcome, we turn to a special (but less extreme) case with particular functional forms. We suppose now that the households in both countries share identical utility functions wherein all of the nonnumeraire goods enter symmetrically and each $u_i(\cdot)$ is quadratic. Then aggregate demand for any good i in country j has the linear form

$$D_i^j(q_i^j) = D - bq_i^j \quad \text{for } i = 1,2,\ldots,n \text{ and } j = A,B. \quad (4)$$

---

[8] We will see that, if the MFN tariffs are the result of a political process similar to the one assumed to precede the negotiation of the FTA, then the joint welfare of the government and the lobby must fall in any import-competing industry where a tariff rate is lowered. This means that no pressured stance could support an FTA if all industries were import-competing and all experienced reduced protection under an FTA.

Also, aggregate world supply of every good is the same, and the supply in each country is inelastic. We assume that $X_i^A = \theta X$ and $X_i^B = (1 - \theta)X$ in a fraction s of the industries, while $X_i^A = (1 - \theta)X$ and $X_i^B = \theta X$ in the remaining fraction $1 - s$ of the industries. In other words, all industries are mirror images, with country A having the larger supply in some industries and country B the larger supply in the others. Here s measures the extent of imbalance in the number of potential export industries and θ measures the imbalance in output in any one sector. Without further loss of generality we take $\theta > \frac{1}{2}$ and $s \geq \frac{1}{2}$.

The viability of an FTA also depends, of course, on the structure of the initial MFN tariffs. So far we have taken these as arbitrary. But it is reasonable to suppose that they too are an equilibrium outcome of a political process. For the purposes of our illustrative example, we will now assume that the MFN tariffs initially protecting the import-competing industries in each country are those that would result from a contribution game similar to the one described here. Assuming that both sets of politicians place the same weight a on aggregate welfare in their objective functions, application of proposition 1 in Grossman and Helpman (1994a) gives

$$\tau_i^j = 1 + \frac{X_i^j}{ab} \quad \text{for } j = A,B \tag{5}$$

for all sectors i that have positive imports in the initial equilibrium.

In this example, different types of outcomes emerge depending on the configuration of parameter values. We will examine three different sets of parameter restrictions. While these possibilities do not exhaust the entire parameter space, they do illustrate all of the different considerations that may come into play.

Restriction 1.

$$\frac{D - b}{X} > 1 + \frac{\theta}{a} .$$

With this restriction on the parameters, all of the nonnumeraire goods are imported in both countries in the initial equilibrium, when the MFN tariffs given in (5) apply. Country A has the higher import tariff in the fraction s of industries where its supply is θX, while country B has the higher tariff in the remaining fraction $1 - s$ of industries. This is because the political processes are similar in the two countries, and the special interests in each country are willing to contribute more in their initial bids for MFN protection when they have more output at stake.

Under an FTA, each country would import from its partners all of those goods on which its MFN tariff is higher. This means that A would import a fraction s of the nonnumeraire goods from B, and B would import the remaining fraction $1 - s$ of these goods from A. Moreover, under restriction 1, the output in the low-tariff country would not suffice to satisfy import demand in the high-tariff country at the latter country's preagreement domestic price. Therefore, recalling Table 1, all industries would experience enhanced protection under the proposed FTA. It is straightforward to calculate the contribution of sector i to the change in aggregate welfare in each country using the formulas from Subsection 1.4. We find

$$\Delta W_i^j = \begin{cases} -\dfrac{\theta(1 - \theta)X^2}{ab} & \text{if } X_i^j = \theta X \\[2mm] \dfrac{\theta(1 - \theta)X^2}{ab} & \text{if } X_i^j = (1 - \theta)X \end{cases} \tag{6}$$

for j = A,B. Notice that what one country gains in aggregate welfare, the other loses.[9]

We can also calculate the profit changes that would result from the FTA. With all industries experiencing enhanced protection, the various import-competing interests in the high-tariff sectors would not suffer any profit losses. Meanwhile, the factor owners in industries that would export under the agreement would all gain. We have

$$\Delta \Pi_i^j = \begin{cases} 0 & \text{if } X_i^j = \theta X \\[2mm] \dfrac{(2\theta - 1)(1 - \theta)X^2}{ab} & \text{if } X_i^j = (1 - \theta)X \end{cases} \tag{7}$$

for j = A,B.

We are now ready to examine the unilateral stances. From (6) we see that an unpressured stance can favor an FTA in country A only if $s = \frac{1}{2}$ (i.e., if the number of potential export industries is exactly the same in each country). If $s = \frac{1}{2}$, the FTA is welfare-neutral, and the government in A could (marginally) support an agreement without any lobbying on its behalf. But if $s > \frac{1}{2}$, the welfare loss from the fraction s of high-tariff industries in country A would exceed the welfare gain from the fraction $1 - s$ of low-tariff industries. Some political activity on the part of the beneficiaries would be necessary for the FTA to materialize.

What about the pressured stances? Using (6) and (7) we find that condition (3) indicates pressured support for an agreement in country B for

---

[9] Joint social welfare in the two countries does not change, because outputs are fixed in each country and consumer prices do not change, so neither do demands. With a fixed allocation of resources in each country, only the distribution of the industry surplus can be affected by the FTA.

all $s \geq \frac{1}{2}$ and that the government of country A will be induced to favor the accord if and only if

$$s \leq \frac{1}{2} + \frac{\theta - \frac{1}{2}}{2\theta - 1 + 2a\theta} < 1. \tag{8}$$

The inequality in (8) will be satisfied for s sufficiently close to $\frac{1}{2}$. Then the potential profit gains to the owners of the fraction $1 - s$ of the specific factors will be sufficiently large in the aggregate to outweigh the cost to the average voter. On the other hand, if s is close to 1, then the contributions by supporters of the agreement will not be sufficient to sway the government in the light of the prospective harm to the average voter. For a given value of s, a pressured stance in A is more likely to support the FTA the smaller is the weight a that the government attaches to aggregate welfare, since welfare in A surely falls under the agreement. Finally, the political viability of a potential agreement increases with the extent of supply imbalance in a representative industry, because the potential profit gains for exporters grow more rapidly with θ than do the social welfare losses in the import sectors.

Restriction 2.

$$1 + \frac{1 - \theta}{a} > \frac{D - b}{X} > \theta + \frac{\theta}{a}.$$

When this restriction holds, all nonnumeraire goods again are imported by both countries in the preagreement equilibrium. But now, using the tariff formula (5), we find that the supply of output in the low-tariff country in each industry is enough to satisfy all demand by the other country at the low-tariff country's price. This means that all industries would experience reduced protection under the agreement.

Again we can calculate the contribution of each sector to the change in aggregate welfare in each country. We find that, for the high-tariff sectors, where there are the offsetting effects of trade creation and trade diversion, the answer depends on the parameter values.[10] Meanwhile, the contribution of the low-tariff sectors in each country to social welfare increases under an FTA, as these all become export sectors.

Summing over all industries, we find that an FTA may increase or decrease aggregate welfare in country A. If the potential export industries are evenly divided ($s = \frac{1}{2}$), aggregate welfare must rise. Then an unpressured stance favors an FTA in both countries as long as no single import-competing industry has sufficient reason to block it. For this, it is sufficient that the total number of specific factors exceeds four. On the

---

[10] The details of this and succeeding calculations may be found in Grossman and Helpman (1994b).

other hand, if $s = 1$, aggregate welfare rises in country A only if the beneficial effect of trade creation in the import-competing sectors is sufficiently large. Thus, even if the special interests that will be hurt by an FTA fail to coalesce into a (noncooperative) coalition, the fate of the agreement remains in doubt.

What if the special-interest groups do become active in the political battle over the FTA? In this case of reduced protection, it is the most politically powerful producers in each country (i.e., those that succeeded in securing high barriers in the initial political equilibrium) that would be harmed by an agreement. Moreover, the potential exporters stand to gain nothing. When we calculate the profit losses for the import-competing industries, we find that for $s = \frac{1}{2}$ the aggregate profit loss in the $n/2$ high-tariff industries exceeds a times the total welfare gain. Therefore, the pressured stance in each country rejects the FTA. As s increases, industry opposition to the FTA grows in country A, while the potential social benefit from the agreement may rise or fall. But even if it rises, the profit losses grow faster with s than a times the welfare gain. It follows that the pressured stance in A rejects the FTA not only when the industries are evenly divided between the countries but for all values of $s \in [\frac{1}{2}, 1]$. The international outcome must be a continuation of the status quo if the special interests in A induce a coalition-proof stance.

Restriction 3.

$$\theta > \frac{D - b}{X} > (1 - \theta)\left(1 + \frac{1}{a}\right).$$

In this case the producers in each country with output θX export their product in the initial equilibrium. Since we rule out export subsidies, they receive only the international price for their goods. Meanwhile, the producers with output $(1 - \theta)X$ cannot satisfy domestic demand at the tariff-inclusive domestic price, when the tariff is given by (5). These sectors are protected in the initial equilibrium. It can be shown that all industries experience reduced protection under the FTA, so that international prices would prevail in all sectors under a trade agreement.

The export sectors again gain nothing from an FTA. But this time, these sectors also contribute nothing to the change in aggregate welfare, as no tariff revenue is collected on the imports that replace diverted sales. The factor owners in import-competing sectors sacrifice profits under an agreement, while the contribution of these sectors to aggregate welfare expands. We must as usual evaluate the sum of $\Delta \Pi_i^j$ and $a\Delta W_i^j$, but now the sum need only be taken over the import-competing industries in country j. In each such industry, tariff revenue falls due to trade diversion and a politically motivated tariff is removed. Since the MFN tariffs in (5) were themselves set to maximize a political objective function, their elimination must reduce the joint welfare of the lobby and the government. It follows that the pressured stance rejects the agreement in both countries.

Let us summarize what we have learned from this example and comment on how the lessons might extend to more general settings. First, we find that the political viability of an FTA requires s to be close to $\frac{1}{2}$. This is the sense in which potential trade between the countries must be balanced: there must be a sufficient number of potential exporters in each country who will lobby for the agreement, or a sufficient number of sectors with assured welfare gains, to offset the potential losses from trade diversion. This result does not rely on the particulars of our example. Any time an FTA would have most trade flows in one direction, political viability in the importing country will be very much in doubt. Viability then requires a predominance of industries facing reduced protection and also that trade creation would outweight trade diversion in many of these, so that aggregate gains would be generated by the agreement. Moreover, since reduced protection implies losses for import-competing industries, it requires a coordination failure among the lobbies who would wish to block the accord. Trade imbalances may explain, for example, why the United States has had more difficulty in concluding trade agreements with several Asian trade partners than it has with partners in North America.

Second, the example suggests that political viability may require a sufficient number of industries that would experience enhanced protection as compared with the number facing reduced protection. In the example, an FTA can emerge as a coalition-proof equilibrium for some parameters satisfying restriction 1, but not for any that satisfy restrictions 2 or 3. In the first of these cases, enhanced protection is in store for all, and the would-be exporters represent a potential source of support for an agreement. In the second and third cases, the import-competing industries face the prospect of reduced protection and are willing to contribute to block it. Recall that enhanced protection generally means joint welfare losses as a consequence of trade diversion (although such losses do not arise in the example with completely inelastic supplies), while reduced protection generally means joint welfare gains stemming from trade creation. The example thus suggests a more far-reaching conclusion: the conditions needed for the political viability of an FTA may contradict those that ensure its social desirability.[11]

The example delivers this message too starkly. Even in our model, there can be efficiency-enhancing agreements that pass political muster

[11] Albert O. Hirschman (1981) made a similar point in his prescient discussion of the dynamics of the European Community.

if demand curves are nonlinear. And our model neglects some additional sources of joint welfare gain that need not imply an absence of extra profits for exporters. We have assumed, for example, that all markets are globally integrated and that international prices set the terms of trade prior to any agreement. If, instead, we allowed some goods to have high transport costs (or high trade barriers in the rest of the world), the markets in A and B might initially be segmented from those abroad. Then exporters in one country could gain from bilateral tariff reductions even as prices fell for consumers in the other (see Paul Wonnacott and Ronald Wonnacott [1981]). Similarly, if products were differentiated by country of origin, the importing country could realize welfare gains while the exporters saw their profits rise. Still, there is an important lesson here that is general. Whenever a trade agreement gives rise to trade diversion, there will be narrow interests that enjoy private gains, while costs will be shared by all taxpayers. To the extent that industry interests are better represented in the political process than are taxpayers' interests, trade diversion will enhance political viability while contributing to an inefficient allocation of resources in the two partner countries.

4 Industry Exclusions

Governments that are considering a free trade agreement have some ability to make a pact palatable to opposing interests. They can do so by providing long periods of adjustment to some sectors and by excluding others from the agreement entirely. However, the national governments are bound to clash on the issue of exceptions, because each seeks to preserve protection for some of its politically powerful industries, while each tries to gain market access for all of its potential exporters. An equilibrium agreement is one that reflects the political pressures on each government and also the give-and-take of the bargaining process.

In this section, we show how industry exclusions might make an otherwise impossible FTA politically viable. We also examine the determinants of the number and identity of excluded sectors. We use "exclusions" here to represent not only the granting of permanent exemptions from an agreement, but also as a metaphor for long phase-in periods. The number of such exclusions should not be so large as to violate the GATT stipulation that an FTA must liberalize "substantially all trade."

4.1 Unilateral Stances

We begin as before by focusing on the political interactions in a single country. We investigate what type of agreement (if any) a government would choose in response to domestic political pressures, assuming that it could dictate terms to its FTA partner. Of course, an equilibrium agreement need not look anything like the *unilateral stance*; but it helps to understand the political process in one country before turning to the two-country bargaining problem.

The lobbies' contribution schedules now must reflect the various positions that their government might take. A government can choose to reject an agreement entirely, it can pursue an agreement calling for the exclusion of certain sectors, or it can seek an agreement with completely free bilateral trade. In principle, the lobbies might link their contributions to the identities of all entries on the list of excluded sectors. However, in our model, the owners of a specific factor care only about the fate of their own industry. An industry facing the prospect of increased competition from partner imports will prefer that its protection be preserved for as long as possible, while an industry that hopes to find a new or expanded export market will not want to see its products among those excluded from the agreement. We can assume without loss of generality that the special interests distinguish their contribution offers only among outcomes that affect their profits. Each lobby i specifies exactly three numbers, denoted C_{iN}, C_{iE}, and C_{iI}, that represent its campaign gift in the event that the government rejects the FTA, in the event that it concludes an FTA but with industry i excluded from the agreement, and in the event that it concludes an FTA with industry i included in the agreement, respectively.[12] Excluded sectors retain their MFN tariffs once an FTA is enacted.

We define a unilateral stance in much the same way as we did in Section 3. In particular, the unilateral stance supports some regime; either the government rejects the agreement entirely ($R = N$) or it opts for an agreement ($R = F$) with a particular set (perhaps empty) of excluded sectors. In an equilibrium stance, the government achieves greater political welfare G than it could under any alternative regime satisfying GATT rules on exclusions. Furthermore, no lobby is able to redesign its offer triplet, given the offers of the other lobbies and the anticipated optimization by the politicians, in such a way as to increase its profits net of contributions.

As McMillan (1993) has argued, GATT rules on the admissibility of free trade agreements are anything but clear. The requirement that an agreement must liberalize "substantially all trade" can be interpreted to place a limit on the number of industries that can be excluded from

[12] In a world with differentiated products and two-way trade, we would need to allow for the possibility that an agreement removes one country's barrier to imports of good i, but not the other's. Here, trade in any one good is unidirectional, with imports going from the low-tariff country to the high-tariff country. In this context, an industry exclusion means that the high-tariff country retains its barrier to imports from its FTA partner.

an agreement, on the fraction of bilateral trade excluded, on the fraction of total trade excluded, or perhaps on something else. We can cover all of the various possibilities by representing the rule as $\int_{i \in \mathcal{E}} T_i di \leq T$, where $\mathcal{E}$ is the set of excluded industries, T_i is the size of sector i according to the indicated measure, and T is the exogenous limit imposed by the constraint. If, for example, the rule places a limit on the number of excluded industries, then $T_i = 1$ for all i, whereas if it places a limit on the fraction of excluded trade, then T_i is the share of industry i in total preagreement trade. By writing the rule as an integral, we of course assume a continuum of sectors. This allows us to avoid "integer problems," which would complicate the exposition without furthering understanding.[13]

In describing the unilateral stances that can emerge as equilibrium government responses to political pressures, it will prove convenient to refer to the *politically optimal set of exclusions,* $\mathcal{E}(T)$. We define this set as follows. First, we order the industries so that $i \in [0,n]$ and $g_i \equiv (\Delta \Pi_i + a\Delta W_i)/T_i$ increases with i. Second, we assign the label i_0 to the sector with the lowest index such that $g_i = 0$. If $g_i > 0$ for all i, then $i_0 = 0$. Finally, we define $\hat{i}$ so that

$$\int_0^{\hat{i}} T_i di = T.$$

DEFINITION 3. The set of *politically optimal exclusions* $\mathcal{E}(T)$ is the set of sectors i such that $i \in [0, \min(i_0, \hat{i})]$.

This definition requires that, for any industry in the set $\mathcal{E}(T)$, the joint gain to the government and the factor owners from liberalizing bilateral trade in good i must be nonpositive and in fact more negative (when normalized by the "size" of the sector) than for any sector not in the set.

Our first result concerns coalition-proof stances.

RESULT 4. There exists a coalition-proof stance with $R = F$ if and only if

$$\int_{i \in \mathcal{E}(T)} (\Pi_{iN} + aW_{iN}) \, di + \int_{i \notin \mathcal{E}(T)} (\Pi_{iF} + aW_{iF}) \, di \geq \int_i (\Pi_{iN} + aW_{iN}) \, di. \quad (9)$$

In this stance, the sectors $i \in \mathcal{E}(T)$ are excluded from the agreement.

The left-hand side of (9) gives the joint welfare of all lobbies and the government under an FTA with excluded sectors $\mathcal{E}(T)$, while the right-hand side gives the joint welfare of these parties in the status

---

[13] Integer problems may arise, because sectors must be excluded wholly or not at all. With large sectors, a ranking of industries according to their (size-adjusted) political clout would not fully determine the list of exclusions, because some potential "last" entry on the list might cause the constraint to be violated while another (smaller) sector would not.

quo. The result follows from theorem 3 of Bernheim and Whinston (1986), which states that every coalition-proof equilibrium in a menu auction selects an action from among those that maximize the joint welfare of the principals and the agent.[14] In the coalition-proof unilateral stance, the constraint on the size of the excluded set will bind if and only if there exists more than a measure T of industries (measured in the relevant way; i.e., by number, trade volume, etc.) in which the factor owners would lose more in profits from being included in the agreement than a times what the average voter would gain. The excluded industries are those that are most politically sensitive, in the sense that their inclusion imposes the greatest cost to specific factor owners and politicians taken together.

The coalition-proof stance can be supported by "truthful offers" in which (i) each lobby bids the same amount for an exclusion as for an outright rejection of the agreement ($C_{iE} = C_{iN} \geq 0$ for all i); (ii) all industries $j \notin \mathcal{E}(T)$ bid for an exclusion exactly what they stand to lose (if anything) by being included in the agreement; and (iii) all industries $i \in \mathcal{E}(T)$ bid for an exclusion at most what they stand to save by having their trade barriers preserved, and exactly what is needed to ensure that they are among those excluded. This stance may be *pressured*, in the sense that at least some of the industries that stand to gain from the FTA contribute actively on its behalf (i.e., $C_{iI} > 0$ for some i). The joint contributions of these (export) industries then are just sufficient to overcome the political resistance to the agreement.

Inequality (9) may hold even when inequality (4) fails for $R = F$. That is, the coalition-proof stance may endorse an FTA with exclusions in cases where the agreement would be defeated in the absence of exclusions. The exclusions allow the government to avoid the biggest political costs associated with an FTA, and the net political gain may be positive once these particularly exposed sectors are sheltered from the agreement.

When inequality (9) does fail, a coalition of industries can form to block any proposed FTA. Moreover, the contributions that block a given proposal require no monitoring (they are best responses) and leave each coalition member at least as well off as under the agreement. However, as before, the interests that oppose the FTA may fail to achieve the required degree of coordination. In this event, the politics may give rise to a unilateral stance in support of an FTA, even though the interests that stand to benefit from the agreement contribute nothing to further its cause. We will refer to such a stance with all $C_{iI} = 0$ as *unpres-*

---

[14] Note that $\mathcal{E}(T)$ maximizes $\int_{i \in \tilde{\mathcal{E}}} (\Pi_{iN} + aW_{iN}) \, di + \int_{i \notin \tilde{\mathcal{E}}} (\Pi_{iF} + aW_{iF}) \, di$ among all sets $\tilde{\mathcal{E}}$ that have $\int_{i \in \tilde{\mathcal{E}}} T_i di \leq T$.

sured.[15] The next result gives the necessary and sufficient conditions for the existence of such a stance.

RESULT 5. There exists an unpressured stance with $R = F$ if and only if

$$\int_{i\in\mathcal{E}(T)} aW_{iN}di + \int_{i\notin\mathcal{E}(T)} aW_{iF}di + C \geq \int_i aW_{iN}di, \qquad (10)$$

where $C = \int_{i\in\mathcal{E}(T)} \max[0, a(W_{iF} - W_{iN}) + \max_{j\notin\mathcal{E}(T)}(-T_jg_j)]di$. In this stance, the sectors $i \in \mathcal{E}(T)$ are excluded from the agreement.

The proof of this result is available from the authors upon request.[16] Intuitively, C represents the total amount of contributions by lobbies that are excluded from the agreement when each such lobby gives the minimum amount that ensures it a place on the list of exclusions (given the equilibrium bids of the others). Each excluded lobby must compensate the government for the political cost of any loss in aggregate welfare that results from its placement on the list of exclusions. This is reflected in the term $a(W_{iF} - W_{iN})$. It must also bid enough to overcome the offers of those lobbies that fail to secure a place on the list. Each lobby j not included in $\mathcal{E}(T)$ bids $C_{jE} = \Pi_{jN} - \Pi_{jF}$ for a potential exclusion, so $-T_jg_j$ reflects the opportunity cost to the government of leaving lobby j off the list. If for lobby i, $a(W_{iF} - W_{iN}) + \max_{j\notin\mathcal{E}(T)}(-T_jg_j) < 0$, then the government would wish to exclude this lobby even without any positive inducement, in which case the lobby contributes nothing (i.e., $C_{iE} = 0$).

Result 5 is analogous to result 1. In each case, the unpressured stance in favor of F can exist because the opponents of the agreement fail to coordinate their political activities to further their common cause. When each lobby expects others to offer little or nothing for a total rejection of the agreement, no single lobby among those slated for inclusion may have enough at stake to warrant its acting unilaterally. Of course, in the case of result 5, the stake of any single lobby is assumed to be small, and so the unpressured stance exists whenever the agreement coupled with the minimal contributions from the excluded sectors is palatable to the politicians.

From results 4 and 5 we see that all unilateral stances in support of an FTA share the same set of (politically optimal) exclusions. It is easy to

[15] It is unpressured in the sense that the government's decision to pursue the agreement elicits no contributions from beneficiaries. The government may, however, collect contributions from some or all of the industries that are granted exclusions.

[16] In Grossman and Helpman (1994b) we proved a similar result for the case of a finite number of sectors, where GATT rules are taken to imply a restriction on the number of elements in the set of excluded sectors. With sectors of finite size, we must allow for the possibility that a single sector may be able to block the agreement even if it does not coordinate its political activities with the others.

see why. Suppose, to the contrary, that there existed a unilateral stance in which some mass of sectors $i \in \mathcal{E}(T)$ were not exempted and that perhaps some others $j \notin \mathcal{E}(T)$ were excluded in their place. First, if there were no such j's, then each such i would be willing to bid up to $\Pi_{iN} - \Pi_{iF}$ in order to secure an exclusion. The government would add i to the exclusion list if the contribution offer were large enough to compensate for the political cost, $a(W_{iF} - W_{iN})$. But according to the definition of $\mathcal{E}(T)$, we must have $\Pi_{iN} - \Pi_{iF} \geq a(W_{iF} - W_{iN})$, because $g_i < 0$ for all $i \in \mathcal{E}(T)$. Second, if there were some mass of j's on the list of exclusions in the place of the i's, choose some subsets of the i's (say $\tilde{I}$) and the j's (say $\tilde{J}$) such that $\int_{i\in\tilde{I}} T_i di = \int_{j\in\tilde{J}} T_j dj$. The j's in $\tilde{J}$ would have bid at most $\int_{j\in\tilde{J}} (\Pi_{jN} - \Pi_{jF}) \, dj$ for their places on the list of exemptions. Again, the definition of $\mathcal{E}(T)$ ensures that the lobbies $i \in \tilde{I}$ could have bid something less than their potential profit gain, and this would have been enough to induce the government to exclude these sectors instead of those in $\tilde{J}$.

4.2 Bargaining over Industry Exclusions

We turn now to the international negotiation of an FTA that might exclude certain industries. We will argue first that the ability to issue some exemptions can save an FTA that otherwise would not be politically viable.[17] Then we will discuss the considerations that determine the number and identity of the excluded sectors.

The fact that exemptions can save an FTA follows almost immediately from the analysis in the previous section. We have seen that the prospects for a unilateral stance in support of an FTA improve when a government has the flexibility to issue exemptions. The exemptions allow the government to capture the support of some potential losers, while winning the favor of exporters (and perhaps voters) who would benefit from the agreement. Of course, in a negotiating situation, neither country is likely to be in a position to dictate the terms of an agreement. Yet the logic of our argument continues to apply. A successful negotiation requires that *some* agreement be identified that both governments prefer on political grounds to the status quo ante. Exclusions improve the prospects for this, because they can be "sold" to some powerful import-competing interests in exchange for their support.

Which sectors will be granted exclusions in an equilibrium agreement? The answer depends on the particulars of the negotiating process. We

---

[17] It appears, for example, that NAFTA was saved by last-minute concessions granted to U.S. sugar producers and citrus growers in the form of exclusions from the agreement.

appeal here to the simple and familiar Nash bargaining solution in order to illustrate some of the considerations that come into play.[18]

Suppose that the equilibrium agreement is designed to maximize a geometric weighted average of the "surpluses" of the two negotiating governments. Moreover, let the lobbies anticipate this bargaining outcome at the time that they make their contribution offers. Since the governments always have the option to walk away from the negotiating table, their surpluses are calculated with reference to the political welfare they would achieve by setting $R = N$. More formally, the equilibrium agreement can be represented by a set of indicator variables, α_i, where $\alpha_i = 0$ implies that sector i is included in the FTA ($i \in I$) while $\alpha_i = 1$ implies that sector i is excluded from the agreement ($i \in E$). The Nash bargaining solution solves expression (11),

$$\max_{\{\alpha_i\}} \sum_{J = A,B} \beta^J \log\left\{ \int_i [(1 - \alpha_i)(a^J W_{iF}^J + C_{i1}^J) \right.$$
$$\left. + \alpha_i (a^J W_{iN}^J + C_{iE}^J)] di - \bar{G}^J \right\}, \tag{11}$$

subject to the constraint that $\int \alpha_i T_i di \leq T$, where β^J is the Nash weight attached to the surplus of government J and $\bar{G}^J \equiv \int (a^J W_{iN}^J + C_{iN}^J) di$ is the political welfare that accrues to government J if it chooses to stay with the status quo.

To find the solution to this problem, we can treat the α_is for the moment as if they could vary continuously between 0 and 1. Then the first-order conditions for maximizing (11) imply

$$\sum_{J = A,B} \frac{\beta^J}{G^J - \bar{G}^J} \left[\frac{(a^J W_{iF}^J + C_{i1}^J) - (a^J W_{iN}^J + C_{iE}^J)}{T_i} \right] \geq -\lambda$$

$$\text{when } \alpha_i = 0,$$

$$\sum_{J = A,B} \frac{\beta^J}{G^J - \bar{G}^J} \left[\frac{(a^J W_{iF}^J + C_{i1}^J) - (a^J W_{iN}^J + C_{iE}^J)}{T_i} \right] \leq -\lambda$$

$$\text{when } \alpha_i = 1,$$

and $\lambda \geq 0$, where $\bar{G}^J \equiv \int_{i \in E} (a^J W_{iN}^J + C_{iE}^J) di + \int_{i \in I} (a^J W_{iF}^J + C_{i1}^J) di$ is the equilibrium political welfare of government J in the Nash bargain, and λ is the Lagrange multiplier associated with the limited-exclusions constraint.

---

[18] In Grossman and Helpman (1994b) we used an alternating-offer bargaining model to establish two propositions. First, we showed that an FTA with exclusions can be an equilibrium outcome in an explicit bargaining model, even if the unique equilibrium when exclusions are prohibited entails a continuation of the status quo. Second, all exclusions may apply to the imports of a single country, if that country's government is the only one that would reject an all-inclusive FTA.

It follows that if industries are ordered according to the term on the left-hand side of the first two inequalities, then the Nash agreement excludes all sectors with indexes less than or equal to some critical cutoff value.

These conditions give the decision rule in terms of the industry-specific contribution offers. It would be more revealing to have an ordering that depends only on aggregates and on the supply and demand conditions in the various industries. To this end, we will establish the following result.

RESULT 6. Let the industries be ordered so that $\omega^A g_i^A + \omega^B g_i^B$ is increasing with i, where $\omega^J \equiv \beta^J / (G^J - \bar{G}^J)$ and $g_i^J \equiv (\Delta \Pi_i^J + a \Delta W_i^J) / T_i$. Then the FTA that solves the Nash bargaining problem excludes all industries $i \in [0, i^*]$, for some $i^* \geq 0$.

The proof relies on the fact that each small lobby takes G^J and $\bar{G}^J$ as constant in constructing its contribution offer. Each industry expects to be included in the FTA if its offer and that of the same industry in the other country are such that

$$\sum_{J = A,B} \omega^J \left[a^J (W_{iF}^J - W_{iN}^J) + C_{iI}^J - C_{iE}^J \right] / T_i < -\lambda$$

and to be excluded if the direction of inequality is reversed. There are several cases to consider.

First, consider an excluded industry ($j \in \mathcal{E}$), where the special interests in the importing country (say A, for concreteness) make a positive contribution to secure the exclusion ($C_{jE}^A > 0$). We know that these contributions must be lowered to the point where the negotiators are just marginally willing to exclude the sector, that is, where

$$\sum_{J = A,B} \omega^J \left[a^J (W_{jF}^J - W_{jN}^J) + C_{jI}^J - C_{iE}^J \right] / T_j = -\lambda$$

The industry's payment does not exceed its profit differential; $C_{jE}^A \leq \Pi_{jN}^A - \Pi_{jF}^A$. We know also that the export interest in country B, which would rather not see its product on the list of exclusions, must bid up to the full profit differential to avoid this outcome ($C_{jI}^B = \Pi_{jF}^B - \Pi_{jN}^B$). Otherwise, a slight increase in its offer will be profitable for this lobby. Combining these facts, we have $\omega^A g_j^A + \omega^B g_j^B \leq -\lambda$ for this excluded industry.

Next, consider an included industry ($k \in I$), where the special interests in the exporting country (again A, for concreteness) contribute positively to ensure that their product is not among those excluded ($C_{kI}^A > 0$). Again, the negotiators must be left indifferent between including this sector in the agreement and not. This time we must have $C_{kI}^A \leq \Pi_{kF}^A - \Pi_{kN}^A$ and (by a similar argument as before) $C_{kE}^B = \Pi_{kN}^B - \Pi_{kF}^B$. So now we find $\omega^A g_k^A + \omega^B g_k^B \geq -\lambda$ for this included industry.

Third, consider an excluded industry ℓ, where the import-competing interests in (say) A make no contribution; $C_{\ell E}^A = 0$. Since this is an import-competing industry, we must have $\Pi_{\ell N}^A - \Pi_{\ell F}^A \geq 0$. Also, we know that the export industry in B does not find it profitable to bid what it would take to ensure that its product is not among those excluded. That is, the bid $C_{\ell I}^B$ that would make

$$\omega^B C_{\ell I}^B + \sum_{J = A,B} \omega^J a^J (W_{\ell F}^J - W_{\ell N}^J) = -\lambda T_\ell$$

exceeds $\Pi_{\ell F}^B - \Pi_{\ell N}^B$. These facts again imply that $\omega^A g_\ell^A + \omega^B g_\ell^B \leq -\lambda$ for this excluded industry.

Finally, the argument for an included industry in which the export interests do not make any positive contribution is analogous to the previous one. So, in each case, if $\omega^A g_i^A + \omega^B g_i^B$ exceeds $-\lambda$, the industry is covered by the FTA, whereas if this magnitude falls short of $-\lambda$ the industry appears on the list of exclusions. Result 6 follows immediately.

The result reveals that the same factors that dictate the politically optimal set of exclusions in a single country also enter into the determination of the set of exclusions in a Nash bargain. In each country, a sector's political "clout" depends upon the effect that the FTA would have on the sum of profits and a times aggregate welfare, normalized for the sector's size (as measured by T_i). If this number (represented by g_i^J) is positive, it means that there is a potential political gain for country J from having the sector included in any free trade agreement. If it is negative, then it would be politically desirable to leave it out. In the unilateral stance, the government excludes only those sectors whose inclusion would be politically damaging and, among those, the ones that would generate the greatest political harm. In the Nash bargain, on the other hand, the politics in both countries must be taken into account.

The Nash solution takes a weighted sum of the political cost/benefit measures for the two countries. The same weights apply in comparing all of the different industries. They reflect the relative bargaining abilities of the two sets of negotiators (as captured in the Nash framework by the weighting parameters β^A and β^B) and the relative surpluses that the two governments attain under the FTA as compared with the status quo. As usual, a government that has a relatively stronger threat point (a high $\bar{G}^J$) finds its interests weighted more heavily in the final bargain. So, for example, the harm that an FTA might bring to some import-competing industries in country A will be given greater consideration, and the gains from improved market access for country B exporters will receive less consideration, the greater is $\bar{G}^A$ and the smaller $\bar{G}^B$. The $\bar{G}^J$'s in turn reflect the aggregate welfare that country J achieves in the status quo with no FTA and the contributions that the government would receive from its import-competing sector if it rejected the agreement entirely. If $\bar{G}^A$ is very large, for example, then ω^A will be large, and only import-competing industries in country A (which may have $g_i^A < 0$) will be candidates for exclusion from the agreement. The same would be true if β^A were large.

When the two governments' bargaining situations are relatively symmetric ($\omega^A \cong \omega^B$), then the agreement compares the political benefit to one country from having an exporting sector included with the possible cost to the other in terms of lost profits and forgone tariff revenue. If, for example, the sector would experience enhanced protection, the potential gains to the exporting industry may be large, while the import-competing industry would suffer no losses at all. Such a sector would probably not find its way onto the list of exclusions, unless the prospective welfare loss for the importing country due to the trade diversion were exceptionally large. By contrast, a sector that would experience reduced protection may well be considered for the exclusion list, especially if the prospective consumer surplus gains in the importing country are modest. Then the political benefit to the exporting country from including the sector would be small (because the export industry reaps no extra profits) while the fallout from losses that would befall the import-competing producers may be great. Finally, note that only industries with $\omega^A g_i^A + \omega^B g_i^B < 0$ are candidates for exclusions, and the constraint on the size of the exclusion set binds only if there is a sufficient mass (appropriately measured) of such sectors.

5 Conclusions

We have examined the conditions under which a free trade agreement might emerge as an equilibrium outcome of a negotiation between politically minded governments. The governments, we imagine, respond to political pressures from industry special interests but also pay some heed to the plight of the average voter.

If an FTA must completely liberalize trade among the partner countries, a particular government might endorse an agreement in two types of situations. The first arises when the FTA would generate substantial welfare gains for the average voter and adversely affected interest groups fail to coordinate their efforts to defeat the accord. The second arises when the agreement would create profit gains for actual or potential exporters in excess of the losses that would be suffered by import-competing industries, plus the political cost of any welfare harm that might be inflicted on the average voter.

A free trade agreement requires the assent of both governments. We have found that this outcome is most likely when there is relative balance in the potential trade between the partner countries and when the agreement affords enhanced protection rather than reduced protection to most sectors. With enhanced protection, an exporting industry captures the benefits of the high domestic prices in the partner country. With reduced protection, an import-competing industry sees its domestic price fall as a result of the duty-free imports from the partner. Whereas reduced protection may involve some trade creation, enhanced protection gives rise only to trade diversion. Thus, the conditions that enhance the viability of a potential agreement also raise the likelihood that the agreement would reduce aggregate social welfare.

If some industries can be excluded from an FTA, the prospects for an agreement improve. Each government would wish to exclude those sectors whose inclusion would impose on it the greatest political costs. Political costs reflect either the fierce opposition of the import-competing interests or the harm that would be suffered by the average voter in the face of inefficient trade diversion. By excluding some sensitive sectors, a government may be able to diffuse the opposition to an FTA.

In a bargaining situation, the equilibrium agreement reflects the political pressures felt by both negotiating governments. We examined the Nash bargaining solution and found that exclusions are granted to industries for which a weighted sum of the political benefit of market access in the exporting country and the (possible) political cost of more intense import competition in the importing country is most negative. Both the political benefit and the political cost are measured by a weighted sum of the change in industry profits and the change in average welfare in going from the status quo to bilateral free trade. The weights on benefits in one country and costs in the other reflect the negotiating abilities of the two governments (i.e., the "Nash weights") and the political welfare that would accrue to the two governments if they rejected the agreement entirely.

We conducted all of our analysis under the restrictive (but somewhat realistic) assumption that governments cannot offer direct, treasury-to-treasury, transfer payments as compensation for any political costs associated with an agreement. It would be a simple matter to redo our analysis for the case in which such transfers are feasible. The more interesting and difficult question in the political economy of international relations concerns the reasons why compensation payments have played such a limited role in most trade negotiations.

APPENDIX

Contributions to Foreign Governments

In the main text we maintained the assumption that an interest group can offer contributions only to its own, native government. Now we relax this assumption and allow lobbies in each country to seek influence over the other's policy. We examine the conditions under which an FTA without exclusions can emerge as an equilibrium outcome, and we compare the scope for such agreements with the case when politicians are prohibited from accepting gifts from abroad.

An FTA can emerge as an equilibrium outcome in one of three different ways. First, both governments may support the agreement as an unpressured stance. Second, both may support it as a pressured stance. Third, one government may favor the FTA as an unpressured position while the other is being pressured into such support. We discuss each of these possibilities in turn.

An FTA can result without pressure in either country if and only if

$$a^J(W_F^J - W_N^J) \geq \max[0, \max_i(\Pi_{iN}^A - \Pi_{iF}^A), \max_i(\Pi_{iN}^B - \Pi_{iF}^B)]$$

$$\text{for } J = A \text{ and } J = B. \qquad (A1)$$

In words, the FTA must offer aggregate welfare gains to both electorates; there can be no single import-competing industry in either country that stands to lose so much under the agreement that it could profitably block the accord with contributions to one government *or the other*. Clearly, this condition is more restrictive than the analogous one in the situation without cross-country contributions [compare (2)]. Without foreign contributions, we required only that it be unprofitable for any lobby to turn its own government against the accord. Now an import-competing industry may succeed politically by offering a big enough gift to the foreign politicians, even if it is unwilling to pay what it would take to win over its own government.

If an FTA emerges as a pressured stance in both countries, then both governments will be left indifferent to the pact. Also, each lobby that will lose under the agreement offers contributions to each government that exhaust its potential to benefit by preserving the status quo. This is because each such lobby could block the pact by swaying either one of the two governments, and no such lobby needs to ante up its offer when both governments actually endorse $R = F$. Finally, no lobby that will benefit from the agreement pays the two governments combined more than what it stands to gain under the FTA. Combining the three equalities and the inequality, we find that an equilibrium outcome with pressured stances in both countries in support of the regime F requires

$$a^A W_F^A + a^B W_F^B + \sum_{i,J} \Pi_{iF}^J \geq a^A W_N^A + a^B W_N^B$$

$$+ \sum_{i,J} \Pi_{iN}^J + \sum_{i \in S_N, J} (\Pi_{iN}^J - \Pi_{iF}^J). \qquad (A2)$$

There are offsetting considerations at play when comparing this condition to the analogous one that applied before. On the one hand, the export interests in each country can enter into the political battle abroad and possibly help their allies to overcome resistance to the agreement that the latter could not defeat alone. The force of this can be seen by noting that, even if (3) does not hold separately for both J = A and J = B, the left-hand side of (A2) may nonetheless exceed the sum of the first three terms on the right-hand side. On the other hand, the import-competing interests in each country have the opportunity to voice their opposition in both. Thus, even if (3) does hold for both J = A and J = B, condition (A2) may fail due to the presence of the fourth term on the right. In short, an ambiguity arises in comparing the alternative political situations: The presence of foreign contributions may make an FTA politically viable that would not otherwise be so, but it also may negate the viability of an agreement that could emerge as a political equilibrium without foreign influences.

The final outcome to consider is one where government J supports the agreement as an unpressured stance, while government K supports the agreement as a result of political pressure. In country J, a condition like (A1) must be satisfied: The FTA must improve national welfare there; and no single lobby representing an import-competing industry in either country should be able to reverse the government's unpressured stance. Again, this condition is somewhat more stringent than the corresponding one that applied without foreign contributions. In country K, the government is left indifferent, the import-competing interests in both countries offer their full profit differential in an effort to block the pact, while the export interests offer at most what they stand to gain. These requirements imply

$$a^K W_F^K + \sum_{i,J} \Pi_{iF}^J \geq a^K W_N^K + \sum_{i,J} \Pi_{iN}^J, \qquad (A3)$$

which may be more or less stringent than the corresponding condition in the absence of foreign contributions. Suppose, for example, that government A would support the agreement in an unpressured stance, and consider the outcome of the political contest in country B. Allowing foreign contributions enhances the prospect for a pressured stance with R^B = F if $\sum_i \Pi_{iF}^A \geq \sum_i \Pi_{iN}^A$ and reduces it otherwise. The cross-border contributions bring foreign interests into play in country B's political battle, which strengthens one side or the other depending upon which interests in country A have more at stake in the decision.

References

Bernheim, B. Douglas, Peleg, Bezalel, and Whinston, Michael D. (1987). Coalition-proof Nash equilibria I: Concepts. *Journal of Economic Theory* 42(1) (June): 1–12.

Bernheim, B. Douglas, and Whinston, Michael D. (1986). Menu auctions, resource allocation, and economic influence. *Quarterly Journal of Economics* 101(1) (February): 1–31.

Cowhey, Peter (1990). "States" and "politics" in American foreign economic policy. In J. S. Odell and T. D. Willett (eds.). *International Trade Policies: Gains from Exchange Between Economics and Political Science* (Ann Arbor: University of Michigan Press), 225–251.

Grossman, Gene M., and Helpman, Elhanan (1994a). Protection for sale. *American Economic Review* 84(4) (September): 833–850.

———. (1994b). The politics of free trade agreements. Discussion Paper in Economics No. 166, Woodrow Wilson School of Public and International Affairs, Princeton University.

———. (1995). Trade wars and trade talks. *Journal of Political Economy* 103(4) (August): 675–708.

Hirschman, Albert O. (1981). *Essays in Trespassing: Economics to Politics and Beyond* (Cambridge: Cambridge University Press).

Krueger, Anne O. (1993). Free trade agreements as protectionist devices: Rules of origin. Working Paper No. 4352, National Bureau of Economic Research.

McMillan, John (1993). Does regional integration foster open trade? Economic theory and GATT's article XXIV. In K. Anderson and R. Blackhurst (eds.). *Regional Integration and the Global Trading System* (London: Harvester Wheatsheaf), 292–310.

Olson, Mancur (1965). *The Logic of Collective Action* (Cambridge, Mass.: Harvard University Press).

Putnam, Robert (1988). Diplomacy and domestic politics: The logic of two level games. *International Organization* 43(3) (summer): 427–460.

Richardson, Martin (1992). Some implications of internal trade in a free trade area. Working Paper No. 92-01, Georgetown University.

———. (1993). Endogenous protection and trade diversion. *Journal of International Economics* 34(3-4) (May): 309–324.

Wonnacott, Paul, and Wonnacott, Ronald (1981). Is unilateral tariff reduction preferable to a customs union? The curious case of the missing foreign tariffs. *American Economic Review* 71(3) (June): 704–714.

Eight

Foreign Investment with Endogenous Protection

1 Introduction

Jagdish Bhagwati coined the phrase "quid pro quo foreign investment" to describe investments undertaken in anticipation of trade policy and perhaps with the intention of defusing a protectionist threat. In a series of papers beginning with Bhagwati (1987), he and several colleagues and

By Gene M. Grossman and Elhanan Helpman. Originally published in *The Political Economy of Trade Policy*, Robert C. Feenstra, Gene M. Grossman, and Douglas A. Irwin, eds., 199–223. Copyright © 1996 by The MIT Press. Reprinted with permission. We thank Rob Feenstra and Kar-yiu Wong for valuable comments and the National Science Foundation and the U.S.-Israel Binational Science Foundation for financial support. Grossman also thanks the John S. Guggenheim Memorial Foundation, the Sumitomo Bank Fund, the Daiwa Bank Fund, and the Center of International Studies at Princeton University. Part of this work was carried out when the authors were visiting Innocenzo Gasparini Institute for Economic Research (IGIER) in Milan and when Grossman was at Laboratoire d'Economie Quantitative Aix Marsailles (LEQAM) in Aix-en-Provence. Needless to say, these were very hospitable environments.

former students explored the role that such direct foreign investment (DFI) might play in shaping tariffs, quotas, voluntary export restraints, and more.[1] These authors typically assumed that the probability of future protection depends on both the extent of import penetration and the stock of DFI, and they viewed DFI as a transfer of capital from one country to another. In this context, firms move their capital and restrict their exports so as to maximize the expected present value of their profits, taking into account the effects of their investment decisions on subsequent policy formation. The foreign government usually was assumed to coordinate investment decisions, although occasionally it has been supposed that foreign oligopolists independently exploit the intertemporal ramifications of their actions (e.g., Dinopoulos [1989]). This literature—motivated in large part by the behavior of Japanese firms in the early and mid-1980s—has produced many interesting insights and has enriched our understanding of the link between foreign investment and the formation of trade policies.

Our aim in this paper is to extend Bhagwati's concept of anticipatory investment to situations where (1) DFI is best seen as the opening of a subsidiary by a multinational corporation and (2) trade policy represents an optimal response by politicians to the pressures applied by special interest groups. We follow Markusen (1984) and Helpman (1984) in modeling multinational investment as the *costly* establishment of a branch plant by a firm that has the exclusive right or the exclusive ability to manufacture a particular product. The foreign owners of such an intangible asset face a choice between bearing the cost of opening a new subsidiary and producing in an existing parent facility. In making this choice, they recognize that their attempts to export may be impeded by subsequent home-country trade barriers. We combine this view of DFI with the approach to policy formation that we developed in Grossman and Helpman (1994a). We suppose that an incumbent government receives offers of campaign contributions that are (at least implicitly) tied to its ultimate policy actions. In setting policy, the government trades off the extra contributions that may be associated with protectionist interventions and the loss of voter goodwill that may be a consequence thereof. At first we assume that there is only one organized interest group attempting to influence policy, namely a lobby representing domestic firms in the industry with DFI. Later we allow for contributions by a lobby that represents domestic workers with skills specific to the industry.

Prospective multinationals anticipate the mechanism by which policy will be set when they make their foreign investment decisions. We treat

[1] See, for example, Bhagwati et al. (1987), Dinopoulos (1989, 1992), Wong (1989), and Bhagwati et al. (1992).

DFI as a decentralized process wherein each foreign company takes the investment decisions of the others as beyond its control. Given the extent of DFI by other companies, each firm forms an expectation about the host country's eventual trade policy and evaluates the profitability of its own potential foreign investment accordingly. A firm establishes a subsidiary if by doing so it can earn greater profits net of investment costs than it can by exporting from its parent facility. It recognizes that the cost of opening a foreign subsidiary cannot be recovered once the investment has been made. Finally, an equilibrium entails a level of DFI and a rate of protection such that the political process supports the particular rate of protection as an outcome in the stage game and the expectations about protection that foreign firms hold when they make their investment decisions are fulfilled.[2]

We develop the basic model in Section 2. This is followed in Section 3 by an analysis of the determinants of equilibrium tariffs and levels of DFI. We show that, if the cost of opening a subsidiary is small and politicians happen to place great weight on the welfare of the average voter, then two stable equilibria may coexist. In one of these equilibria no multinational investments are made, while in the other all foreign firms establish offshore production facilities. For all other parameter configurations there exists a unique stable equilibrium. In this equilibrium typically some foreign firms choose to build plants in the home country. In the event, an increase in the fixed cost of foreign investment reduces the number of multinationals while a decrease in the home government's concern for the plight of the average voter expands the multinational presence. We find also that when the politicians' concern for the average voter is great and the cost of DFI is low, an increase in the weight attached to average welfare results in a higher rate of protection.

In Section 4 we examine whether direct foreign investment serves the interests of the average voter in the home country. This issue is particularly interesting when manufacturing costs in the home country happen to be higher than those abroad. Then the entry of foreign multinationals diverts production from the lower-cost location to the higher-cost location, and this would reduce home welfare if trade policy were fixed. But here the presence of multinationals also changes the political environment, so that special interests find it more difficult to lobby for

---

[2] Horstmann and Markusen (1992) have studied how protection affects the equilibrium level of DFI under the assumption that home-country trade policy is exogenously given. Hillman and Ursprung (1993) examined how the extent of multinational investment influences the determination of trade policy, given the numbers of national and multinational firms. Our analysis is distinguished by the fact that we treat both multinational investment and trade policy as endogenously (and jointly) determined.

protection. When the political response is factored in, DFI may in fact benefit the average voter.

In Section 5 we extend the model to account for the interests of workers with skills specific to the sector with DFI. We show that the interests of these workers are closely aligned with the interests of the domestic manufacturers on the issue of trade protection. Given the level of DFI, both wage earners and profit recipients gain from an increase in the tariff. However, on the issue of policy toward foreign multinationals, the two interest groups are bound to conflict. Domestic manufacturers stand to gain from restrictions on DFI, whereas the workers with specific human capital are harmed by such impediments. If elected officials can regulate entry by multinationals, the extent of DFI in equilibrium depends on the relative political strengths of the two competing interest groups. We examine the determinants of "political strength" in this context.

2 Basic Model

The home country produces a numeraire good with unskilled labor alone. One unit of labor is required per unit of output. Thus the equilibrium wage equals 1. The home country also manufactures various brands of a differentiated product. Each brand requires a fixed amount of unskilled labor per unit of output. For the time being, we assume that no other inputs are needed. The number and types of the domestic products are treated as given throughout.

The domestic manufacturers of differentiated products compete with a fixed set of foreign brands. Each foreign supplier faces a choice. It can assemble its product in an already-existing plant in its native country or it can build (or purchase) a new production facility in the home country. The choice between exporting and foreign investment is made based on a comparison of expected profits, where profits from a potential subsidiary are calculated net of the fixed costs of acquiring the facility. These costs, which must be borne before the home country finally sets its trade policy, cannot be recouped in the event that the plant is not used. Thus each foreign company must form some expectations about the likely outcome of the home country's political process.[3] We focus on equilibria with self-fulfilling expectations.

After the foreign investment takes place, the home government sets a tariff on imported varieties of the differentiated product. The height of

---

[3] We choose this order of play in order to emphasize that investments in plant and equipment are often irreversible, whereas policy can be changed by the government at will. In these circumstances foreign firms must realize that long-run trade policy will reflect political conditions prevailing after all decisions regarding DFI are made.

the tariff reflects the conflicting political pressures it faces. On the one hand, the government is concerned with the welfare of the average voter, because its prospects for reelection depend on the standard of living it provides. On the other hand, it values the campaign contributions that it collects from special interest groups. We assume that the domestic lobbies—which, to begin with, constitute only a single group representing the domestic manufacturers of brands of the differentiated product— offer donations that are contingent on the tariff imposed by the government. Presumably a higher tariff will elicit a larger contribution from the domestic industry, although the interest group is free to design its contribution schedule in any way it chooses. Faced with the contribution schedule, the government sets the policy that maximizes its own political objective function. We take the latter to be a simple weighted sum of total campaign gifts and average welfare.[4] All of this is well understood by the foreign companies at the time that they make their entry decisions.

We now describe the domestic economy in more detail.

2.1 Consumption and Production

The home country is populated by a continuum of individuals with measure 1. The utility function of each individual is given by

$$U = x_0 + \frac{\theta}{\theta - 1} x^{(\theta-1)/\theta}, \qquad \theta > 1, \tag{1}$$

where x_0 represents consumption of the numeraire good and x is an index of consumption of the differentiated products. The consumption index takes the form

$$x = \left[\int_{j \in N_h} x(j)^{(\varepsilon-1)/\varepsilon} \, dj + \int_{j \in N_f} x(j)^{(\varepsilon-1)/\varepsilon} \, dj \right]^{\varepsilon/(\varepsilon-1)}, \qquad \varepsilon > 1,$$

where $x(j)$ denotes consumption of brand j, and N_h and N_f are the sets of brands manufactured by home and foreign firms, respectively (the latter either in a native plant or in a subsidiary located in the home country).

As is well known, this structure of preferences yields constant-elasticity demand functions for each brand, with ε being the elasticity of demand. In fact, given the two-tier structure of preferences, the demand for any brand j can be represented by

$$x(j) = p(j)^{-\varepsilon} q^{\varepsilon-\theta},$$

[4] This political objective function can be derived as a reduced form of a game in which the incumbent government competes in an election with an opposition party. See Grossman and Helpman (1994b).

where $p(j)$ is the price of brand j and q is a price index for all differentiated products. We assume that $\varepsilon > \theta$, which implies that the different brands substitute more closely for one another than they do for the numeraire good. This assumption ensures a positive cross-elasticity of demand.[5]

Each manufacturer of a brand of the differentiated product maximizes profits by equating marginal revenue to marginal cost. In doing so, the firm treats the price index q as beyond its control. A foreign firm manufacturing in its native facility faces the constant marginal cost c_f. In the home country, c_h units of labor are needed to produce a unit of any brand of the differentiated product. This means that the marginal cost for home firms and foreign subsidiaries is also c_h, since the wage rate equals 1. The mark-up pricing rule then implies

$$p(j) = \begin{cases} p_h \equiv \dfrac{\varepsilon}{\varepsilon - 1} c_h & \text{for } j \text{ manufactured in the home country,} \\[2ex] p_f \equiv \dfrac{\varepsilon}{\varepsilon - 1} c_f \tau & \text{for } j \text{ manufactured in the foreign country,} \end{cases} \tag{2}$$

where p_i, $i = h, f$, denotes the consumer price of a variety manufactured in country i and τ represents one plus the *ad valorem* tariff rate. We denote by n_h the number of brands owned by home-country firms (the measure of the set N_h) and by n_f the number of brands owned by foreign firms (the measure of the set N_f). In addition we let m denote the number of brands controlled by foreign firms that have established production facilities in the home country. Then the price index for x can be written as

$$q = [(n_h + m) p_h^{1-\varepsilon} + (n_f - m) p_f^{1-\varepsilon}]^{1/(1-\varepsilon)}, \tag{3}$$

assuming that all foreign firms with subsidiaries in the home country actually use these facilities to produce their output.[6] Finally we calculate output levels and operating profits (i.e., revenue minus manufacturing costs) for firms producing in each location, which gives

$$x_i = p_i^{-\varepsilon} q^{\varepsilon - \theta} \qquad \text{for } i = h, f, \tag{4}$$

---

[5] An increase in the price of competing brands always causes substitution from these brands to variety j. At the same time it raises the price index q, which causes consumers to substitute the numeraire good for the entire group of differentiated products. When $\varepsilon > \theta$, the former effect dominates and the demand for good j increases.

[6] If this is not the case, then m in (3) should be replaced by the number of multinationals that supply the home market with output produced in their subsidiaries. Of course, in an equilibrium with fulfilled expectations, all firms that make costly investments in foreign plants will use these plants for production.

$$\pi_i = \frac{1}{\varepsilon \tau_i} \, p_i^{1-\varepsilon} q^{\varepsilon-\theta} \qquad \text{for } i = h, f. \tag{5}$$

Here π_i represents the operating profits derived from a single brand, and we use the notational convention that $\tau_h = 1$ and $\tau_f = \tau$.

For the time being we assume that the tariff is the only policy instrument available to the government. The government redistributes any tariff proceeds to the voters on an equal, per capita basis. We can now use (1) to express the average (gross) welfare of a citizen in the home country as a function of the tariff rate and the number of products supplied by subsidiaries of multinational corporations. We have

$$W(\tau;m) = L + n_h \pi_h + \frac{\tau - 1}{\tau} (n_f - m) p_f x_f + \frac{1}{\theta - 1} q^{-(\theta-1)}, \tag{6}$$

where L is average labor income in view of an assumed inelastic supply and the fact that the wage rate is equal to 1. The remaining terms on the right-hand side represent average profit income, the average tariff rebate, and the average surplus derived from the consumption of differentiated products, respectively. The complete functional dependence of W on τ and m is obtained by substituting equations (2)–(5) into (6).

2.2 The Special Interest Group and the Government

The government chooses the rate of protection τ to maximize its political objective function, which we take to be a linear combination of political contributions and the average welfare of voters. In selecting a trade policy, the government faces a contribution schedule $C(\tau) \geq 0$ that has been proposed by the domestic lobby group. We write the governments' objective function as

$$G = C(\tau) + aW(\tau;m), \tag{7}$$

where $a > 0$ is the weight that the government attaches to (gross) voter welfare relative to political contributions.

The lobby represents all of the home-country manufacturers of differentiated products. Somehow they overcome Mancur Olson's "collective-action" problem (see Olson [1965]) and coordinate their efforts to influence policy. Multinational corporations with subsidiaries in the home country do not participate in lobbying for protection. We assume for simplicity that the set of voters who own shares in companies that produce brands of the differentiated product is of measure zero. In the event, owners of home firms instruct their lobby to design a contribution schedule that maximizes their joint profits net of campaign contributions. In short, we take the lobby's objective to be the maximization of $n_h\pi_h - C$.[7]

The lobby's leaders know that once a contribution schedule has been proposed to the politicians, the latter will set policy to maximize (7). Moreover, they know that they cannot drive the politicians' welfare below the level that the latter could attain by declining all contribution offers. The government's reservation welfare level is given by $aW^*(m)$, where

$$W^*(m) = \max_\tau W(\tau;m). \tag{8}$$

The curve G^*G^* in Figure 1 depicts the combinations of contributions and tariff levels that yield the government a value of G equal to $aW^*(m)$. Curves above G^*G^* represent government indifference curves with higher welfare levels. If the lobby designs a contribution schedule that is located everywhere below G^*G^*, the government will choose τ^*, which secures its reservation welfare. In view of this, the best the lobby can do is to induce the government to choose point A, where the lobby's own indifference curve L^*L^* is tangent to the government's indifference curve. Clearly there are many contribution schedules that will generate this outcome; one example is a contribution schedule that coincides with the horizontal axis to the left of the lowermost point of L^*L^* and coincides with L^*L^* to the right of that point.

Our argument suggests that the lobby implicitly solves the problem

$$\max_{\tau,C} n_h\pi_h - C$$

$$s.t.\ C + aW(\tau;m) \geq aW^*(m) \text{ and } C \geq 0.$$

Thus the political equilibrium is characterized by a tariff that maximizes the joint welfare of the lobby and the government (i.e., $\tau^p = \text{argmax}_\tau[n_h\pi_h + aW\{\tau;m\}]$)and a level of contributions that satisfies the participation constraint with equality (i.e., $C^p = a[W^*\{m\} - W\{\tau^p;m\}]$).

Using (6), we can express the equilibrium tariff as

$$\tau^p = \text{argmax}\left[(1 + a)n_h\pi_h + a\frac{\tau - 1}{\tau}(n_f - m)p_f x_f + a\frac{1}{\theta - 1}q^{-(\theta-1)}\right]. \tag{9}$$

When written in this way, we see that the political tariff maximizes a weighted sum of profits, tariff revenue, and consumer surplus. Whereas

[7] If the set of shareholders were nonnegligible in the voting population, then the lobby's members would receive a nonnegligible share of any redistributed tariff revenue and would enjoy a nonnegligible share of aggregate consumer surplus. In the event they would share in any deadweight loss caused by the tariff policy. In Grossman and Helpman (1994a) we show how these considerations (slightly) affect the formula for the equilibrium tariff.

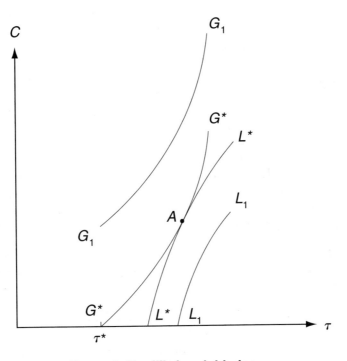

Figure 1. Equilibrium lobbying

these components would receive equal weight from a benevolent social planner, the political process gives greater weight to the profits, which accrue to an organized interest group, and relatively less to the tariff revenue and consumer surplus, which go to the general public. Next we can use the first-order condition for (9) together with (2)–(5), to derive an implicit formula for the equilibrium tariff, namely

$$\frac{\tau^p - 1}{\tau^p} = \frac{1 + a}{a\varepsilon} \frac{(\varepsilon - \theta) n_h}{\varepsilon (n_h + m) + \theta (n_f - m) (\tau^p c_f / c_h)^{1-\varepsilon}}. \tag{10}$$

This formula applies provided that $m < n_f$ and so long as the equation has a solution with $\tau^p > (c_h / c_f)^{(\varepsilon-1)/\varepsilon}$. The latter condition ensures that foreign multinationals who have invested in subsidiaries will use these facilities to serve the home market. Otherwise, the multinationals leave their subsidiaries idle and the home government sets the tariff $\tau^p = (c_h / c_f)^{(\varepsilon-1)/\varepsilon}$. Finally, when all foreign companies establish subsidiaries in the home country (i.e., $m = n_f$) any tariff level $\tau^p \geq (c_h / c_f)^{(\varepsilon-1)/\varepsilon}$ solves the maximization problem, because variations in the tariff rate have no real effects as long as the tariff is high enough to induce the multinationals to make use of their offshore production facilities.[8]

2.3 Multinationals

We turn now to the first stage of the game, when each foreign firm must decide whether to establish a foreign subsidiary. We will assume that the entry process is decentralized; that is, each firm makes its own decision, taking those of all of the other companies as given. Given its beliefs about aggregate DFI, each firm forms expectations about the tariff rate using (9).[9] Then it calculates the difference between expected profits from operating a subsidiary and expected profits from exporting. Finally, it compares this difference with the fixed cost, ϕ, of establishing an offshore facility.

Using (2)–(5), we can calculate the difference in operating profits as a function of the tariff level and the number of subsidiaries. The result is

$$\pi_h - \pi_f \equiv \delta(\tau;m) = \frac{B(c_h^{1-\varepsilon} - \tau^{-\varepsilon}c_f^{1-\varepsilon})}{[(n_h + m)c_h^{1-\varepsilon} + (n_f - m)(\tau c_f)^{1-\varepsilon}]^{(\varepsilon-\theta)/(\varepsilon-1)}}, \quad (11)$$

where $B = \varepsilon^{-\theta}(\varepsilon - 1)^{\theta-1} > 0$. A foreign company expecting the tariff rate to be τ, and observing a measure m of foreign firms establishing sub-sidiaries in the home country, will itself invest if $\delta(\tau;m) > \phi$. If $\delta(\tau;m) < \phi$, the company will certainly not open a branch plant, while if the two are equal, it is indifferent between the two options.

An alternative to our specification would allow coordinated entry by foreign multinationals. This would be appropriate if foreign companies could collude in making their investment decisions or if the foreign gov-ernment were inclined to regulate DFI. In either of these cases, m would be chosen to maximize $(\delta - \phi)m + n_f\pi_f$, recognizing the dependence of the endogenous tariff rate on the choice of m—via (9). This alterna-tive setup would be closer in spirit to the formulation suggested by Bhag-wati (1987) and explicitly analyzed in Bhagwati et al. (1987). We will not pursue it any further here.

---

[8] Our discussion in the text ignores one last possibility. It may happen that, given m, a choice of $\tau^p < (c_h/c_f)^{(\varepsilon-1)/\varepsilon}$, which is low enough to make the multinationals export to the home market, provides higher joint welfare to the lobby and the government than any policy with $\tau^p > (c_h/c_f)^{(\varepsilon-1)/\varepsilon}$. This case cannot arise in equilibrium, however, because foreign firms would not bear the positive cost of DFI if they expected such a low tariff.

[9] With a continuum of firms, the aggregate amount of DFI is independent of the decision of any one firm.

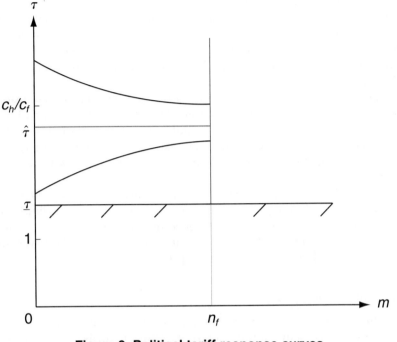

Figure 2. Political tariff response curves

3 DFI and Protection

We seek to characterize perfect-foresight equilibria. In what follows we assume that manufacturing costs are higher in the home country; that is, $c_h > c_f$.

3.1 Tariff Response Curves

Figure 2 depicts two *tariff response curves*, each describing the political tariff as a function of m for a particular set of parameter values. These curves are derived from (9).[10] It is easy to verify that all curves above the horizontal line at $\hat{\tau} = (c_h/c_f)(\theta/\varepsilon)^{1/(\varepsilon-1)}$ slope downward and that all curves below this line but above the horizontal line at $\underline{\tau} = (c_h/c_f)^{(\varepsilon-1)/\varepsilon}$

---

[10] Equation (10) does not always provide a unique solution for τ^p as a function of m. Two solutions exist, for example, when $m = 0$, $a = 0.217$, $\varepsilon = 2$, $\theta = 1.1$, $c_h = 5$, $c_f = 1$, $n_h = 1$, and $n_f = 1$. In this case neither one of them solves (9); the solution to (9) instead is an infinite tariff. Equation (10) can be inverted, however, to express m as a function of τ^p.

slope upward.[11] Tariff response curves below $\underline{\tau}$ are horizontal because, with such low tariffs, any multinational that happened to own a subsidiary in the home country would not use its local plant to supply the home market in any case. We restrict our attention to parameters that give a political tariff at least as high as $\underline{\tau}$. Notice that the figure is drawn under the assumption that $\hat{\tau} > \underline{\tau}$, but this need not be the case. If $\hat{\tau} < \underline{\tau}$, then all tariff response curves slope downward. Finally, recall the discussion following equation (10), where we argued that in the limiting case where $m = n_f$ (i.e., when all foreign companies establish subsidiaries in the home country), the political tariff can take any value at least as large as $\underline{\tau}$ because all of these tariffs solve (9) and all result in the same allocation of resources.

We note for later reference that, when the parameter a rises, the tariff response curve shifts down. In other words, were the political climate to change in such a way as to make the government place relatively greater weight on per capita welfare, the equilibrium tariff would be lower for every (given) degree of multinational presence.

3.2 Profit Differential Curves

We show in Figure 3 five *profit differential curves*, each one representing a given difference between the operating profits of a firm manufacturing in the home country and one manufacturing in the foreign country, as described by (11). A higher curve corresponds to a greater profit differential. When one plus the tariff rate equals the cost ratio c_h/c_f, the profit differential does not depend on the number of multinational firms m (i.e., the curve is a horizontal line). For higher tariffs than this, the curves slope upward, whereas for lower rates they slope downward. A very large differential that might arise when $m = 0$ may not be possible even with an infinite tariff for some positive values of m. This is reflected in our depiction of the uppermost curve in the figure.

3.3 Entry

Each foreign company compares the profit differential with the fixed cost ϕ, after forming some expectation about the eventual tariff. Let $\tau^e(m)$ describe (one plus) the tariff rate that a foreign firm expects when the number of multinationals equals m. Then there are three possible equilibrium configurations:

---

[11] We should emphasize the ambiguity in the slope of the tariff response function. Most of the literature that follows Bhagwati assumes a priori that an increase in the number of multinationals reduces the expected rate of protection.

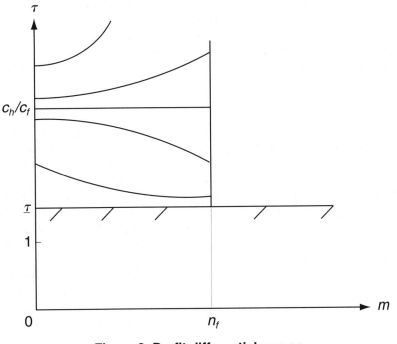

Figure 3. Profit differential curves

(i) $m = 0$ and $\delta[\tau^e(0), 0] \leq \phi$;
(ii) $0 < m < n_f$ and $\delta[\tau^e(m), m] = \phi$;
(iii) $m = n_f$ and $\delta[\tau^e(n_f), n_f] \geq \phi$.

In the first case, no DFI occurs and no firm finds it profitable to enter on its own. In the second case, some multinationals form and net profits for firms that establish subsidiaries are the same as for ones that do not. In the third case, all foreign firms form subsidiaries and net profits are at least as high as the profits that a single firm would attain if it refrained from investing in the home country.

As we will see in a moment, occasionally more than one of these types of equilibria can exist for given parameter values. When this happens we will select among them on the basis of a stability criterion. We adopt the following (ad hoc, but intuitive) adjustment process:

$$\dot{m} = M(\delta[\tau^e(m), m] - \phi) \quad \text{for } 0 < m < n_f, \tag{12}$$

where $M(0) = 0$ and $M(\cdot)$ is everywhere an increasing function. This process presumes that whenever the existing number of subsidiaries is such that it would be profitable for a single firm to invest, the number of subsidiaries rises, and that whenever it would be profitable for a single firm to refrain from investing, the number of subsidiaries falls. Of course this "adjustment" does not take place in real time; recall that the fixed costs of purchasing a subsidiary are assumed to be sunk, once incurred.

3.4 Equilibrium DFI and Protection

We now combine these elements in order to characterize the stable, perfect-foresight equilibria. Figure 4 depicts a case with a high fixed cost of entry ϕ and a low value of a. The latter means that the government is primarily concerned with amassing campaign contributions. As a consequence of these parameter restrictions, the tariff response curve and the profit differential curve corresponding to a value of ϕ both lie everywhere above the cost ratio c_h/c_f for all relevant values of m. This means that the tariff response curve TT slopes downward while the relevant profit differential curve $\Pi\Pi$ slopes upward.

The point A in the figure represents a perfect-foresight equilibrium. So do all points on the vertical line above point B. In the former case, penetration of foreign multinationals is partial, and a firm that invests in the home country enjoys the same net profit as one that serves the home

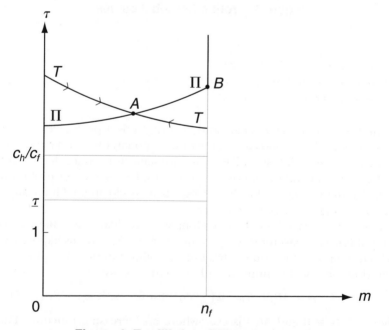

Figure 4. Equilibrium DFI and protection

market with exports. In the latter case(s), all foreign firms establish subsidiaries, and the ensuing political tariff causes none of them to regret its decision. Note, however, that these latter equilibria are all unstable. If, for example, the number of multinationals were slightly less than n_f, then the expected tariff would be on the tariff response curve below B, causing a reduction in the number of multinationals, an increase in the expected tariff, and so on, until the economy converged (following the arrows) to the equilibrium at point A.

To clarify the source of the instability, it may help to think as follows. Each foreign firm knows that if all others establish subsidiaries, the home government will be indifferent among all tariffs above $\underline{\tau}$. In consequence the government would indeed be willing to choose a tariff above the one at point B, which would sustain an equilibrium there. But the firm also knows that if a single other foreign firm were to refrain from investing in the home country, the political tariff would be well below that at point B. If this were to happen, the firm would very much regret any decision to invest. So it might decide not to take the risk. If all firms think in this way, they will all be led to expect the tariff at A and to make their investment decisions accordingly.

We now can examine the effects of varying the underlying parameters slightly. We focus on the cost of entry and the degree to which the government cares about the average voter. First consider the parameter a. The less weight the government attaches to per capita welfare (lower a), the higher is the tariff response curve and the higher is point A on the profit differential curve. The result is a higher rate of protection and a greater presence of foreign multinationals. Now consider the cost of entry. When ϕ is lower, so too is the relevant profit differential curve and the location of point A along the tariff response curve. It follows that DFI is greater and protection lower the lower the costs of foreign entry.

Figure 5 depicts another possible situation, which can arise when the government cares significantly about welfare, entry costs are low, and $\hat{\tau} < \underline{\tau}$.[12] In this case, point A again represents the unique, stable equilibrium (as before, the arrows indicate the adjustment path). Here again lower entry costs imply a greater number of foreign subsidiaries and a lower rate of protection. But, unlike in the previous case, now if the government were to concern itself more with contributions and less with per capita welfare, the tariff rate would *fall*.

A comparison of the two cases depicted in Figures 4 and 5 shows that there is no clear-cut relationship between a government's willingness to cater to special interests and the degree of protection that ultimately obtains. The reason is that foreign firms make their investment decisions

---

[12] This requires that $c_h/c_f < (\varepsilon/\theta)^{\varepsilon/(\varepsilon-1)}$.

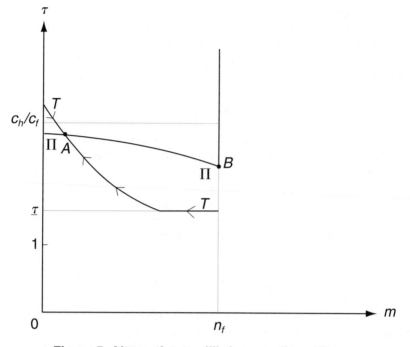

Figure 5. Alternative equilibrium configurations

in anticipation of policy formation and their decisions can alter the political climate in which the tariffs are eventually determined. In both cases the direct effect of a decrease in a (given m) is to generate an incipient increase in the expected tariff; in both cases this induces more foreign firms to enter; and in both cases recognition of this entry causes expectations of the tariff increase to moderate. In the case depicted by Figure 4, the entry of multinationals does not cause the tariff to fall below its initial level. But in the case depicted in Figure 5, the assumed adjustment process indeed causes this to happen.

Figure 6 depicts still another possibility. This situation can arise when the politicians place a great weight on voter welfare and when fixed costs of forming a subsidiary are low. It also requires $\hat{\tau} > \underline{\tau}$. Here there are two stable perfect-foresight equilibria, at points A and C (whereas the equilibrium at point B is unstable). If all foreign firms were to refrain from investing, as at point A, the political tariff would be reasonably low. Then the firms that had expected this low tariff would be happy that they had chosen to export from their home plants. On the other hand, if all foreign firms were to form subsidiaries, as at point C, then the political

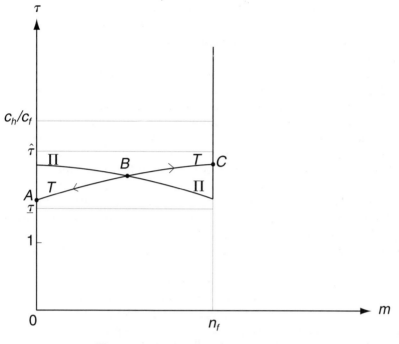

Figure 6. Multiple stable equilibria

tariff would be high, and the firms would be glad to have their production facilities inside the protected market.

The comparative statics are simple in this case. Neither a small change in the government's utility weights nor a small change in the fixed cost of entry has any effect on the existence of the two extreme equilibria. If a were dramatically lower, however, the TT curve would lie everywhere above the $\Pi\Pi$ curve, and then the unique equilibrium for firms expecting very high tariffs (at all m) has entry by all. Similarly, if ϕ were dramatically lower, the $\Pi\Pi$ curve would lie below TT, and again all would enter. Finally, if either a or ϕ were much higher than the values depicted by the figure, the unique equilibrium would have low tariffs or prohibitive entry costs, and no multinationals in either case.

4 Does DFI Benefit the Average Voter?

Our analysis has focused on the joint determination of direct foreign investment and the rate of protection when domestic companies lobby for protection. The resulting equilibrium has of course implications for the well-being of the general electorate. There are many welfare questions that one could address with our model. In this section we concentrate on one that may be particularly interesting. Namely, we examine whether foreign investment serves the interests of the average voter.

In our model there is no efficiency rationale for such investment. After all, foreign firms must bear an extra (fixed) cost to open a plant in the home country and, moreover, manufacturing costs are higher at home than abroad. The foreign firms' motivation for DFI comes entirely from the anticipated protection of the home market; by opening a subsidiary in the home country, these firms can "jump" the eventual tariff barriers. When Brecher and Díaz-Alejandro (1977) studied the implications of DFI (viewed as international capital flows) that is induced by a *fixed* tariff, they found that such investments always reduce aggregate host-country welfare. Thus restrictions on foreign investment into protected markets would be desirable in their context. But the same need not be true here because the rate of protection may vary endogenously with the extent of multinational presence.

To demonstrate the possibility that impediments to DFI may harm the average voter, we consider a situation where the government attaches very little weight to the public interest and the fixed cost of establishing a subsidiary is relatively low. In that event, the unique stable equilibrium when DFI is tolerated has entry by all foreign firms ($m = n_f$) and a tariff high enough to ensure that all these firms actively use their subsidiaries. Moreover, once all foreign firms have built their plants in the home country, gross welfare of the average voter does not depend on the tariff rate (provided that $\tau > c_h/c_f$). This means that the government would be happy to provide the equilibrium protection without contributions from the interest group. Then net welfare (which is gross welfare less any political contributions) would equal gross welfare, which in turn could be expressed, using (2)–(6), as

$$\tilde{W}(q) \equiv L + \frac{n_h}{\varepsilon} p_h^{1-\varepsilon} q^{\varepsilon-\theta} + \frac{1}{\theta - 1} q^{-(\theta-1)}$$

$$\text{for } q = (n_h + n_f)^{1/(1-\varepsilon)} p_h. \tag{13}$$

Now compare this outcome with the one that would obtain if foreign investment were prohibited. A government that cared little about average welfare would cater readily to the interest group. It would be induced by the group to choose the tariff that maximized domestic profits, which in this case is a prohibitive one. Moreover it would require only a minuscule contribution to provide such protection. It follows that net welfare again would equal gross welfare and that the latter would again be given

good. In this case, the indirect effect on the wage also is positive, and the wage rate must rise as the number of multinationals expands. On the other hand, if domestic goods are cheaper than imports, q falls with m and so does x_h. Then DFI has an adverse, indirect effect on the demand for skilled labor. But the direct effect always dominates, and so the skilled wage always rises when the number of foreign subsidiaries increases.[15]

Now let us return to the politics of the situation. Given the number of foreign multinationals m, both π_h and w increase with τ. So, if both the capitalists and workers are politically organized, both will have an incentive to lobby for protection. In contrast, while domestic profits certainly fall with an increase in m, the skilled wage rises in response to an inflow of foreign firms. So domestic firms and industry workers will find themselves in conflict concerning policy toward multinationals.

How will such a conflict be resolved? To gain some insight into this issue, we focus on the extreme case where a is close to zero. In the event, the government puts no weight on consumer surplus or tariff revenue and so is willing to accede to workers' and firms' demands for a prohibitive tariff. Indeed home interest groups need pay only a tiny political contribution in order to secure a fully protected market. Foreign firms should expect an infinite tariff no matter what the degree of multinational presence.[16] Accordingly we know that some foreign firms will wish to establish subsidiaries provided $\pi_h > \phi c_h(w)$ when $m = 0$. It remains to be seen only whether a government that can set investment barriers will choose to impede this foreign investment.

Suppose that the lobbies compete to influence the government's policy toward multinationals. Let each propose a contribution schedule linking the political gift to the number of foreign firms allowed to enter. We focus on Nash equilibria—in which each group's contribution schedule is optimal given the schedule of the other—and, among these, on equilibria that are not Pareto dominated for the two lobby groups. There is in fact a unique, Pareto-undominated Nash equilibrium in the situation we have described; namely the lobby groups induce the government to

---

[15] We calculate that

$$w_m = \frac{w}{m} \frac{\left(1 - \dfrac{n_h}{n_h + m}\, l_x\right) + \eta\, \dfrac{\varepsilon - \theta}{\varepsilon - 1}\, \dfrac{m}{n_h + m}\left(\dfrac{p_f^{1-\varepsilon} - p_h^{1-\varepsilon}}{p_h^{1-\varepsilon}}\right) l_x}{\sigma_s + \beta_s l_x [\eta\theta + (1 - \eta)\varepsilon]},$$

which is non-negative, because $l_x \le 1$ and the terms multiplying l_x in the numerator of the second fraction sum to something less than or equal to one.

[16] An infinite tariff with an infinitesimal contribution is the unique Nash equilibrium when both interest groups independently set their contribution schedules. It is also the outcome if only one of the groups lobbies for protection.

choose m so as to maximize the sum of the skilled wage bill and domestic profits.[17]

What does this tell us about investment restrictions in the ensuing political equilibrium? To answer this question, we define $J \equiv n_h \pi_h + wS$, and calculate that

$$J = \varepsilon^{-\theta}(\varepsilon - 1)^{\theta-1} n_h (n_h + m)^{(\varepsilon-\theta)/(1-\varepsilon)} c_h(w)^{1-\theta} + wS,$$

when the tariff is prohibitive. Also (14) reduces to

$$s(w) [\varepsilon^{-\theta}(\varepsilon - 1)^{\theta}(n_h + m)^{(\theta-1)/(\varepsilon-1)} c_h(w)^{-\theta} + m\phi] = S$$

as $\tau \to \infty$. From these two equations we can evaluate how the joint (gross) welfare of the interest groups is affected by the entry of foreign firms. We find that

$$\frac{dJ}{dm} \frac{m}{J} = - \frac{(1-\omega) m (\varepsilon - \theta)}{(n_h + m)(\varepsilon - 1)} + [\omega - (1-\omega)(\theta - 1)\beta_s]$$

$$\times \frac{(1 - l_x) + l_x [m(\theta - 1)/(n_h + m)(\varepsilon - 1)]}{\sigma_s + \theta\beta_s l_x}, \tag{15}$$

where $\omega = wS/J$ is the share of skilled wages in the aggregate income of members of the two interest groups.

Inspection of (15) reveals that joint income falls with m when ω is close to zero. In the event, the political equilibrium entails a complete ban on all foreign investment. Intuitively, when $\omega \cong 0$, the sector-specific factor has only a (relatively) modest stake in the policy toward multinationals. Meanwhile the owners of domestic firms are more seriously affected by DFI. So the firms' lobby outbids the workers' lobby in the competition for the government's favor. Of course the situation is just the reverse when ω is close to 1. Then an inflow of multinationals boosts the income of skilled workers, and these workers have the most at stake in the outcome of the policy. In this case the workers win the political battle and all foreign firms are free to enter. Finally, if ω is not so extreme, the political contest may give rise to compromise. The political limit to foreign entry can be found by maximizing J with respect to m. This number will be greater, the larger are skilled wages in comparison to the profits of the domestic industry (large ω), the less elastic are firms' demands for

[17] This conclusion follows from theorem 2 of Bernheim and Whinston (1986). They have shown that all coalition-proof equilibria in menu-auction games maximize the joint welfare of the principals and the agent. Here the government is the agent and its welfare is just a transfer from the principals when $a = 0$. So m must maximize $n_h \pi_h + wS$ in any coalition-proof equilibrium. Finally, the set of coalition-proof equilibria coincides with the set of equilibria that are Pareto undominated for the principals, when there are only two principals bidding for influence.

the skilled labor (small σ_s), and the larger are the fixed costs of establishing a facility (large ϕ, which implies a small l_x for a given m).

6 Conclusions

We have developed a model of anticipatory foreign investment that resembles in some respects the quid pro quo foreign investment described by Bhagwati (1987). In the model, foreign investment is assumed to be irreversible, while trade policies can be more readily changed. Therefore, foreign firms must base their investment decisions on their expectations about subsequent policy formation. The firms bear the extra cost of establishing subsidiaries because they fear the eventual imposition of import barriers by the home country.

In our model there is no simple relationship between the number of multinationals and the politically determined tariff rate. In an equilibrium with endogenous trade policy but no impediments to DFI, the stock of foreign investment increases with the home government's taste for campaign contributions and decreases with the fixed cost of entry. But a government that is willing to cater more to special interests does not necessarily provide a higher rate of protection in equilibrium; this depends on how many foreign firms respond to the anticipation of a government with more protectionist proclivities by relocating their production to the home country.

We have shown that DFI can be welfare improving, even if domestic manufacturing costs exceed foreign costs, so that "'tariff-jumping" is the sole motivation for the investment. This conclusion is somewhat at odds with prevailing wisdom in the literature (e.g., see Brecher and Díaz-Alejandro [1977]). Our result can be reconciled with the earlier literature in view of the assumed endogeneity of protection; that is, DFI may be harmful for a given tariff rate but still beneficial if it induces a more liberal trade-policy outcome.

Finally, we have examined the possibility that the home government might regulate inward foreign investment. When policy toward DFI is endogenous, the politics may generate a conflict between domestic firms wanting investment restrictions and domestic workers with industry-specific skills wanting free entry by multinationals. The resolution of this conflict depends on the elasticity of the industry demand for the skilled labor, the ratio of the skilled wage bill to industry profits, and the size of the fixed cost of establishing a multinational facility.

References

Bernheim, B. Douglas, and Whinston, Michael D. (1986). Menu auctions, resource allocation, and economic influence. *Quarterly Journal of Economics* 101: 1–31.

Bhagwati, Jagdish N. (1987). Quid pro quo DFI and VIEs: A political-economy-theoretic analysis. *International Economic Journal* 1: 1–14.

Bhagwati, Jagdish N., Brecher, Richard A., Dinopoulos, Elias, and Srinivasan, T. N. (1987). Quid pro quo foreign investment and welfare: A political-economy-theoretic model. *Journal of Development Economics* 27: 127–138.

Bhagwati, Jagdish N., Dinopoulos, Elias, and Wong, Kar-yiu (1992). Quid pro quo foreign investment. *American Economic Review* 82: 186–190.

Brecher, Richard A., and Díaz-Alejandro, Carlos F. (1977). Tariffs, foreign capital, and immiserizing growth. *Journal of International Economics* 7: 317–322.

Dinopoulos, Elias (1989). Quid pro quo foreign investment. *Economics and Politics* 1: 145–160.

Dinopoulos, Elias (1992). Quid pro quo foreign investment and VERs: A Nash bargaining approach. *Economics and Politics* 4: 43–60.

Grossman, Gene M., and Helpman, Elhanan (1994a). Protection for sale. *American Economic Review* 84: 833–850.

Grossman, Gene M., and Helpman, Elhanan (1994b). Electoral competition and special interest politics. Woodrow Wilson School Discussion Paper in Economics 174. Princeton University.

Helpman, Elhanan (1984). A simple theory of multinational corporations. *Journal of Political Economy* 92: 451–471.

Hillman, Arye L., and Ursprung, Heinrich W. (1993). Multinational firms, political competition, and international trade policy. *International Economic Review* 34: 347–363.

Horstmann, Ignatius, and Markusen, James R. (1992). Endogenous market structures in international trade. *Journal of International Economics* 32: 109–129.

Markusen, James R. (1984). Multinationals, multi-plant economies, and the gains from trade. *Journal of International Economics* 16: 205–226.

Olson, Mancur (1965). *The Logic of Collective Action* (Cambridge, Mass.: Harvard University Press).

Wong, Kar-yiu (1989). Optimal threat of trade restriction and quid pro quo foreign investment. *Economics and Politics* 1: 277–300.

Index

Page numbers followed by "fn" indicate footnotes; those followed by "f" indicate figures; "t" represents tables.

A

Abramowitz, A. I., 75fn
Advertising, political, 1; campaign, 49fn
Agenda setter, 6
Aggregate welfare, 9, 11, 12, 13, 14, 15, 16, 18, 19, 35, 36, 37, 63, 85, 92fn, 96–98, 99, 113, 115, 119, 126, 134, 136, 179, 180, 187, 192, 195, 207, 208, 215, 217
Alternating-offer bargaining model, 225fn
Anderson, K., 126fn
Aranson, P., 49fn
Austen-Smith, D., 46

B

Baldwin, R. E., 126fn, 168, 169
Ball, R., 78
Bandyopadhyay, U., 18–19
Baron, D. P., 46, 49fn, 55, 58fn, 77
Bayes' rule, 83, 87–88, 93
Bayesian equilibrium (PBE), 82
Becker, G. S., 40, 152fn
Benthamite social welfare function, 26

Berg, L., 74
Bernheim, B. D., 7, 26, 46, 62fn, 116, 119, 122, 150, 161, 189, 204, 222, 254fn
Bhagwati, J. N., 16, 181fn, 184, 233, 234fn, 242, 244fn, 255
Binmore, K., 165
Bohara, A. K., 20
Branstetter, L., 20
Brecher, R. A., 242, 250
Brock, W. A., 13, 15, 47fn, 112, 141, 142, 184

C

Cameron, C. M., 78
Campaign contributions, 4, 5, 9, 11, 18, 19, 35, 37, 44, 46, 47, 51–53, 52fn, 55–56, 59, 67, 68, 71fn, 112, 113, 114, 115, 116, 118, 119, 126–132, 134, 135, 184, 185, 194, 234, 237, 239, 246; importance, 77; influence-driven, 186–191; with only an influence motive, 56–59; by PACs, 1; schedule, 142–143

Campaign spending, 6, 8, 9, 47, 49, 50fn,
    54, 59, 68
Campbell, A. A., 74
Coalition-proof equilibrium, 195, 211,
    218
Coalition-proof stance, 212, 221
Coate, S., 41fn
Common agency, 5, 7, 9, 11, 13, 25–40,
    116, 132, 150, 164; application to
    government policy making, 35–40;
    no unified party in power, 6
"Compensating" payment schedule, 8
Contribution schedules, 6, 9, 12, 30, 45,
    52–54, 62, 64, 65, 70, 116, 119, 120,
    125, 126, 143, 145, 146, 147, 148,
    149, 204; designed by lobbies, 240;
    differentiable, 52, 63, 121, 122, 123,
    125, 126, 150–151, 159, 160, 161,
    162, 170, 209, 240, 253; linking
    political gifts to, 253; lobbies, 220;
    locally truthful, 38, 121, 122, 122f,
    123, 124, 127, 129, 131fn
Contributions to foreign governments, 7,
    16, 17, 20, 142fn, 153fn10, 204fn,
    229–231
Converse, P. E., 74
Coughlin, P. J., 49fn, 185
Cowhey, P. F., 140, 200
Crawford, V., 98fn
Crémer, J., 53fn
Customs unions, 202

D
Delegation game, 149
Denzau, A. T., 49fn
DFI (direct foreign investment),
    234–236, 245, 247, 253; benefits to
    average voter, 249–251; welfare
    improving, 20, 255. See also "quid
    pro quo" foreign investment.
Diamond, P. A., 27, 37
Díaz-Alejandro, C F., 250
Differentiable contribution schedules,
    52, 63, 121, 122, 123, 125, 126,
    150–151, 159, 160, 161, 162, 170,
    209, 240, 253
Dinopoulos, E., 234, 234fn, 242
Direct democracy, 175–178
Direct foreign investments. See DFI.
Dividing-line rules, 85–88, 87f, 93, 94
Dixit, A. K., 7, 8, 40, 41fn, 46, 59fn
Donnelly, H., 74–75, 75fn

E
Electoral competition: and special
    interest groups, 8–9, 43–71
Electoral motive, 6, 9, 44, 45, 47, 56,
    59–61, 66–68, 184, 186
Endogenous protection, 233–255
Endorsements, political: competition for,
    74–106; effective, 85–95; enhance
    political efficiency, 99; group
    members unaware, 97–99;
    information from, 87f; labor unions
    and, 74; literature on, 77–79;
    mechanical, 86–92; neutral, 84–85;
    parties not competing for, 98; process
    and political efficiency, 96; role in
    election process, 73–106; role in
    policy determination, 88; role in
    referendum voting, 78; simultaneous,
    99; special interest groups and
    policies, 94; strategic, 92–95; votes for
    party based on, 9–11, 94
Enelow, J. M., 46, 49fn
Enhanced protection, case of, 206, 207,
    207t
Equilibria, 28–32; alternative
    configurations, 248f; coalition proof,
    195; electoral, 83; with one lobby,
    54–61; perfect-foresight, 243, 246;
    political, 52–54; political
    contributions and policy, 119–126;
    with several lobbies, 61–67; truthful,
    32–34; and lobbies, 38–39
Equilibrium agreements, 212–219
Equilibrium contributions, 128, 129f,
    130, 131–132, 134; locally truthful
    schedules, 162; voters represented as
    special interests, 130–131
Equilibrium DFI: protection and,
    246–249, 246f
Equilibrium rate of protection, 176
Equilibrium tariffs, 240–241; levels of
    DFI, 243–249
Equilibrium trade agreements, 160, 161,
    163
Equilibrium trade policies, 125, 152, 192
Equilibrium vote shares, 105f
European Union (EU), 26, 199, 200
Evans, P., 192

F
Feenstra, R. C., 20, 181fn, 183–184
Fershtman, C., 149

Findlay, R., 13, 141fn, 181
Fixed positions, 3, 9, 76, 77, 79
Flam, H., 174
Foreign interest groups, 20, 153fn, 164, 231
Foreign investments: effect on formation of trade policy, 233–255
Foreign multinationals: and trade policy, 235–236
Foreign subsidiaries, 235, 242
Free trade, 111, 114, 130
Free trade agreements (FTAs), 14–20, 194–197; economic equilibrium under, 205–207; effects on economic interests, 207–208; effects on the welfare of agents, 201–208; equilibrium agreement, 212; as equilibrium outcome, 230; industry effects of, 205–206, 206f; industry exclusions, 219–228; bargaining over, 224–228; outcomes under, 207t; political viability, 218; politics of, 199–231; profit changes from, 215
Free trade areas, 202
Freeman, J., 75, 75fn
Fremdreis, J. P., 44

G
Garber, P. M., 174
GATT (General Agreement on Tariffs and Trade), 175, 194, 201, 202, 219, 220
Gawande, K., 17fn, 18–19, 20
Germond, J. W., 75
Goldberg, P. K., 17–19
Goldenberg, E. N., 116fn
Green, D. P., 115fn, 116fn
Grofman, B., 77, 78
Grossman, G. M., 26, 35, 40, 46, 59, 152, 186, 189–190, 191, 192, 195, 200, 203, 204, 234, 237fn

H
Hammond, P. J., 41fn
Helpman, E., 26, 35, 40, 46, 59, 152, 186, 189–190, 191, 192, 195, 200, 203, 204, 234, 237fn
Hillman, A. L., 13, 14, 112, 141fn, 142, 178, 235fn
Hinich, M., 46, 49fn
Hirschman, A. O., 218fn
Horstmann, I., 235fn

I
Import-penetration ratio, 169
Impressionable voters. See voters, impressionable.
Influence motive, 9, 44, 56–59, 66, 68, 186, 189
Informed voters. See voters, informed.
Insiders (voters), 80–81; and endorsements, 93; updating of beliefs, 86, 87f; votes as function of party position, 90f
Interest groups. See Special-interest groups

J
Jacobson, G. G., 115fn
Jacobson, H., 192
Johnson, H. G., 136, 140, 152, 192
Johnson equilibrium, 152, 155f, 156, 156fn, 165
Jones, R. W., 181
Judd, K. L., 149
Jung, J. P., 78

K
Kats, A., 49fn
Katz, M. L., 149
Kau, J. B., 44
Kennan, J., 140
Kennedy, E., 75
Kornhauser, A., 74
Krasno, J. S., 115fn, 116fn
Krishna, P., 17fn, 20
Krueger, A. O., 206
Kuga, K., 140
Kuklinski, J. H., 74

L
Lavergne, R. P., 169, 170
LeRoy, M. H., 74
Li, J., 185
Lindbeck, A., 46, 50fn, 69fn
Lobbies, 3–4, 27, 38–40, 47, 69, 113, 125fn, 127, 128, 131, 132–133, 134–135, 142, 159, 163–165, 185, 205, 209–210, 212, 223, 225, 230, 241f; antiprotectionist, 182–183; application to government policy making, 36; attempting to influence policy, 234; contributions, 36–38; contribution schedules, 70, 116, 125, 145–146, 148, 150, 160–161, 220, 237;

Lobbies *(continued)*
  contribution schedules and trade
  talks, 193–194; contributions to
  foreign governments, 229–231;
  cooperation between, 149; deviate,
  40; equilibria with one, 54–61;
  equilibria with several, 61–67;
  foreign, 150, 154fn, 156; influence-
  driven contributions, 186–191, 195;
  political contributions to set trade
  policy, 114; 132–133; and pressured
  stances, 210; proprotectionist,
  182–183; truthful contribution
  schedules, 127; and truthful
  equilibria, 38–39, 130; and
  unpressured stances, 209
Local truthfulness, 62fn, 71, 121, 122f,
  124, 151, 162
Londregan, J. B., 41fn, 46, 59fn
Long, N. V., 123, 142, 180fn
Lupia, A., 74, 78, 84fn

M
Magee, S. P., 13, 15, 47fn, 112, 141, 142,
  184
Magelby, D. B., 115, 168, 186
Maggi, G., 17–19
Majority rule, 69–71
Markusen, J. R., 234, 235fn
Martinez, G., 75
Mayer, W., 13, 136, 140, 163fn, 175–176,
  185
McCalman, P., 19–20
McKelvey, R., 77
McMillan, J., 202, 220
Median voters. *See* voters, median.
Menu auction, 26, 46, 116, 119, 204, 211,
  222, 254fn
MERCOSUR (Southern Common
  Market), 20, 200
MFN. *See* "most favored nation"
Mirrlees, J. A., 27, 37
Mitra, D., 19
Mondale, W., 75
Morris, S., 41fn
Morton, R., 64fn
Moser, P., 141fn
"Most favored nation" (MFN), 201, 202,
  213
Multilateral negotiations, 13, 17, 200
Myerson, R., 64fn

N
NAFTA, 139, 174, 196fn, 200, 212, 224fn
Nash bargaining problem, 226, 227
Nash bargaining solution, 159, 225
Nash equilibrium, 82, 84, 151, 181, 185,
  211, 253; contributions, 141;
  multiple subgame perfect, 32;
  Pareto-undominated, 253;
  platforms, 141; subgame-perfect,
  52–53, 120, 212
Nelson, C. J., 115, 168, 186
Nitzan, S. I., 49fn
Norrander, B., 77, 78
North American Free Trade Agreement.
  See NAFTA.

O
O'Brien, D. P., 53fn
Olson, M., 50, 118, 178, 203, 239
Ordeshook, P., 49fn, 77
Outsiders (voters), 81; votes as function
  of party position, 90f

P
PACs (political action committees), 18,
  19, 115, 186; campaign contributions
  by, 1
Particularistic policies, 55
Payment function, 29; truthful, 32–33.
  See also Truthful contribution
  schedules.
Peleg, B., 211
Peltzman, S., 14, 142
Pliable policies, 8, 9, 10, 44–45, 48, 49,
  50, 51, 52fn, 54, 55, 57, 58, 66, 67, 68,
  69, 80–81, 89, 92–93, 96, 97, 98, 104,
  105–106
Pliable positions, 76, 79, 82, 86, 91
Political Action Committees (PACs), 18,
  19, 115, 186; campaign contributions
  by, 1
Political endorsements. *See*
  Endorsements, political
Political equilibria, 52–54, 240; nature
  of, 143–147
Political-support function, 13–14,
  112–113, 142; relation to choice of
  tariff rate, 178–180
Political tariff response curves. *See* Tariff
  response curves.
Politically optimal set of exclusions, 221

Pressured stances, 209–212, 215, 216, 217, 222, 230
Probabilistic voting, 46
Probabilistic voting theory, 185
"Protection for sale," 11–12, 92, 111–138
Putnam, R. D., 140, 175, 192, 200

Q

Quasi-linear preferences, 34–35
Quasi-linearity, 26–27
"Quid pro quo foreign investment," 16–17, 233, 251, 255

R

Ramsey rule, modified, 114
Rapoport, R. B., 75fn
Reduced protection, case of, 206, 207t, 208
Richardson, M., 202fn, 205
Riedel, J. C., 169
Riezman, R., 140
Riordan, M. H., 53fn
Robbins, M., 20
Rodrik, D., 132fn, 191
Rubenstein, A., 165
Rubinstein bargaining model, 165
Rubin, P. H., 44

S

Sanguinetti, P., 20
Shaffer, G., 53fn
Shapiro, C., 49fn
Shepsle, K. A., 175
Single-market program, 174
Snyder, J. M., 49fn, 58, 168
Sobel, J., 98fn
Social-welfare function, 9, 26, 35fn, 44, 55fn, 68, 123
Southern Common Market (MERCOSUR), 20, 200
Special interest groups, 1–6, 50–52, 58fn, 111; active in free trade agreements, 217; competition between, 133; conditions for endorsements, 74; contribution schedules, 204; effect on trade policies, 174; and electoral competition, 43–71; gifts to influence government policy, 134; and government, 239–242; government responses to equilibrium behavior, 208–210; incentives for giving during election campaign, 6; influencing policy, 140, 142; motivation for campaign contributions, 51–52; political competition among, 135; political contributions and influencing policy, 168; and trade policy formation, 141; and trade talks, 139
Special Interest Politics, 2–6, 7, 8, 11
Special interest politics: and international trade relations, 139–170
Srinivasan, T. N., 242
Stackelberg leaders, 141
Stigler, G. J., 14, 112, 142, 178
Stone, W. J., 75fn
Subgame-perfect Nash equilibrium, 120, 212
Sutton, J., 166

T

Tariff-formation function, 13–14, 141fn, 180–184
Tariff levels, 175, 234, 240–242; determined by direct voting, 176–177; equilibrium in direct democracy, 178. See also Trade taxes and subsidies.
Tariff response curves, 243–244, 243f, 246, 247
Tariffs: equilibrium, 240–241; MFN, 213; "optimal," 13; political response curves, 243–244, 243f; theory of discriminatory, 208. See also Trade taxes and subsidies.
Terms-of-trade motives, 152
Textile Bill of 1985, 168
Thomakos, D. D., 19
Tosini, S. C., 44, 168
Tower, E., 44, 168
Trade Act of 1974, 168
Trade diversion, 207, 219
Trade negotiations: predictions of outcome, 169
Trade policies, 111–136, 174, 184, 191, 193; efficiency properties, 173–174; electoral competition, 184–186; instruments, 173; noncooperative equilibrium, 151; political economy approaches to formation, 175–191; political economy of, 112; politics and, 173–197; role in income redistribution, 144; role of electoral

Trade policies *(continued)*
    motive for campaign contributions,
        185–186
Trade relations, 139–170; between two
    countries, 143
Trade talks, 193–194; between politically
    motivated governments, 158–168
Trade taxes and subsidies, 26, 46, 113,
    116, 117, 124, 126, 132, 143, 144,
    145, 147, 159
Trade war equilibrium, 155f, 165; two
    governments at bargaining table,
    165–167
Trade wars, 12, 146, 147–157, 192–193
Trefler, D., 169
Truthful contribution schedules, 122,
    123, 124, 127, 129
Truthful equilibria, 32–35; and lobbies,
    38–40
Truthful Nash equilibrium (TNE), 123,
    127, 130, 133
Two-country policy games: international
    negotiations, 148–168; non-
    cooperative policies, 147–157

U
Ulubaşoğlu, M. A., 19
Unilateral stances, 208–212, 213,
    219–224; definition, 209; pressured,
    209–212, 215, 216, 217, 222, 230;
    unpressured, 209–212, 216, 222–223,
    230
Uninformed voters. *See* voters,
    uninformed.

Unpressured stances, 209–212, 216,
    222–223, 230
Ursprung, H. W., 112, 235fn
Uruguay Round, 139, 174, 175

V
Voters, 47–49; DFI serving interest of,
    249–251; impressionable, 6, 8, 45, 48,
    67, 77, 187fn; informed, 47–48;
    insiders [*see* Insiders (voters)];
    median, 13, 44, 57, 141, 176, 177,
    178, 205fn; outsiders [*see* Outsiders
    (voters)]; partisan, 3; uninformed,
    47–48, 49fn, 55fn, 58fn, 59, 62, 63,
    67, 68, 74, 96, 98, 99, 187fn
Voting equilibrium, 13
Vousden, N., 123, 142, 180fn

W
Waterman, R. W., 44
Weibull, J. W., 46, 50fn, 69fn
Wellisz, S., 13, 141fn, 181
Whinston, M. D., 26, 46, 62fn, 116, 119,
    122, 150, 161, 189, 204, 211, 254fn
Wilson, J. D., 132fn
Wolinsky, A., 165
Wong, K., 234fn
Wonnacott, P., 219
Wonnacott, R., 219
Wotcover, J., 75

Y
Young, L., 13, 15, 47fn, 112, 141, 142, 184